EISENHOWER DECIDES TO RUN

EISENHOWER DECIDES TO RUN

*Presidential Politics and
Cold War Strategy*

WILLIAM B. PICKETT

Ivan R. Dee
CHICAGO 2000

EISENHOWER DECIDES TO RUN. Copyright © 2000 by William B. Pickett. All rights reserved, including the right to reproduce this book or portions thereof in any form. For information, address: Ivan R. Dee, Publisher, 1332 North Halsted Street, Chicago 60622. Manufactured in the United States of America and printed on acid-free paper.

Library of Congress Cataloging-in-Publication Data:
Pickett, William B. (William Beatty), 1940–
   Eisenhower decides to run : presidential politics and Cold War strategy / William B. Pickett.
      p.   cm.
   Includes bibliographical references (p.) and index.
   ISBN 1-56663-325-7 (acid-free paper)
      1. Presidents—United States—Election—1952.   2. Eisenhower, Dwight D. (Dwight David), 1890–1969.   3. United States—Politics and government—1945–1953.   I. Title.
   E816.P53 2000
   973.921'092—dc21   00-031534

For Robert H. Ferrell

CONTENTS

ACKNOWLEDGMENTS

BOOKS HAVE A WAY of taking longer from conception to press than the author expects. This one, though I did not know it at the time, began in the late 1980s at the Eisenhower Library in Abilene, Kansas. My purpose for being there was to put the finishing touches on a brief biography of the former general turned president. One of the helpful archivists brought me a box of materials from the Edwin Norman Clark papers. In the box was a long diary with previously undisclosed information about Eisenhower's entry into the partisan political arena. That discovery, it turned out, was the origin of this book.

Now, more than a decade later, I gratefully acknowledge those who helped bring this book to fruition. They include, first and foremost, Robert H. Ferrell, distinguished professor emeritus at Indiana University. A teacher, friend, and colleague for almost thirty years, he recommended in 1982 that I do a book on Eisenhower. And when that task was complete, he provided important materials that he had come across—in his research on a biography of Truman—on Truman's efforts to get Eisenhower to run on the 1952 Democratic ticket. The individual who directed me to the Edwin Clark papers at the Eisenhower Library was James Leyerzapf, senior archivist there. Leyerzapf became a constant source of assistance on this project during my visits to Abilene, in the summers and during a sabbatical leave. Others who helped include the Eisenhower scholar Fred Greenstein, at the Woodrow Wilson School at Princeton University, who took a personal interest in my research and provided several books and documents re-

[ix]

lated directly to the topic. Wilson Miscamble, chair of the department of history at the University of Notre Dame, read and made numerous helpful suggestions on an early draft. Tom Deligiannis and Robert Wampler provided copies of their conference papers on nuclear weapons and NATO strategy. James T. Patterson, professor of history at Brown University, also provided early encouragement. Michael Birkner, professor of history at Gettysburg College, provided documents from several sources, including the Norris Cotton papers at the University of Vermont.

General Andrew J. Goodpaster, Eisenhower's White House staff secretary, adviser on international and security affairs, and later himself supreme allied commander of the North Atlantic Treaty Organization, allowed an interview, read the manuscript, offered suggestions for improvement, and supported my efforts to find a publisher. Abbott Washburn, deputy director of the United States Information Agency during the Eisenhower presidency and a participant in the 1952 campaign, also provided helpful context. William Bragg Ewald, who mentioned Clark's activities without attribution or annotation in a book that he published in 1981, directed me to the remainder of Edwin Clark's personal papers. Herbert Brownell, at the Eisenhower centennial conference at Gettysburg College in 1990, shared with me his memories of Eisenhower's entry into politics.

William Robinson's widow, Ellen R. Reynes, gave permission to use her late husband's papers and oral history at the Eisenhower Library and provided photographs. Daniel Holt, director of the Eisenhower Library, and Martin Teasley, assistant director, helped in a variety of ways. Professor John P. Burke of the University of Vermont corresponded with me about Herbert Brownell. Leila Sussman and Joan D. Goldhamer shared memories of their work with Robert Merton at Columbia University analyzing the letters that in 1948 urged the general to run. John E. Wickman, retired director of the Eisenhower Library, shared his knowledge of the role of Jackie Cochran. The staff at the Massachusetts Historical Society helped find the numerous useful documents in the Henry Cabot Lodge, Jr., papers. Edwin Clark's nephew, Campbell L. Searle, professor emeritus at the Massachusetts Institute of Technology, invited me to his home in Weston, Massachusetts, and, after a delightful dinner and an evening of inventory work, turned over to me all remaining correspondence between his uncle, Edwin N. Clark, and Dwight D. Eisenhower—files that, after photocopying, I transferred to the Eisenhower Library.

Rose-Hulman Institute of Technology provided a sabbatical leave, a special leave, and financial support for several trips to Abilene. I am especially indebted to the former head of the department of humanities and social sciences, Peter Parshall; the current head, Heinz Luegenbiehl; the former vice president for academic affairs, James Eifert; and the current holder of that office, Barry Benedict. My colleagues in the department (notably my political scientist colleague, Thad Smith) offered valuable advice at a department seminar during the early stages of writing. The Institute's librarian and archivist, John Robson, provided constant encouragement, and the interlibrary loan librarian, Amy Harshbarger, was available whenever I needed her services. One of my history students, Eric Panhorst, with work/study financial support, entered my revisions to the manuscript and organized footnote citations. Finally, the Institute print shop, under the management of Jack Bagley, printed and duplicated numerous copies of the manuscript.

The most important contributions during this journey came from my family and friends. They tolerated my absences and preoccupations but also shared the small discoveries that, as they accumulate, become large findings and result in a new way of thinking about past events. My brother-in-law, William Toner, provided a place to stay during research trips to the east coast. My parents-in-law, Ida and Gordon Hollingsworth, were their usual encouraging selves during my drafting summers in Minnesota and Christmases in Terre Haute. My friend and college roommate, William K. Johnson, remained interested, with questions about what I had discovered. And my wife, Janet, listened patiently and provided essential emotional balance, as did our two sons, Robert and Jeff.

Finally, I would like to thank the most recent Eisenhower biographer, Geoffrey Perret, for recommending that I contact a friend of his, Clyde Taylor, literary agent *par excellence*. I am grateful finally to Ivan R. Dee for his superb editing and publishing skills.

W. B. P.

Terre Haute, Indiana
June 2000

PREFACE

THE ELECTION OF Dwight David Eisenhower in 1952 marked a dividing line in the history of the American presidency. With the close of the Truman administration and the defeat of Adlai Stevenson, twenty years of Democratic dominance of the executive branch ended. Presidents Eisenhower, Nixon, Ford, Reagan, and Bush, all Republicans, occupied the White House during twenty-eight of the next forty years. Eisenhower's successors in the White House, John F. Kennedy and Lyndon B. Johnson, continued to draw upon the support of the so-called New Deal coalition that had supported Franklin D. Roosevelt, and in doing so brought still more social and economic reform legislation that increased the role of government in American life. But after Eisenhower such legislation faced an undercurrent of opposition. Kennedy barely defeated Nixon in the election of 1960 and trimmed his reform efforts in response to a growing American middle class that supported conservative, individualistic, budget-balancing views. In addition, the victory of Eisenhower, the only professional soldier and strategist to be elected president in the twentieth century—after the outbreak of cold war, the explosion of the first Soviet atomic bomb, the advent of communist China, and the outbreak of war in Korea—ended the uncertainty that had existed in American foreign relations since 1898 about whether the United States would play a continuing role in world affairs.[1]

The popular view of Eisenhower's entry into politics is that he succumbed to pressure and was thus the first individual since George

Washington to receive a presidential draft. The 1952 victory was, according to this view, the result of an outpouring of support for the most popular man in America—a beaming, genial, five-star general, symbol of victory over Hitler in World War II. Both parties had tried to woo him, each sensing that his lack of partisan baggage would sweep the elections. The Republicans won out as a result of spontaneous, irresistible pressure . . . at least this is how the story goes.

It is now clear that pressure for a draft—a great deal of it and much of it spontaneous—did exist. It came from the rank and file of both parties and from certain leaders. It did not, however, come from the Republican party organization, which by 1951 supported the candidacy of the Ohio senator and Senate minority leader, Robert A. Taft. What the general and his closest supporters concealed from the public and, until recently, went undiscovered by historians—was that, despite his popularity, he worked behind the scenes to encourage a popular movement for his candidacy. Indeed, he and his supporters felt that such activity was the only way he could overcome the apparent stranglehold of Taft on the 1952 GOP nomination.

Eisenhower would have preferred to separate himself from what he saw as the grasping and demagogy of partisan politics, and, at age 62, to retire. But the circumstances rendered this impossible. As a public servant and expert in national security policy, he came to believe that the values for which the nation had fought in two world wars and perhaps even the peace of the world were in jeopardy. As international tensions increased in the postwar years, along with confusion in the United States over what to do about them, he determined, beginning in mid-1948, that if Dewey were defeated that year he might have to make himself available for election to the office of commander-in-chief. If tensions with the Soviet Union and the People's Republic of China had somehow diminished, or if another candidate with understanding and stature had surfaced as a national leader, he might have decided otherwise. They did not.

Eisenhower was aware of his political potential as a war hero. He also knew something about the hazards faced by any presidential candidate but especially by generals who run for high office in the United

States. As a master of strategy—an art that he knew was as applicable in party politics as in war—he decided that if he proceeded in the correct fashion, he might be successful. One important element of his approach—and a luxury that, given his popularity, he might be able to achieve—was to be the sought rather than the seeker.

The common wisdom that Eisenhower had responded to a draft was plausible. He had renounced any intentions for political office in 1946 and again, at least so the public thought, before the January 1948 New Hampshire primary. And the evidence is abundant that he was ambivalent about the partisan arena, which in many ways he considered alien. Despite such examples as George Washington and Ulysses S. Grant, he had misgivings about crossing the constitutional barrier of civilian supremacy. Other generals had tried and failed. As late as the New Hampshire primary in March 1952, according to the published memoirs of his political strategist and later attorney general, Herbert Brownell, Eisenhower was still trying to make up his mind.[2] The general's public statements, and many private ones as well, seemed to indicate that only after entreaties by scores of prominent individuals persuaded him it was his duty to run, and that he could win, did he give in to pressure.[3] His biographer Stephen Ambrose concluded in 1983 that the hero from Abilene did not seek the presidency. "There is not a single item in the massive collection at the Eisenhower Library prior to late 1951," Ambrose said, "that even hints that he would seek the job or that he was secretly doing so."[4]

Recently discovered documents at the Eisenhower Library, however, say otherwise. Soon after the end of World War II, people who were Eisenhower's friends or ambitious for him began politicking in his behalf.[5] The historian Blanche Wiesen Cook, in a 1981 book, referred to Eisenhower's position as logical successor to Dewey for the Republican presidential nomination after Truman's victory in 1948, and asserted, based on an examination of the general's correspondence files, that Eisenhower "while at SHAPE was running for president."[6] It turns out that Cook was correct and that Eisenhower was more deeply involved in promoting his presidential fortunes than even she knew. By the summer of 1948 the general believed that the nation again needed his experience and knowledge. His awareness of an increasing national anxiety—and an accompanying yearning for the confidence his fellow Americans felt only he could provide—combined with a belief that the most likely GOP candidate, Senator Robert A. Taft of Ohio, could not supply the leadership the nation needed. In July 1948, Eisenhower authorized activities to explore the feasibility of a 1952 presidential candidacy.

By mid-1950, foreign relations had turned markedly for the worse. The Soviet Union had exploded an atomic bomb. The Communist party had triumphed in China. North Korea had invaded South Korea. With national security policy uncertain, Eisenhower was concerned about the danger to American democracy of either excessive military spending or a return to isolationism. Although he agreed with the direction and thrust of Truman's foreign policy, he remained concerned over the lack of faith of the American people and their European allies in American leadership, especially after the war in Korea began to go badly for the allies in November 1950 and in the following spring. Far from remaining aloof and waiting for a draft, Eisenhower began to work closely with the partisan efforts that created the appearance of a public seeking him.[7]

The factors underlying Eisenhower's decision to run for the presidency appear perhaps most vividly in the contrast between him and General Douglas A. MacArthur, another general with presidential aspirations. Why, one might ask, was it Eisenhower rather than MacArthur who followed a select few other American military commanders, including—in addition to Washington and Grant—Andrew Jackson, William Henry Harrison, and Zachary Taylor, into the White House? MacArthur, after all, was senior. In the early 1930s Eisenhower had served as his aide in the War Department when MacArthur was army chief of staff, and as his chief of staff from 1935 to 1939 when MacArthur was military adviser to the Philippines.[8] And MacArthur, on September 2, 1945, had accepted the surrender of Japan. For many observers this was more newsworthy than V-E day because it ended World War II. Finally, the Far Eastern supreme commander, certainly more than Eisenhower, yearned to be president.

The two generals differed in their view of the line between military affairs and partisan politics, the role of a theater commander, and the proper cold war strategy for the United States. While on active duty MacArthur was willing to criticize publicly the commander-in-chief; Eisenhower saw such action as counterproductive and unconstitutional. MacArthur believed that even in the nuclear age a theater commander should have unfettered freedom to plan and carry out military operations and that, just as in World War II, there was "no substitute for victory." Eisenhower, for his part, believed that nuclear weapons signaled a new era of warfare and demanded a new way of thinking about world affairs. Wars had to be prevented or contained, and national interests protected. Unlike MacArthur, Eisenhower established and maintained a continuous flow of correspondence and reports to both the chairman of the joint chiefs of staff and the president. By 1951 the two generals were clearly at odds on specific strategy: MacArthur determined that he, rather than the president, should establish the mission of the United Nations forces he commanded in Korea; that the main theater of the cold war was Asia. Eisenhower, one of the architects and implementers of the Europe-first strategy during World War II and now NATO supreme commander, believed that American security and world peace rested chiefly upon a revitalized and unified Europe. Finally, MacArthur was openly ambitious for the presidency. Essentially a loner, he increasingly surrounded himself with a staff that was more obedient than advisory. He thought he could elicit "spontaneous" popular support, which never came. Eisenhower denied interest in political office but carried on an active—indeed, voluminous—correspondence with prominent individuals and enjoyed the company of friends and influential acquaintances. In this way he quietly but systematically established a network of supporters.[9] In sum, Eisenhower's approach succeeded because, unlike that of his former boss, it was both appropriate to the situation and in harmony with the outlook of a majority of his countrymen.

EISENHOWER DECIDES TO RUN

☆ **1** ☆

WAR HERO

DWIGHT D. EISENHOWER'S JOURNEY from professional soldier to candidate for the presidency, though he did not know it at the time, began in 1943. In November 1942 an allied expeditionary force under his command, in a dangerous amphibious operation—the Germans largely controlled the European continent and the Mediterranean Sea—landed in North Africa. By the following May, with the help of the British Eighth Army in the east, Eisenhower's forces had defeated the brilliant German field marshal Erwin Rommel's Afrika Korps.[1] In September, General George Van Horn Moseley, who had been Eisenhower's friend in the early 1930s at the War Department, wrote a letter to the American commander. The occasion was a broadcast comment by Walter Winchell, the columnist and popular radio personality, that if the "Republicans ran MacArthur for President, Mr. Roosevelt would take Eisenhower as his running mate." Moseley urged Eisenhower to "adopt the position that you are so intimately engaged in your battle problems that you have no time for anything else."[2]

Eisenhower, Moseley knew, had served as aide to General Douglas A. MacArthur from 1930 to 1934, when MacArthur was army chief of staff. Later he had been MacArthur's chief of staff in the Philippines, where MacArthur was military adviser. The general from Abilene, Moseley also knew, considered his former boss an enigma, his brilliance offset by an egocentrism and ambition that blinded him to the Constitution's strict mandate for civilian supremacy over the military. MacArthur seemed to have no concept, for example, that the regulation barring professional military men from participating in partisan politics applied to him. For a long time Eisenhower accepted Mac-Arthur's foibles as part of his aura and mystery, but finally he had begun to find such ambition (and accompanying vanity) distasteful. By the time Eisenhower left the Philippines in 1939, their private relationship had broken down.

The episode that began the friction occurred in 1936. Eisenhower at first struggled to keep things in perspective. In his diary he recorded that MacArthur "has the capacity to undertake successfully any position in government" but doubted that "he has any real political ambition and in these days of high powered publicity and propaganda I do not expect to see him ever prominently mentioned for office outside the War Department."[3] Then MacArthur decided, largely as a result of wishful thinking and partisan sentiment, that the Kansas Republican Alf Landon was about to defeat Franklin D. Roosevelt in the presidential election. The American military adviser proceeded to broadcast his prophesy, telling not only his staff but Philippine president Manuel Quezon. Such political advocacy was distasteful to Mac-Arthur's staff. If it became known in the United States, Eisenhower knew it could jeopardize congressional appropriations for Philippine defense. Roosevelt's defeat of Landon in a landslide, proving Mac-Arthur wrong, only added to the embarrassment.[4]

By October 1937, the relationship between General MacArthur— who had asked for and accepted the rank of field marshal in the Philippine army—and his American chief of staff had fractured. Eisenhower found especially intolerable the senior's tendency to blame subordinates when things went badly. He scorned MacArthur's "egotism, exclusive devotion to his own interests, including a 66,000 peso salary plus penthouse and expenses." No longer able to overlook past events, he recalled the time in Washington when a message to report to the president "led MacArthur to conclude, in the greatest seriousness, that he was to be invited to be the President's running mate in the succeeding election." It was this trait, Eisenhower now determined, "that seems to have destroyed his judgment and led him to surround himself with people . . . who simply bow down and worship."[5]

By the end of July 1939, with MacArthur insisting that the islands could be defended against a Japanese invasion (and seeking himself to be appointed successor to Paul V. McNutt as U.S. High Commissioner to the Philippines), their relationship was at an impasse. In October, MacArthur relieved Eisenhower from duties as his chief of staff. Eisenhower remained in a staff position, at least in part because of his close relationship with President Quezon and his mastery of the intricacies of Philippine-American relations. But he had few hopes that the Philippine defense plan as then constituted would work, and MacArthur seemed unaware of the need to educate public opinion to support a different one.[6] Eisenhower's efforts to obtain reassignment back to the United States having finally succeeded, in mid-December 1939 he departed with his family for the United States.[7]

Now, in 1943, Eisenhower took time to reply to Moseley's letter. "No one," he said, "has had the temerity to mention the possibility that I might become interested in a political career." When Winchell brought up the subject, Eisenhower added brusquely, he was, "to say the least, badly misinformed."[8]

The events following the victorious North Africa campaign proved Moseley's concern to be justified. Eisenhower could not escape his new status. With the surrender of hundreds of thousands of Italian and German soldiers in North Africa in May 1943, world leaders congratulated, decorated, and promoted him. Journalists and historians looked to chronicle his life and career. Henry Cabot Lodge, Jr., of Massachusetts, whose grandfather had been chairman of the Senate Foreign Relations Committee in the first decade of the century and who was himself one of the Republican party's bright young leaders—at the time serving as a tank corps officer—told Eisenhower after his North African victory that the general "had the confidence of the average American." His handling of the complex political factors involved in the campaign, Lodge told him, had been "realistic, energetic, and smart."[9] (Lodge spoke French and after D-day at Normandy would become the supreme commander's liaison with the French commanders.) By that time, North Africa and Sicily having fallen to allied forces under Eisenhower's command and Rome having been liberated, President Roosevelt had awarded Eisenhower (now a four-star general) the Legion of Merit for his command of Allied mobilization and preparation for the North Africa invasion, and the Distinguished Service Medal with oak leaf cluster.[10]

The adulation was just beginning. Eisenhower's brother Edgar expressed his amazement at the family's "place in the esteem of most of the world now, due entirely to your accomplishment."[11] The historic D-day landing at Normandy on June 6, 1944, brought praise from, it seemed, everywhere—even from the brooding Soviet ally in the east. Averell Harriman, U.S. ambassador to Moscow, told the supreme commander that in the weeks following D-day two hundred senior Soviet officers had watched a film of the landing. Americans in Moscow, including himself, were living, he said, in "the reflected glory of what you are doing." Generalissimo Joseph Stalin had called the assault "an unheard of achievement the magnitude of which had never been undertaken in military history."[12] (Eisenhower replied that he was tracing the Red Army's progress in the east on a map and getting a great "thrill out of the rate in which they are demolishing the enemy's fighting power." He conveyed to Stalin and his commanders "very deep admiration and respect.")[13] After the German surrender, Eisenhower, now wearing on his uniform jacket the circled, five-star insignia of general of the army, attended celebrations in Moscow. The Communist dictator complimented him on his human, friendly, kind, and frank nature. General Eisenhower was not, said Stalin, "*gubyi* (coarse, brusque) like most military men."[14]

After the liberation of western Europe by the Allied forces under his command, and, on May 8, 1945, his acceptance of the German surrender at Reims, Eisenhower's smiling countenance and upraised arms waving from his motorcade became for the Western nations a symbol of the Allied victory. Ticker-tape parades in Washington, D.C., and New York City marked a hero's return. He addressed a joint session of Congress, and President Harry S Truman (Roosevelt having died on April 12) held a stag dinner for him at the White House. News of that event brought a flurry of speculation that Democratic leaders might want to "run Ike for President."

The rumormongers, it turned out, were onto something. We now know that Truman told his wife, Bess, at the time that a Democratic presidential ticket led by Ike "was fine with him."[15] The following month, during the Potsdam summit conference, while on an automobile tour of the former enemy capital, now in rubble (Potsdam is a suburb of Berlin), the president leaned over and told Eisenhower that he could have anything that it was in his [Truman's] power to give, including the presidency in 1948.[16] Caught off guard and embarrassed by what appeared to be an impulsive overture, Eisenhower quickly demurred. But he was enormously flattered, recalling the event in his war memoirs. His boyhood hero had been Theodore Roosevelt, but until 1940, having served only in training commands and staff positions, the general from Abilene, Kansas, had doubted that he would ever become a general, much less command troops in war.[17] He had entered a new universe of opportunity or, from a different point of view, of duty.

After a brief time as military governor of the U.S. zone in Germany, Eisenhower in the autumn of 1945 accepted a different offer, appointment as U.S. army chief of staff. Eisenhower was the obvious choice as his boss's successor. General George C. Marshall, organizer of the Allied victory against the Axis nations, wanted to retire, but at the president's request he agreed to go to China and try to mediate the conflict there between the nationalist forces of Chiang Kai-shek and the Communists of Mao Tse-tung.[18]

Eisenhower's appointment did little to silence the pundits. Six months into his new post, Winchell again was touting him for president in his newspaper column.[19] Adulation also came from other sources. Thomas J. Watson, president of the IBM Corporation, for example, published an article in his company's publication entitled "General of the Army Dwight D. Eisenhower: Representative American Soldier." It chronicled the supreme commander's victorious return from Europe and spoke of his "faith in the cause of democracy . . . as he devotes his unwavering ability to the task of effecting and maintaining a program for permanent peace and prosperity."[20] Winchell and Watson, capturing the sentiments of a large number of Americans, were certain that their urgings were in their nation's interest.

Eisenhower's patriotism and sense of professional responsibility were strong, his ideas about the national interest well articulated. Both were moving him—protests notwithstanding—away from Moseley's advice.[21] His success as supreme commander was now on the record. Eisenhower later recalled that the historian and biographer of Robert E. Lee, Douglas Southall Freeman, explained to him in late 1943 that in his research on Lee he had had little trouble discovering what had happened but had had "hell's own time finding out why." The historian pleaded with Eisenhower to write a "contemporary memorandum of the reason for [his] important decisions."[22] A student of history himself, Eisenhower replied that he was pleased to hear from "a person of Freeman's distinguished standing." As for the memoranda in question, he said "he already was writing them."[23] Eisenhower, who admired Lee as a military strategist, may also have considered the fact that his own career more nearly paralleled that of the Union commander and later president, Ulysses S. Grant. "Politics," Eisenhower later recalled, "had been suggested to me by Virgil M. Pinkley [a newspaper reporter] as early as 1943." Pinkley told him, "You just can't get away, as long as you've been a successful general here in Africa, from being considered as a possibility for the Presidency." Eisenhower's reply was, "Forget it." But in an oral history interview years later, he confessed that "this was when the damned thing began."[24]

☆ 2 ☆

LESSONS
IN POLITICS

GENERAL GEORGE C. MARSHALL, addressing a meeting of the American Historical Association at the onset of World War II, observed that "the dominating influence on the organization of a nation for war is its politics." In a democracy, "where the government is truly an agent of the popular will, military policy is dependent upon public opinion, and our organization for war will be good or bad as the public is well informed or poorly informed regarding the factors that bear on the subject."[1] Supreme command necessarily put Eisenhower at the place where military and political affairs merged.

The North African invasion—Operation Torch—of November 1942 provided a case in point. After the German blitzkrieg overran northern France in the early summer of 1940, the French set up a collaborationist government at Vichy under Marshal Philippe Pétain. German troops occupied northern and central France; Pétain controlled the south along with the French colonies in North Africa under Admiral Jean Darlan. In 1942, Darlan established an anti-Semitic police regime later memorialized in the classic movie *Casablanca*. Eisenhower knew Darlan was a thug, but he also knew the Allied mission, Operation Torch, was dangerous. The Prussian philosopher of war, Karl von Clausewitz, whose writings Eisenhower had mastered as a young officer, had warned that amphibious landings on hostile shores were the most difficult of military maneuvers. And this, he implied, was especially true when the forces that conducted the landing were from different countries. Darlan's troops might fire on the force when it landed, or attack from the rear as it began to move against Rommel. Eisenhower preferred the political hazards of dealing with a fascist to the prospect of losing troops to French (rather than German) gunfire. After discussions, the French admiral promised not to resist the landing; in exchange, Eisenhower promised not to remove him from power.

News of the agreement brought outrage. In Washington the Republicans stepped up their attacks on President Roosevelt (and on his supreme commander in North Africa), asking what the nation was fighting for. The landing in the Mediterranean also irked the Soviet Union, an essential ally against Germany. The previous December, the *Wehrmacht* had reached the outskirts of Moscow and by late 1942 was headed into the southeastern part of the Soviet Union, beyond Stalingrad toward the Baku oil fields in the Caspian. Stalin had sought an early cross-channel invasion by the British and Americans to relieve German pressure on him, but to no avail. The North Africa landing was thus to him a poor substitute for a diversionary second front. Eisenhower's arrangement with Darlan, not surprisingly, brought intense criticism from the Kremlin. (A few months later, Darlan's assassination relieved the situation somewhat.)

Stung by the criticism, Eisenhower wrote to his son John: "It is easy enough for a man to be a newspaper hero one day and a bum the next . . . One reason why we train people all their lives to be soldiers, is so that in a moment of emergency they can get down to essentials of situations and not be too much disturbed about popularity or newspaper acclaim" (and, by implication, criticism).[2] He said he hoped never again to hear the word "politics" but admitted the feeling "of a crusader in this war and every time I write a letter or open my mouth." He told his childhood friend, Swede Hazlett, that "in no other war in history has the issue been so distinctly drawn between the forces of arbitrary oppression on the one side and, on the other, those conceptions of individual liberty, freedom and dignity under which we have been raised in our great democracy."[3]

Eisenhower also knew that war required politics of a very practical sort—leadership. "The idea is to get people to working together . . . because they instinctively want to do it for you. You must be devoted to duty and be sincere, fair and cheerful." "The men," he told his son, "must trust you and instinctively wish to win your approbation."[4] "The average American," he said, "will respond to intelligent and sympathetic instruction and will absolutely admire a leader that takes all the blame on his own shoulders and gives the credit to the sergeants and the corporals."[5] Theater command, he told John (then a cadet at West Point), "is partly politics, partly public-speaking, partly essay-writing, partly social contact, onto all of which is tacked the business of training and disciplining an Army."[6]

It also meant shunning the appearance of ambition. He told Edgar that he disliked mention of his name as a "logical candidate for political office" because "I can think of nothing that could more definitely damage a soldier's effectiveness than to have people at home begin to believe he was interested in political preference."[7] "Some publicity is mandatory," he wrote, "otherwise American soldiers would not know they had an American commander interested in their welfare." The "500 newspaper and radio men accredited to this organization are my friends." But while they served his purposes at the time, "the vast majority of them will eventually turn upon a man who shows any indication of acting in his own self interest."[8]

This concern became an issue in early 1944 when four of Eisenhower's five brothers, Arthur, Earl, Edgar, and Milton, found themselves collaborating with a biographer. Milton, now president of Kansas State University, was their contact with the author, Kenneth S. Davis, a member of the faculty there.[9] The publisher was Doubleday. If they would relate their memories of the supreme commander's boyhood, Davis promised, he would not identify them. The general protested anyway.[10] Any biographer, he said, "naturally hopes to make a piece of change for himself."[11] But the project went ahead and ultimately received Eisenhower's approval. Davis interviewed him at Supreme Headquarters Allied Expeditionary Forces Europe [SHAEF] in May 1944.[12] When the book, *Soldier of Democracy*, was published in

1946, the general read it carefully, making notes in the margins. Davis had written that "what he [Eisenhower] did in the military sphere seemed so easily, almost casually, done that it was easily underrated."[13] The supreme commander jotted beside the passage: "If this is true, it is highest possible praise—all commanding officers should strive for it."[14]

But cooperating with a biographer was as far as he would move toward the personal spotlight. By placing too many restrictions on the project, he halted an effort by Samuel Goldwyn in July 1944 to make a movie about his life, this despite a script by the playwright Robert Sherwood that would be approved by the War Department.[15] Milton had agreed to serve as his brother's representative to the moviemakers, and Eisenhower had asked his former subordinate commanders in Europe for their cooperation. But he insisted that the movie "glorify democratic principles and methods" and tell how the European war was won by "an allied Anglo-American team devoted to common political concepts." Any proceeds, he said, would have to go to two foundations, the first to establish exchange scholarships between British colleges and an American university and the other to educate against racial discrimination. The project went no further.[16]

The postwar era began, it is possible to say, with the death of President Roosevelt on April 12, 1945. During the previous three years, Eisenhower had briefed the president several times, both at the White House and during summit conferences.[17] Now, suddenly, FDR's enormous presence was gone. That evening, April 12, in the occupied area of central Germany, Eisenhower returned with his generals, Omar Bradley and George S. Patton, from viewing the horrific Nazi death camps that their troops had liberated. Shaken by what they had seen, and now by the loss of their commander-in-chief, the three generals sat down together. Bradley confessed that he did not think Vice President Truman, the former senator from Missouri, qualified to "fill Roosevelt's big shoes." His fellow West Point graduates agreed.[18]

The most destructive war in human history—well over 55 million dead—was almost over. Hitler committed suicide on April 30. American nuclear explosions at Hiroshima and Nagasaki on August 6 and 9, 1945, and—in between—the Soviet declaration of war on Japan, brought Allied victory on August 14. Popular euphoria replaced the grim determination of the three years and eight months since Pearl Harbor. Everywhere soldiers, sailors, and civilians celebrated.

Eisenhower, as army chief of staff, discovered himself at the fulcrum of the problem of national security in a democracy—a form of government that is inherently distrustful of military power and militarism. He was among the professional soldiers who recalled a previous German surrender, in 1918. Peace, he realized, was considerably more difficult to achieve than war; but the stakes now, in an age of mass population bombings and nuclear weapons, were huge. He pointed to the lack of preparedness and a resulting weak diplomacy that had led to Japanese, Italian, and German aggression in the 1930s. Most Americans now, however, believed their security guaranteed by possession—an American monopoly, they called it—of the atomic bomb. American science and technology, they hoped, had made war and the need for standing armies obsolete.

Eisenhower knew better. Troops were necessary to defend or to occupy territory, and therefore to coerce or change governments or policy, which invariably was the purpose of war. The atomic bomb, even if enough of them existed (which they did not), was usable only in situations in which the United States felt justified in killing tens of thousands of noncombatants at once. In a democracy, he said, such a weapon was usable only to strike at "an enemy's heart and capacity" after tensions had reached such a level that war had broken out.[19] And there was no reason to believe that an atomic monopoly would last, that the United States would itself not be deterred from using it by fear of reprisals in kind. There was no such thing, after all, as "American science." While the Manhattan Project that produced the bomb was certainly American, the scientists who worked there had learned nuclear physics in their native countries—Hungary, Italy, and Germany. Indeed, the scientific theory that underlay their work, $e=mc^2$, was that of Albert Einstein, a Jewish refugee from Nazi Germany.[20]

The public reaction to the end of the war and to possession of the bomb, in other words, was for Eisenhower a call to action. He "would be unworthy of those who gave their lives to gain the victory," he said, "if I failed now to do everything in my power to protect it." World War II, he knew, resulted in large measure from a breakdown of international responsibility on the part of the great powers, including the United States. Even had it desired to stand tall against international lawlessness, the United States had lacked necessary strength and accompanying respect—whether from an army in being, or, like Switzerland, from a reserve of armed citizens produced by a system of universal military training. He reported to Congress in January 1946 that the Pentagon was discharging soldiers and sailors "as quickly as possible and to the limit of available shipping, with priority on those with the longest and hardest service." The "five millionth," he said, "had passed through one of the separation centers last week." This would mean that by July 1 the total of those released from active duty would number 7.75 million. Fourteen months later only 500,000 of the 8.3 million serving at the time of V-E day would remain. It would be, said Eisenhower, the "most rapid and broad scale demobilization in history." The problem, he said, was that American occupation responsibilities and its foreign policy obligations required an army of at least 1.5 million.[21]

He was alarmed by what he saw happening, Eisenhower told the congressmen and senators solemnly. For him the security of the United States was a matter of "personal trust." In the post–World War II era, as General Lucius D. Clay—Eisenhower's close friend since their service together in the Philippines in the late 1930s and his successor as military governor in West Germany—later recalled, Eisenhower had recommended ten divisions of Western occupation forces in 1946. "We wound up with one and a half."[22] Eisenhower voiced to friends his sense of "drifting back to unreadiness, which is very disheartening and uncalled for."[23]

As army chief of staff, Eisenhower was thus immersed in national security policy and, inexorably, politics. And while he believed that generals should mark carefully the constitutional subordination of military to civilian power, he also knew that retired generals could be qualified by personality and experience for civilian leadership positions. He commented to Hazlett, for example, that appointment of his former SHAEF chief of staff, Lieutenant General Walter Bedell Smith, as U.S. ambassador to Moscow was a blow to Smith because "his ambitions do not lie along diplomatic and political lines." Yet he added, "I know of no one better qualified for the job." As Eisenhower's personal representative, after all, Smith had negotiated the surrender of the Italian government in 1943 and participated in the surrender of the German army at Reims. As for himself, though aware of his new stature and his qualifications based on his experience of leadership, he characteristically buried in hyperbole any suggestion that he seek political office. He "could not imagine," he told Hazlett, "any set of circumstances that could ever drag out of me permission to consider me for any political post from Dog Catcher to Grand High Supreme King of the Universe."[24]

Nevertheless his outlook, it is now clear, was political. He was deeply concerned about the nation's postwar security and how it would be affected by military demobilization. In 1946, during an inspection trip to the Pacific, he visited MacArthur, now United Nations commander in the Far East, United States Far Eastern commander, and military governor of Japan. When he notified MacArthur's command that he was coming out for a visit, the Far Eastern general privately told a staff member that the new chief of staff was "up to no good. . . . Got the roar of the crowd in his ears, that boy. Can't sit still and do his job. Got to junket around." The professional courtesy (and West Point bonds), however, remained intact. The older general wrote to his former subordinate cordially that he "looked forward with greatest pleasure and anticipation to your visit."[25]

One must assume that during their visit, as they reminisced about the war just past (Eisenhower had admired MacArthur's campaigns in New Guinea and the Philippines) and the conversation drifted to policy and then to politics, the two men warmed to each other. According to records of their conversation, MacArthur reminded his former aide of the similarity between civil-military relations in 1946 and those they had encountered in the early 1930s, when the two of them, working together in the War Department, had tried "to save the remnants and nucleus of the services." He then admonished the army chief of staff in a fatherly way not to "let it get you down and don't worry about losing many of the skirmishes." As for presidential politics, MacArthur asked him—only half in jest—how his candidacy for the presidency was coming. Eisenhower replied that he was not a candidate. MacArthur responded with a hearty and mischievous, "That's fine. That's the best way to get it."[26] The joshing continued, each man urging the other to throw his hat in the ring. MacArthur said he was too old and that Eisenhower should run instead. MacArthur's biographer, Geoffrey Perret, concluded that both men "were fascinated by the idea of running for the Presidency, but neither was prepared to admit it to the other."[27]

Upon his return to Washington, Eisenhower revisited the purpose of his Far East trip by dictating a letter to his host in Tokyo. Accepting the dictum (attributed to Marshall) that a "responsible officer had the right (perhaps duty) to question a policy he considered wrong or mistaken and to discuss a proposal thoroughly," Eisenhower took issue with the path of American defense policy.[28] Political pressure groups bent upon getting their relatives out of the military, he told Mac-Arthur, had generated a kind of "hysteria." The chief of staff asked the Far Eastern commander for a letter that he might use in congressional testimony supporting the proposition that the army was figuring manpower requirements at a "bare minimum," and that "American prestige, best interests, and even safety in the Pacific depended upon military strength."[29] MacArthur, interestingly, failed to respond.[30]

President Truman, for his part, knew he needed help. Before Eisenhower had left for the Far East, Truman had asked him to visit General Marshall in China, to "feel him out" about the possibility of returning to the United States for a new assignment. The president wanted to replace James F. Byrnes as secretary of state and wanted to know, before making a formal request, whether Marshall would take the job. In China, Eisenhower discovered that his former boss was more than willing to meet with the president's wishes. Frustrated by his inability to stop the civil war, Marshall remarked that he would "do almost anything to get out of this place. I'd even enlist in the Army!"[31] Truman was enormously relieved. This gave him "a wonderful ace in the hole," he said. "I have been terribly worried."[32]

Sometime after Eisenhower's return, Truman again raised the issue he had mentioned in Potsdam. If Eisenhower would run on the Democratic ticket in 1948, the president would step aside . . . even take the vice presidency.[33] Eisenhower again declined.

What Truman did not know was that Eisenhower had become frustrated with and critical of American policy. His attitude appears in conversations with close friends. Even to MacArthur he wrote, revealingly, that he "would be truly happy if I could get completely out of official life so that, without inhibition or the restraint of governmental policy, I could really shout from the housetops what we are doing to ourselves in the international world and in the occupied areas."[34]

☆ **3** ☆

COLD WAR

AS WORLD WAR II ENDED, Eisenhower was hopeful about relations with the Soviet Union. Stalin had cooperated with the Western allies against the *Wehrmacht*—notably on D-day, keeping the German high command distracted by launching an offensive in the east. Field Marshal Georgi Zhukov, the hero of the eastern front, was Eisenhower's Russian counterpart and had been the American supreme commander's host at the victory celebration and sports parade at the Kremlin in August 1945.[1] (Photographers recorded Eisenhower standing next to Stalin viewing the parade from atop Lenin's tomb in Red Square.) "Warm personal friendships between officers of different nations," Eisenhower later said, "is one thing that offers some hope for the future." Eisenhower sent Zhukov a letter introducing his former chief of staff, Bedell Smith, as the postwar U.S. ambassador to the Soviet Union. Zhukov responded with a large trove of gifts, including a polar bear rug.[2] The American general thought that good relations could continue. Alas, Stalin soon transferred Zhukov to the Soviet provinces, away from contact with Eisenhower and for that matter, any other Westerner.

General Clay too recalled the initial harmony with the Russians. But at the beginning of 1946, he noted, the Soviets began "tearing their zone to pieces for reparations without reaching any agreements for the dividing of these reparations among the nations," and became "uncooperative in Berlin."[3] They failed to keep their promise to withdraw their troops from northern Iran, and that summer directed a troop buildup and diplomatic campaign to gain concessions from Turkey. As the historian Eduard Mark has shown, this initiative toward Turkey resulted in "Anglo-American agreements on how to fight World War III, the earliest plans for a strategic air offensive against the USSR, and the first efforts at covert paramilitary operations in the Balkans."[4]

The growing split with the former Soviet ally became obvious in early March 1946 to Western intelligence agencies. They estimated that in three months the Soviet armed forces, even after demobilizing 9 million men, would still total between 4.5 and 4.8 million.[5] In response to a request from the secretary of state for an appraisal of Soviet pressures on Turkey, the joint chiefs of staff replied that the Soviet Union desired to "dominate the Middle East and eastern Mediterranean." The Communist purpose, they said, was to impede communications between Great Britain and its possessions in the Far East and threaten the sources of oil—threatening the disintegration of the British empire, the "last bulwark of resistance between the United States and Soviet expansion." Soviet pressures on Turkey, in other words, might tip the balance of world power.[6] The situation seemed more perilous in the months that followed because of a Communist-led insurgency in the mountains of Greece.

On March 12, 1947, Truman—drawing upon the thinking of the State Department's Soviet expert, George F. Kennan, who urged Western "countermeasures short of war" to prevent Soviet territorial expansion, and responding to Britain's decision to withdraw its forces from Greece and the Mediterranean for financial reasons—issued his so-called Truman Doctrine in a speech to Congress. Truman's immediate need was $400 million from Congress for aid to Greece and Turkey—to replace British power in the eastern Mediterranean. But he also hoped to rally the American people and their representatives in Congress to the need for an active role in the postwar world—at a time when Republicans controlled the Eightieth Congress and, under the leadership of Senator Robert A. Taft, sought to cut spending for foreign aid. Truman's speech divided the world into two camps, the slave and the free, and declared that it would be the policy of the

United States to go anywhere in the world to assist countries being threatened by Communist expansion. The following month, at a conference of foreign ministers in Moscow, Secretary of State Marshall became convinced that Stalin had stopped cooperating. Soviet-American relations were now best described, in the words of one journalist, as cold war.[7]

Before the announcement of the Truman Doctrine, Eisenhower had begun considering ways to support the nation's interests abroad and at the same time prevent war. Recalling his frustration with American demobilization, isolationism, and national impotence following World War I, and feeling a special responsibility as supreme commander of the Allied forces that had defeated Mussolini's Italy and Hitler's Germany, he had become critical of both Congress and Truman. In fact Truman agreed with Marshall's and Eisenhower's assessment of the problem of national security, and Eisenhower knew it. But all too often after 1945 the administration's national security proposals went down to defeat in Congress. The problem, he decided, was lack of leadership—the "state of confusion, doubt, and hazard following upon global war." No one seems to have a "sane, comprehensive program behind which one people as a whole can get together," he told his son.[8] National strength, he insisted, required "a peacetime military doctrine and a strong, consistent foreign policy."[9]

One high-ranking German general, Bodo Zimmermann, in postwar testimony, had pointed to what he believed was the single most important reason for German defeat. The unitary command of Allied forces in the west, he said, enabled the Americans, British, Canadians, Poles, and French and all three branches of their services to act as a team.[10] No one knew this truth better than the man who had directed that team. If ever he had "the energy to do any crusading after this war is over," Eisenhower had said in May 1944, "I am going to recommend the abolition of several of the combat branches as we now know them in favor of an overall divisional combat organization." The "traditional differences in the training of combat officers of the various arms [land, sea, and air]," Eisenhower told his son, "are going to disappear."[11] With the war over—despite demands by Congress and the American public for demobilization and budget reductions, and by the armed services for a return to the old system of separate arms—Eisenhower worked to obtain a unified defense establishment with a broad annual program for the three services.[12] On November 16, 1945, he testified to that aim at a hearing of the Military Affairs Committee of the United States Senate. "As a soldier to whom was entrusted the command of the greatest combined force ever brought to bear against an enemy . . . and as one who has experienced (with my thousands of comrades in arms) the successful conclusion of a great enterprise based on unity of command," he said he could "not perceive the logic behind the objections which are voiced against the proposal before you."[13] Eisenhower's ideas, though in modified fashion, became part of the deliberations that led to the Department of Defense.

Even more important for national strength than unification of the services, he believed, was a sense among the people of citizenship and an accompanying willingness to sacrifice for one's country. American weakness, he had seen, had led to defeat by Rommel at the Kasserine Pass in North Africa. As supreme commander he had had to get rid of the lazy, slothful, indifferent, or complacent. "Get rid of them if you have to write letters the rest of your life," he had told his subordinate commanders.[14] The army's foremost intellectual, General John McAuley Palmer, after World War I had proposed an idea, obtained from his study of the Swiss system of citizen soldiers, that Eisenhower felt would have prevented such a fiasco. His proposal was universal military training (UMT) in which every eighteen-year-old male would undergo six months of military training and then return home, renewing his skills during summer training in subsequent years. Such a program, Marshall agreed, would create with relatively low cost a ready reserve force of 600,000 to 700,000 to supplement the expensive full-time standing army of 886,000 and go far toward "the free, independent, and interested actions of individual citizens that would be the foundation of national strength."[15] A deterrent to potential aggressors, it would be the "keystone in the arch of our national security and international responsibility."[16] Truman, after a valiant effort beginning in 1945 to obtain passage of UMT, in the spring of 1948 finally gave it up.

Critics of UMT in Congress, influenced by exhortations that ranged from Senator Robert A. Taft on the right to leaders of organized labor such as Walter Reuther on the left, preferred selective service and, if necessary, reliance on American air power.[17]

But Eisenhower continued to work on the problem and arrived at what he felt was the best solution, given international and domestic realities. During the war, Harvard University president James B. Conant had been chairman of the scientific committee, the National Defense Research Council, that oversaw the Manhattan Project. In October 1946 the respected scientist wrote and distributed a secret study entitled "The Atomic Age."[18] The "greatest assurance for postponing a 'superblitz' [surprise attack] by Russia after she has made one bomb," he concluded, would be the "certain knowledge on her part that she would take on the whole western world once the attack began." In addition to an international consensus that would make any nation that used the bomb an outcast, Conant's study advocated retention by the United States of its own nuclear arsenal. No one in American government was advocating that it do so, but Conant's article nonetheless asserted that the Soviet nuclear potential required that the United States not unilaterally dismantle its own nuclear arsenal. Eisenhower agreed. In the next war, he believed, the United States would itself be vulnerable to devastating attack. It therefore had to anticipate a time when the Soviet Union had a sufficient number of atomic bombs to launch a surprise attack.[19] For the United States, relinquishing the atomic bomb without gaining anything in return would be giving away the ability to balance Soviet "strategic strength."[20] To address the possibility of surprise attack, Eisenhower also recommended "mutual disarmament," with free inspection and verification, and called together a group of Pentagon planners—the so-called superblitz group—to design ways of ensuring "ourselves against future surprise."[21]

What Eisenhower found especially appealing about Conant's article was not its advocacy of nuclear weapons but its implied recommendation for U.S. support in the rebuilding of western Europe. "It is vital," he told Bedell Smith, "that we decide upon the general plan we must follow but that we determine also the areas in which we can concentrate most advantageously."[22] He was talking about economic aid and political support "before the development of a crisis." "Fore-handed action," he told the joint chiefs, "would be both less costly and more likely to insure international stability."[23] He was not alarmed. Indeed, he disliked the stark tones of the president's Truman Doctrine speech. "Study, patience, open-mindedness and at least a modicum of optimism," he said, "are necessary in these conflicting times."[24] The Soviet Union, Eisenhower believed, posed a short-term danger because of its willingness to use "political pressure and subversive tactics" in places such as Greece and Turkey.[25] But if it stood "before the world as friends of all people who really long for freedom," the United States had the advantage, because in the long term the truly subversive force in the world was the desire of people to be free of domination.[26] He supported the Marshall Plan and U.S. aid for European economic recovery, the European Recovery Program (ERP). His particular focus was on France and Italy, where the Communists were the strongest political parties. "No use to save Greece and Turkey," he said, "if these two should go."[27]

In the few moments of reflection available to him in 1946 and early 1947, Eisenhower thought about retirement—perhaps to a small college where he could reminisce, write his memoirs, and teach. The position he decided to accept in the spring of 1947 bore small resemblance to those reflections. In February he and Marshall both received honorary degrees from Columbia University. In the weeks that followed, Thomas J. Watson of IBM, the Columbia trustee who was heading the search for someone to replace the retiring Nicholas Murray Butler as president of this Ivy League university located in upper Manhattan, approached Ike. The general hesitated but Watson persisted, and on June 14 the fifty-seven-year-old army chief of staff, having talked it over with the president, accepted his first nonmilitary position.[28] Truman concurred in Watson's conviction that the position would enable Eisenhower to "render a worthwhile public service."

Some of his friends were puzzled, but they should not have been. No small college had made an offer. More important, Columbia,

Eisenhower had come to realize, would give him a better chance to maintain his contacts in Washington and a better forum from which to speak out on issues of public concern. "People began to insist," he later recalled, "that it was my duty to undertake the job." These efforts "finally descended on me in such intensity and [were] backed by so much pressure," he told Bedell Smith, "that I had to give a 'Yes' or 'No'."[29] "World order," he told his friend, Hazlett, "can be established only by the practice of true cooperation among sovereign nations." He did not "look upon the Columbia detail as any final severance of my connection with the Army," he assured air force chief of staff General Hap Arnold. "Going to Columbia is merely to change the location of my headquarters" and "the method by which I will continue to strive for the same goals . . . merely a flank position from which to support our security efforts conducted from Washington."[30]

Eisenhower knew that, by law, army officers with the rank of general of the army could not retire. Although he would be officially a civilian, the president still could call on him (and other five-star generals and admirals, including Marshall and MacArthur) for assistance on matters affecting the national security. He was a public servant without portfolio. (Acknowledging this, he took with him to Columbia his military aide, Colonel Robert L. Schulz, his Pentagon speechwriter, Kevin McCann, and his personal valets, Sergeants Moaney and Dry.)[31] He elaborated his view of his new situation on October 12, 1948, in his inaugural address as president of Columbia. Rather than a "weapon of tyranny or aggression," he said, the military profession "in our nation, is the servant of the people, designed and trained exclusively to protect our way of life. Duty in its ranks is an exercise of citizenship. Hence, among us, the soldier who becomes an educator or the teacher who becomes a soldier enters no foreign field but finds himself instead engaged in a new phase of his fundamental life purpose—the protection and perpetuation of basic human freedoms."[32]

Eisenhower left active military duty on February 7, 1948. He used earned leave from that date until June to write his war memoir. William F. Robinson, vice president of the nation's largest and most influential Republican newspaper, the *New York Herald Tribune*, smoothed the way for the publication of Eisenhower's war memoirs. This involved, first, overcoming the famous general's scruples about profiting from his military service by telling him that too many erroneous stories were in print about how the allies had defeated Hitler. He had an obligation to "set the record straight." Eisenhower worried that having a literary agent would "put him in the position of wanting to sell something," though he admitted that he faced "the necessity of making something out of such a venture, if I should decide to resign from the Army [and therefore lose his regular pay check] in order to publish it." At the urging of Robinson, he contacted several publishers and wrote an outline.[33] Publicity for a book, Robinson knew, would put the general's name and photograph in full-page ads and on the sides of newspaper delivery trucks in every large city.[34] And there was the possibility that the book would catch on, sell a great many copies, and make its author a literary figure. A contract with a publisher would also provide Eisenhower with a substantial sum of money in advance.

The details of publication were worked out by Robinson, Milton Eisenhower, New York attorney Edwin Clark, and another friend of Ike's, Joseph Davies, a prewar ambassador to the Soviet Union, now a wealthy Washington attorney. Together, they found a publisher, Doubleday, and drafted a contract. Davies arranged with the Internal Revenue Service to count the author's royalties as capital gains rather than income. Robinson persuaded Doubleday publisher Douglas Black and Helen Reid, publisher of the *Herald Tribune* (which would have syndication rights), together to pay Eisenhower the largest advance ever paid for a book, $635,000. Combined with his army pension of $15,000 a year and, later, his salary from Columbia University of $25,000, this sum with wise investments would enable Eisenhower to become a moderately wealthy individual.[35] For three months during his "terminal leave in quarters," and with the help of a clerical and research staff, he dictated and edited copy furiously. *Crusade in Europe* was published in the autumn of 1948 and soon had met all of Robinson's expectations, selling in the hundreds of thousands (later millions) of copies. Praised by reviewers and translated into several foreign languages, it remains in print today. Taking leave from his military duties was a simple but not an easy thing to do. When the book, *Crusade in Europe*, was finished and it came time to leave the chief of staff's residence at Fort Myer, Virginia, Quarters #1, "Ike, clad in a battle jacket, stepped from the quarters, as an army band sounded a salute and a small detachment of troops snapped to attention. A soldier stepped forward and presented Mamie with a large bouquet of yellow roses. Old friends and acquaintances were standing on the lawn. Mamie and Ike said goodbye and waved. People lined the route all the way to the gates of the Fort Myer military installation."[36]

He relished his new life in New York. Proceeds from the sale of the book brought him financial independence. After he and Mamie moved into the Columbia University president's mansion at 60 Morningside Drive in Manhattan, he insisted on more time for recreation. Constant decisions involving life and death and, ultimately, the fate of nations had taken their toll. Without time away from the job he sensed he would not survive emotionally, and perhaps not physically. So he scheduled golf, fishing, and hunting into his routine. On Monday evenings he played bridge with friends at home.[37] He took up oil painting. And he accepted invitations to go hunting or fishing.[38]

Yet before long, and little by little, international tensions and the demands of Columbia once again made his stress almost unbearable. Within days of their arrival at the renovated four-story Columbia University presidential mansion, Ike and Mamie discovered how little time they had to themselves. The university, with a resident student body of 27,000, employed 8,200 faculty and 3,000 staff.[39] Mamie found herself organizing teas and dinners for university officials, faculty, and donors. She accepted the honorary chairmanship of a concert to benefit the Manhattanville Neighborhood Center, an activity that brought her into contact with new friends, including W. Alton "Pete" Jones, president of Cities Service Oil; William S. Paley, president of CBS; and Arthur Hays Sulzberger, publisher of the *New York Times*.[40]

Eisenhower's activities now brought him in contact with the elite of the American business and financial community, some of whom (as he already knew) were members of the Columbia board of trustees.

McCann recalled that the general "made more friends at Columbia in two and a half years than he had made in all his life until that time." Not long after his arrival, for example, Eisenhower found himself the guest of Winthrop W. Aldrich, chairman of the board of the Chase National Bank (later the Chase Manhattan), at a special meeting of the bank's board of directors, in conjunction with a white-tie dinner for the New York Chamber of Commerce.

The son of Republican Senator Nelson Aldrich of Rhode Island, who had served in the United States Senate from 1881 to 1911, Winthrop was born in 1885 in Providence. He grew up surrounded by privilege and influence, learning at an early age, in the waters of Narragansett Bay, his lifetime hobby of yachting. He attended Harvard and Harvard Law School and, because of family and marital connections, soon found that his wealth and influence had increased substantially. His elder sister, Abby, married John D. Rockefeller, Jr., the son and namesake of the nation's richest individual; Winthrop married Harriet Alexander, the daughter of Charles B. Alexander, a prominent lawyer and trustee of Princeton University, and Harriet Crocker, daughter of San Francisco railroad and banking magnate Charles Crocker.[41] Aldrich had served as a naval officer in World War I and, upon returning to New York, at the suggestion of Rockefeller, joined Murray, Prentice & Howland, a law firm whose principal clients were the Rockefeller corporate and family interests, notably the Equitable Trust Company. Aldrich soon became personal adviser to Rockefeller, helping establish Colonial Williamsburg, Rockefeller Center, and the Rockefeller Foundation. In 1929 he became president of the Equitable Trust Company. After it merged with the world's largest bank, the Chase National, with deposits of $2 billion, fifty branches, and control of the American Express Company (with thirty-four domestic and sixty-six overseas branches), Aldrich became president of the new corporation as well.[42]

By the time Eisenhower arrived at Columbia, Aldrich was chairman of the board at the Chase and an outspoken critic of the New Deal. But, interestingly, he was also chairman of President Truman's Advisory Committee for Financing Foreign Trade, chairman of the

Committee on International Economic Policy, a member of the National Advisory Council, and a member of the executive committee of
the Citizens' Committee for the Marshall Plan. In these advisory positions he served with Paul G. Hoffman, former president of the Studebaker Corporation and later administrator of the Marshall Plan for
European economic recovery. As the founder and chairman of the
American Heritage Foundation, Aldrich persuaded Eisenhower to
join the board of that organization.[43]

In the months following his arrival at Columbia, Eisenhower also
became an honorary member of the prestigious Bohemian Club in
San Francisco. Its members included corporate chief executives, writers, and politicians, including former president Herbert Hoover.[44]
Eisenhower attended its annual encampment at Bohemian Grove
among the redwood trees in northern California in 1950 and, in the
words of one member who was there, made "a tremendous impression."[45]

Eisenhower's most important initiative at Columbia, drawing
upon support from his new acquaintances and friends, was the American Assembly, a forum whose purpose was to create a better-informed
and more productive public debate. At weekend conferences held
once a year, representatives from business, finance, government,
labor, the professions, and academia discussed questions such as how
to "determine the dividing line between the responsibilities and rights
of the individual, on the one hand, and the necessary controls of the
central government, on the other."[46] Assembly staff published tran-
scripts and summaries of the conferences and made them available to
the public. Eisenhower persuaded his wartime acquaintance and
longtime Columbia benefactor, Averell Harriman, to allow the use of
his Hudson River estate, Arden House, as the conference center. With
help from Wall Street investment bankers William Burnham and Cliff
Roberts, Eisenhower secured numerous individual donations. These
included, among others, L. F. "Mc" McCollum of the Continental
Oil Company of Houston, and Harry Bullis, chairman of the board of
the General Mills Corporation of Minneapolis.[47]

A good many of Eisenhower's activities, not surprisingly, reflected events on the international scene. Among his colleagues in the Association of University Presidents were Brown University president Henry Wriston (also the president of the Manhattan-based Council on Foreign Relations) and Harvard University president Conant. At Paul Hoffman's request, in late 1948 the Council on Foreign Relations, with funding from the Rockefeller and Ford foundations, established a study group on the economic and political effects of the European Recovery Program which included some of the more prominent public thinkers of the era. Among them were Allen W. Dulles, Edward Mead Earle, George S. Franklin, Walter H. Mallory, Stacy May, Isidor Rabi, Graeme Howard, R. C. Leffingwell, Jacob Viner, John H. Williams, and Tracy Voorhees. Eisenhower agreed to be its chairman. By the end of 1950 the general also asked George F. Kennan and Richard Bissel, who had just returned from being Hoffman's deputy in Europe, to join.[48] In his initial letter to members, Eisenhower noted that the purpose of the study group was to "inform the American people" of the progress of the Marshall Plan, which he characterized as a program "in the foreign field without parallel in our peacetime history."[49] The group's first report argued that European recovery required, first of all, a stable flow of exports from Europe to the United States. In the first half of 1949, it noted, U.S. imports had fallen by 14 percent as a result of economic recession at home. Exports from Great Britain, France, and Italy, however, had fallen 23 percent, 28 percent, and 31 percent respectively.[50] After the North Atlantic Treaty Organization was established in the spring of 1949, the group discussed possible alternatives to the Marshall Plan. One side, led by former army undersecretary Voorhees, argued for conversion of the Marshall Plan's assistance to purely military aid. The other side, with staff member William S. Dieboldt, Jr., as spokesman, recommended continuing the existing program. By the end of 1950 the committee proposed using NATO as the basis for the political unification of western Europe and German rearmament.[51]

Yet another influential figure in American foreign relations called on the Eisenhowers not long after they moved to New York. Henry Robinson Luce, publisher of *Time* and *Life* magazines, was the son of missionaries and had spent his childhood in China. He attended Yale, with time off to serve as a second lieutenant in World War I. Luce understood the power of public opinion as well as any individual of his generation. He and a Yale classmate, Briton Hadden, founded America's first national news magazine, *Time*. After its success he founded *Life*, a pictorial news magazine, and *Fortune*, a magazine about business and the American economy. Like Aldrich, Luce had watched from the sidelines during the 1930s as economic disintegration, social chaos, and isolationism led to fascist tyranny and aggression overseas. Luce determined to do everything in his power in the postwar era to prevent the United States from again being helpless on the world stage. After 1945 his magazines urged economic and, where necessary, military aid to friendly, including anti-Communist, governments. His special interest was Chiang Kai-shek's Nationalist regime in China.

A lifelong Republican, Luce articulated a program that sought to explain past disasters and avoid future ones. By 1948 the problems facing the nation, Luce advised, stemmed from the policies of Franklin Roosevelt and his successor. Nothing good could be accomplished until the Republican party again occupied the presidency. In 1940, Luce and his editor at *Fortune*, Russell Davenport, helped orchestrate the campaign by which Wendell Willkie won the GOP nomination; they also supported Thomas E. Dewey in 1944 and again in 1948.

With Dewey's defeat, the publisher once again set out to find a candidate. Party regulars favored Robert A. Taft, but Luce concluded that the senator from Ohio had not learned the lessons of the 1930s and reminded him too much of a bespectacled, balding college professor. Luce believed such a candidate could not win. At the urging of one of his vice presidents, the managing director of Time-Life International, C. D. Jackson, Luce decided to meet the famous general.[52]

By this time Eisenhower—with help from a New York attorney, West Point graduate, and former deputy chief of staff for supply at SHAEF, Brigadier General Edwin Norman Clark—had established still another innovative program at Columbia. "No American university has undertaken the continuous study of the causes, conduct, and consequences of war—the greatest ill to which our civilization is heir," said Eisenhower. This failing, he remarked, was "almost incomprehensible." In his March 1950 Gabriel Silver Lecture for International Peace, Eisenhower admonished his audience to study war as a tragic social phenomenon. The public needed to understand "war's origins, its conduct, its impact and particularly its disastrous consequences upon man's spiritual, intellectual and material progress."[53] After receiving the support of the Columbia history faculty, he authorized Clark to begin discussions, ultimately successful, with officials of the American Military Institute, a private, nonprofit organization and publisher of the scholarly journal *Military Affairs*. His objective was to bring the AMI to Columbia. The proposed institute was to have an endowed chair, and among the potential donors Clark contacted was Henry Luce.[54] Thus Clark invited the publisher to join the institute's board of governors and arranged for him to have lunch with Eisenhower.[55] Before the arrangements for the institute were completed in the summer of 1950, Clark would confer with Luce at least three more times.[56]

Columbia University opened its Institute for War and Peace Studies in late December 1951. Under the leadership of its director, Professor William T. R. Fox (whom Eisenhower had hired away from Yale's Institute of International Studies), the institute proposed to investigate "the function of war as a 'method of protecting values considered even more precious than the values which war places in jeopardy'" and "attempt to find 'less costly ways of protecting those things for which we are willing to fight.'"[57] Its consultants included Professor Frederick S. Dunn, director of the Center for International Studies at Princeton University; Professor Edward Mead Earle, director of the Institute of Advanced Study at Princeton; George F. Kennan, (now also affiliated with the Institute for Advanced Study); and Pendleton Herring, author of the book *The Impact of War* and president of the Social Sciences Research Council. The twenty-seven-member board of governors ultimately included Luce, Clark, General Clay, Douglas Southall Freeman, the columnist Walter Lippman, Walter Reuther, and David Sarnoff, president of NBC.[58]

In 1948 the global situation appeared to worsen. The joint chiefs of

staff, in their efforts to gauge Soviet capabilities, had discovered in
1948 that the Red Army had a ground force of 2.5 million in 175 divisions. While less than an earlier estimate of 4.5 million, this force was
formidable because of the Soviets' capacity, learned from hard lessons
in two world wars, quickly to mobilize their reserves. Not only did the
Soviet Union have some 10 million combat veterans, they also continued to induct 750,000 men annually into the armed forces and to
release a similar number into the reserves (a Soviet UMT). Consequently they would be able, within thirty days after an outbreak of hostilities, to field an additional 145 ready divisions for a total of 320, with
another 25 divisions in basic training. Western intelligence agencies
put Soviet ground force strength thirty days after mobilization at 8 million men, well equipped.[59] The Soviets had stored rather than
destroyed weapons produced or captured during World War II, and
by 1948 were producing 1,000 to 2,000 planes a month. This would
enable them within six months of mobilization to employ 20,000
combat planes. In November 1948 the Anglo-American Joint Intelligence Committee estimated that, with their supplies of artillery, self-
propelled guns, and at least 28,000 tanks (over 7,000 of them in
Eastern Europe), 175 Red Army divisions would be at full strength
within five days after mobilization, with an additional 145 at full
strength twenty-five days later. The joint chiefs had no doubt that the
Soviets could send 50 divisions into Western Europe very quickly, followed shortly by 50 more.[60]

Thus it was not surprising that no sooner had Eisenhower settled
in at Columbia than he turned his attention once again to activities in
Washington in response to alarms from Europe. Just before passage of
the Marshall Plan in early March 1948, he had advocated a Western
European economic union and a political accord based upon establishment of a "Consultative Combined Chiefs of staff to study common defense problems."[61] At about the same time, on March 5,
General Clay cabled from West Berlin that for the first time he felt
"war was possible and that it might come with dramatic suddenness."[62]
Three months later the Soviet Union — as part of a stiffening of its position throughout Eastern Europe and in specific response to the cre-

ation by the Western occupation governments of a single currency in the Western zone—blocked western ground access routes to Berlin. By early autumn Eisenhower feared that the Russians were "so sure of themselves" that they might push the rest of the world beyond endurance. "The time," he said, "is clearly here to reduce our planning to concrete problems and to be ready to act on a week to week basis."[63] In November he sent a message to the new Secretary of Defense, James Forrestal: he could "scarcely think of any chore that I would refuse to do wherever people in responsible positions feel that I might be able to help."[64]

In January 1949, Forrestal accepted his offer. Truman officially requested that Eisenhower come to Washington to preside at meetings of the joint chiefs of staff. The former supreme commander's vision, energy, and prestige, he said, were needed to get the services to stop squabbling and agree on a strategic concept. Eisenhower began spending two days each week at the Pentagon. It was the beginning of a difficult time.

☆ **4** ☆

THE
FINDER
LETTER

WHILE WELL-WISHERS AND POLITICIANS—including President Truman and General MacArthur—had ideas about whether Eisenhower was running or should run for the presidency after his appointment as army chief of staff, he did his best to avoid public comment. His appointment as commander of the European theater of war in early 1942 had come as a result of General Marshall's appraisal of his enormous abilities. He had performed consistently well and almost always impressed his superiors. Considering the lack of opportunity in a peacetime army for promotion to rank above lieutenant colonel or direct command of troops, this strong performance demonstrated character. He thought it possible, especially after fighting broke out in Asia and Europe, that if he handled himself well he might sometime reach higher rank or a combat command. But this ambition was never overweaning. His upbringing in a small Kansas community emphasized the importance of humility and team play; the importance of cooperation and hard work as necessary for a family's sustenance and harmony. And he learned on the baseball diamond and football field the importance of common effort as essential to success against the opponent.[1] Lack of humility was something he deplored in MacArthur, whom he said "had a proclivity for the vertical pronoun." In *Crusade in Europe* he revealed the qualities that were his ideal. Appointment as European theater commander, he recalled, gave him feelings of considerable pride, "what any soldier would have wanted." But "the weight of responsibility involved was so great as to obliterate any thought of personal elation and so critical as to compel complete absorption in the job at hand."[2] As army chief of staff he considered both unseemly and inappropriate any actions on his part to put himself forward as a candidate for the presidency.

As early as December 1946 a story appeared in the *Washington Times Herald* that Eisenhower had informed friends he was "ready to run for President in 1948 if the people wanted him." To counter the report, members of his staff, including generals J. Lawton Collins, Alexander Surles, Floyd Parks, Wilton Persons, and Lieutenant Colonel James Stack, drafted a news release. "This sort of talk," it read, "is most harmful to the army and to me as Chief of Staff of the Army. . . . I have completely divorced myself from national and local politics and I shall continue to do so. I do not desire nor will I seek any public office. I have not, nor will I in the future, authorize anyone to promote my name for public office. All of my time," he said, "will be devoted to the establishment of a sound national security."[3]

The release went out but the speculation continued; and it is now clear that it was justified. An article written by Professor Charles Toth in the spring of 1952 asserted that the "starting point" of Eisenhower's candidacy was October 12, 1948, "the date upon which General Eisenhower officially assumed his duties as president of Columbia University and upon which date he became a private citizen in the eyes of the public." Eisenhower's characteristic way of thinking and acting, he said, was to maximize his flexibility. "It seems clear from the record that Eisenhower did not know whether he wished to stand for election until late 1951 or 1952."[4]

While it is difficult to pinpoint a date when Eisenhower's candidacy began—indeed, one must begin by defining "candidacy"—materials available at the Eisenhower Library confirm this appraisal. For example, in the midst of one furor about a possible candidacy, which continued into the early autumn of 1947, he wrote a letter marked "personal and confidential" to Bedell Smith in Moscow. It spoke of the history of presidential drafts.[5] "So-called 'drafts,'" Eisenhower said, "at least since Washington's time, have been carefully nurtured, with the full, even though under cover, support of the 'victim.'" He had no "immediate plans" to give such support, but declaring a year in advance of such a faint possibility that even under such an "unmistakable call" he would not run [in the nominating conventions of 1948] would be the same thing "as a soldier refusing to go forward with his unit." "Few people outside the armed services and the higher echelons of the State Department," he said, "are giving their full attention to American interests as a whole and refusing to color their conclusions and convictions with the interests of party politicians." What circumstances, he asked, could cause him to believe it was a duty to run for public office? A deadlocked convention would not. But he could not refuse "being named by common consent."[6]

Eisenhower had come to believe by late 1947 that a decline of American world influence stemmed from demobilization and from Truman's inability to persuade Congress of the value of military strength and consistent public resolve. The Soviet Union, while intent on expanding its influence, would not, he believed—if the United States played its cards properly—launch a military attack. It would look for opportunities to take advantage of American weakness.[7]

Having been out of the White House since 1933, the Republicans were seeking a presidential candidate for 1948, and Eisenhower's stature as a war hero made him an obvious choice. Except for the president, he was perhaps the most sought-after figure in American public life. Between June 1, 1945, and December 31, 1948, he gave some 124 formal addresses. His message invariably was of peace, freedom, patriotism, duty, teamwork, unity, and the common good. He especially emphasized cooperation. "Allied unity and cooperation had won the war; the same qualities were necessary to keep the peace."[8] In the words of one historian, for Eisenhower the American constitutional republic was the superstructure that allowed for human freedom— moral, ethical, political, religious, and economic. The perpetuation of that superstructure, not just of an American army or industrial capacity, was his mission. This entailed defending the nation from armed attack as well as internal subversion "through paternalistic [government] destruction of individual enterprise and initiative or weakening of the social bonds of family, school, church, and neighborhood."[9] In retrospect it is clear that for Eisenhower, national security was inseparable from a sense of community and cooperation for the common good, the basis for a sound economy and a strong foreign policy. The threats he saw to these values stirred in him a sense of responsibility and, with the growth of an apparently spontaneous effort to promote his candidacy for the presidency, of ambition as well.

Eisenhower had recorded in his diary in July 1947 that "a number of scattered people—some friends, some strangers—continue to argue that I should get into the political field, at least to the extent of making myself 'available' for a presidential nomination."[10] In September, Bedell Smith wrote that a mutual friend had told him that if Dewey were not nominated in the first few ballots at the 1948 Republican convention, the delegates probably would put forward Eisenhower's name, and it would "sweep the convention." Smith applauded such a possibility. The "international picture," he said, was "discouraging," with the Kremlin exerting its influence in Greece and northern Iran and "banking heavily" on an economic collapse in the United States in 1948.[11]

The following month William E. Robinson came to see Eisenhower in his office at the Pentagon. Robinson had met the general first in France in late December 1944, during the war. After the liberation of Paris he had come to SHAEF to request permission to resume publication of the Paris edition of the *Tribune*. His conversation with the supreme commander so impressed Robinson that he decided to work through the *Herald Tribune* syndicate and its contacts throughout the United States toward what he called a "leadership position for Eisenhower."[12]

Reintroducing himself to the general in October 1947 was the first step in Robinson's self-assigned task. As it turned out, this was a fateful meeting. The newspaper executive later recalled that Eisenhower was "a little appalled at what now seemed to be the terrible demands upon his time" of being president of Columbia University. In the ninety minutes they talked, neither man referred to the possibility of a run by the general for the presidency. "The whole subject," Robinson wrote, "is distasteful to him. It is apparent that he will not move a finger to promote himself for the nomination." Nevertheless Eisenhower was "completely free, unguarded to the point even of indiscretion . . . natural, alive, alert, spirited, and gave the impression of having an intense amount of unloosened energy." Above all, Robinson concluded, Eisenhower "desired to be helpful to the country . . . he loves."[13] If one of the major political parties could demonstrate a preponderance of opinion in his favor, Robinson wrote in his memorandum of the meeting, Eisenhower "would accept the nomination, and make a vigorous and strong campaign."[14]

Robinson began "quietly and behind the scenes"—but persistently—to keep the former supreme commander's name in the public eye.[15] Eisenhower's efforts to dampen the political fires, evidenced by the purposes driving Robinson and the others who helped see his book *Crusade* into print, thus seemed destined to fail. "I'd like to see you in the White House," Hazlett had written again in October 1947. "I'm convinced no one else could offer the same leadership, common sense, and sanity."[16] The general replied that he could not conceive of "any set of circumstances that would ever convince me that it was my duty to enter such a hectic arena." "Without artificial stimulus," he said (in retrospect revealingly), "all these 'boomlets' for particular individuals sooner or later collapse."[17]

An article appeared in *Life* magazine implying that he might be a political "stalking horse" for General MacArthur.[18] Despite the distance between Tokyo and Washington, D.C., MacArthur had not been able to restrain his partisan self, and as the 1948 presidential campaign approached, had written to a friend about his political interests. He "certainly," he said, did not "covet or actively seek any other office, but should the movement become more expressive of the desire of good and loyal friends and well-wishers, and take on the character of popular will, I should be left no alternative but to consider it a mandate which I could not in good conscience ignore."[19] Leaders and potential candidates on both sides of the partisan divide now desired to know Eisenhower's intentions; so in January 1948 he used the occasion of a New Hampshire newspaper editorial urging him to run to give a carefully worded public reply. His so-called Finder letter was a way of responding to a possible MacArthur candidacy and, while keeping his future options open, to bow out of the 1948 race.

Eisenhower had met Leonard Finder, publisher of the *Manchester Union* and *Evening Leader*, in October 1947. At the publisher's invitation he had participated in the Manchester Community Forum, a speakers' series that included such prominent individuals as Joseph E. Grew, former ambassador to Japan; David Lilienthal, Atomic Energy Commission chairman; General Carl Spaatz of the air force; Minnesota governor Harold Stassen; and Franklin D. Roosevelt, Jr.[20] Like Robinson, Finder had become intrigued by Eisenhower's presidential possibilities and had organized a citizens' movement to draft him for the presidency.[21] On January 12, 1948, he had sent Eisenhower a clipping of a front-page editorial from the *Evening Leader* endorsing him for president. "While we appreciate that you are not for political aspirations," Finder had written, "we are equally confident that you will not resist or resent a genuine grassroots movement. That is exactly what we have here in New Hampshire . . . As you once told me [perhaps referring to their conversation of the previous October], no man should deny the will of the people in the matter such as this."[22]

Eisenhower drafted a reply with the help of Kevin McCann, Colonel Pete Carroll, and Secretary of Defense Forrestal, and sent it on January 22.[23] Failure until now to say he would not accept the nomination, he wrote, had stemmed from a desire not to be presumptuous about the wishes of his fellow countrymen. But his candidacy might corrupt the system of promoting military officers. The services and their civilian heads must select their commanders based on "their military abilities rather than their future political potential." "Nothing in the international or domestic situation," he added, "especially qualifies for the most important office in the world a man whose adult years have been spent in the country's military forces. At least this is true in my case." He promised to work more diligently for America, but "My decision to remove myself completely from the political scene is definite and positive."[24]

Finder made the letter public on January 24, and it stopped the draft-Eisenhower movement. Wall Street investment banker William H. Burnham, who helped Eisenhower raise money for Columbia, was at this time chairman of the National Draft Eisenhower League, an organization that claimed a national membership of 150,000 and included among its leaders Senator Charles W. Tobey of New Hampshire; publisher Stuart Scheftel; businessmen George P. Converse and Antonio Ponvert; and NBC broadcasting executive Tex McCrary. Burnham responded to publication of the Finder letter by writing the general that while the Willkie campaign in 1940 had been "planned spontaneity, the enthusiasm for you [Eisenhower] and the willingness to work are in the people's heart and souls."[25] Finder, for his part, had his own interpretation of the letter. The office of the *Union Leader*, he informed the general, was "piled high with letters from strangers," and only one of them was pleased he had withdrawn his name. "Normally, I would abhor the thought of a military man in the Presidency," he said, "but you just do not fit the category." The American people were praying that Eisenhower would "accept a new command and a new duty for their sake." He asked the general to meet with him privately.[26]

Mail also poured into Milton's office at Kansas State University. One letter, from Tom Campbell of the Campbell Farming Corporation in Hardin, Montana, disagreed with Eisenhower's assertion that politics was not a job for career soldiers. "Every day we see the hazard of appointees for political reasons." Campbell, who had been a GI in North Africa, told Milton that his brother had demonstrated his ability as a statesman, administrator, and executive. The general's "popularity, character and integrity are sweeping the country like a prairie fire," he said. "He is the one man on whom the people of this country would unite. . . . Eisenhower's election would be like magic in the Russian situation."[27]

Eisenhower was beginning to feel the heat. He sent a copy of his Finder letter to Bedell Smith on January 28, describing it as the means by which he had "completely and finally removed himself from the national political picture" and restored a "great sense of personal freedom that I was rapidly losing."[28] Smith, disappointed, humored his former boss. "I am sorry in a way that you came down flat-footed on the question of the Presidential nomination," he replied, "although I know how you feel about it. . . . I really believe that you would have been nominated if you wanted it and . . . would have been elected." He reiterated his discouragement about Soviet-American relations. Smith did not, he said, envy any individual who would be in the White House during the next four years. "The future looks dark, indeed, from where I sit."[29]

Eisenhower's political supporters were everywhere. Even General Howard Snyder, his personal physician, considered him a potential presidential candidate. After Eisenhower's return from Europe, Snyder had decided—in part from his belief that his only patient was a potential candidate for the presidency—to try to protect this man, especially from the effects of smoking four packs of cigarettes a day.[30] Walter Winchell, in late March, sent Eisenhower the results of a presidential nomination poll of 95,000 of his listeners. Eisenhower had won with 36,007 to 19,374 over Henry Wallace, the runner-up; Dewey received 10,221, Truman 5,060.[31] Douglas Black of Doubleday went to the general's office in March 1948 for a wide-ranging discussion (Robinson and McCann were also present) and an informal celebration of the completion of the manuscript for *Crusade in Europe*. Eisenhower suggested that the efforts of the Democrats to draft him for the nomination indicated that they were "desperately searching around for someone to save their skins." When Black mentioned that MacArthur might receive the GOP nomination, Eisenhower exclaimed, "My God, anything would be better than that." "If there seemed to be a chance of MacArthur's getting the nomination as a result of a stalemate between Dewey and Taft," Robinson recorded in his diary, "Eisenhower would be more than eager to accept the bid."[32]

Two days later an editorial written by Robinson appeared in the *Herald Tribune*. It laid out the newspaper's interpretation of Eisenhower's position. Only "some obvious and overriding reason," it said, could "shake his [Eisenhower's] conviction that a professional military man should not seek high political office." Such a reason would "have to be a national and not merely a party crisis and it would have to point compellingly to Eisenhower as the one man best fitted to meet its responsibilities. . . . If the country clearly, demonstrably needed him in high political office, who believes he would refuse?" Privately Robinson praised Eisenhower's aloofness, writing him that the Finder letter and a Pentagon reiteration that he was not a candidate had "had a marked beneficial effect here," dispelling "a lot of silly rumors that might have been harmful."[33]

But the Berlin blockade of June 1948 stirred new interest. Indeed, the *Herald Tribune* editorial was virtually a setup. Robinson wrote his boss, Helen Reid, that the blockade and airlift had created a new world situation. "No man since George Washington has ever had the degree of support and confidence from the American pubic as has General Eisenhower," he said. "No man living in the world today can bring to Western Europe the unity of purpose, the cohesion and the complete confidence in ultimate victory—if a shooting war becomes necessary—as can General Eisenhower. . . . The Russians respect and fear no American so much. . . ."[34]

The general's letter to Finder, while relieving him of responsibility for efforts in his behalf and reducing expectations in 1948, had only confirmed his supporters in their conviction that a time would come when their wishes would be fulfilled. Robinson now told Ike and Mamie that he had arranged for them to vacation at Augusta National Golf Club. He would fly them there in the *Herald Tribune*'s Lockheed Lodestar. They would stay in a cottage where "all their needs would be cared for by the finest corps of servants I have ever gathered to-gether," and Ike would be able to play golf with, among others, Bobby Jones, the designer of the course; Cliff Roberts, investment banker, co-founder (with Jones) and chairman of the club; and Robert Woodruff, chairman of Coca-Cola.[35] This, it turned out, would be yet another key step, orchestrated by Robinson, in Eisenhower's movement toward the partisan political stage.

☆ 5 ☆

BEHIND
THE SCENES

TO MOST OBSERVERS, the election of 1948 appeared to offer the GOP a prime opportunity to recapture the White House from the Democrats. Harry Truman lacked the Roosevelt mystique, his speeches seemed cool compared to FDR's, and his party was in disarray. Roosevelt's previous vice president, Henry Wallace, recently fired by Truman as secretary of commerce because of his opposition to the growing hard line against the Soviet Union, had formed the Progressive party and welcomed to it those who felt that he, not Truman, was the proper heir to Roosevelt. Southern Democrats, after Truman supported a strong civil rights plank in the Democratic platform (their delegates actually walked out of the convention), either joined Governor Strom Thurmond's Dixiecrat party or voted for Senator Richard Russell of Georgia.

As for the remaining Democrats, the members of the Americans for Democratic Action (ADA) led by Senator Hubert Humphrey of Minnesota and historian Arthur Schlesinger of Harvard, agreed with Truman's foreign policy, but a number of them began casting around for another candidate—one who could win if the Republicans, as expected, nominated Dewey. The New York governor, after all, had come close to defeating Roosevelt in the 1944 general election. In the words of the historian William E. Luechtenburg: "With both wings of his party broken off, Truman seemed so certain a loser that a vigorous effort would be launched by the Roosevelt element to deny Truman the presidential nomination." Interestingly, even FDR's widow, Eleanor, doubted that Truman could be elected president. Perhaps not surprisingly, both the ADA and Roosevelt's sons, Franklin Jr. in New York and James in California, initiated a movement to draft Eisenhower as the Democratic candidate.[1]

When he wrote to Finder in January 1948, Eisenhower had decided against a move toward the presidency. But it is now clear that he intended to remain in the political arena. What no one knew at the time was that just days after mailing his January 22 letter, he sent the New Hampshire publisher a second letter. It said that he considered abstention in 1948 a "necessary move on my part" to keep the army—whose health, efficiency, and strength he considered essential—separate from partisan politics. He was, he said, flattered and proud of Finder's interest. He then issued a carefully worded disclaimer. "So long as I remain active there will never be any diminution of my readiness to work for the good of the country. My decision merely inhibits me from directing these efforts to the strictly political field."[2]

In Tokyo, MacArthur was angry, suspecting (probably correctly) that the remarks about the unsuitability of generals for political office were aimed at him. Eisenhower's letter was, he told the British ambassador to Japan, a "slur on the army," and was "the reason I felt obliged to offer my own candidacy." The Far Eastern supreme commander then issued a statement: "I would be recreant to all concepts of good citizenship were I to shrink . . . from accepting any public duty to which I might be called by the American people."[3]

Eisenhower surely thought (and no doubt hoped to ensure) that the draft movement MacArthur sought would never materialize. Most observers in 1948 felt that Dewey could defeat Truman. *Time* reported that while Eisenhower was the only Republican nominee who seemed to have a sure chance of beating the president, not one member of the GOP national committee had announced for Eisenhower.[4] MacArthur, for his part, won eight of twenty-seven delegates to Stassen's nineteen in the Wisconsin primary, and did worse in Nebraska. At the GOP convention in Philadelphia, he received only eleven of the eleven hundred votes cast for the nomination.[5] The Finder letter, one might say—to use a metaphor from Eisenhower's favorite card game, bridge—had drawn the MacArthur trump while making the general from Abilene appear direct, sincere, and, most important, lacking in personal ambition. In Forrestal's view, the Finder letter put Eisenhower in a position of "tremendous influence, above the battle."[6] *Kansas City Star* publisher Roy Roberts said it had clarified a confused GOP nominating situation. With Eisenhower out of the picture, the convention could give the nomination to Dewey rather than Taft and the conservative wing of the party. Roberts told delegates that Eisenhower preferred Dewey, Stassen, Senator Arthur Vandenberg, and Governor Earl Warren, and that the others were unacceptable.[7]

Eisenhower wisely remained quiet (thereby allowing his friend Roberts to speak for him), refusing publicly to support any candidate and turning down suggestions by *Newsweek* writer Ernest Lindley that he support Vandenberg or issue a statement in favor of an internationalist foreign policy.[8] At the last minute both the Taft and Stassen forces—realizing the nomination was about to go to Dewey instead of Vandenberg, and perhaps encouraged by a letter to the editor drafted by Robinson but signed "an American citizen" saying that "if the American people wanted Ike Eisenhower to do a job, he'd do it regardless of his own inclinations"—tried to persuade Eisenhower to allow his name to be entered. The general said "no" once again.[9]

The Democrats, meanwhile, also courted the general. On March 26 the former president's son, Franklin Roosevelt, Jr., started a movement to draft Eisenhower. The general again balked, telling Roosevelt that "any action of this kind now, in the middle of very delicate situations in various countries abroad, could have the most dangerous consequences and might negate American policy."[10]

But initiatives persisted. Seeking to create a bipartisan mandate, Finder contacted Democratic Senator Claude Pepper of Florida, who replied in a way that revealed yet another effect of the Eisenhower factor. A delegation should "go see the general" and "put the question squarely to him," Pepper said. "If he does not now say he would accept the nomination, all Democrats and all those who are against what Republicanism would mean under Dewey will have to get behind President Truman."[11] Finder replied that he had spoken with Eisenhower on June 19, the day before the opening of the Republican convention, and that his mind was not made up. The general's obligation to accept a draft, said Finder, "would be increased in the event of a reactionary Republican ticket." Yet he was not necessarily "out of the picture in the event of a liberal ticket." He said he had talked with key Democrats and felt "we have nothing to lose and everything to gain by trying to draft General Eisenhower."

Democratic leaders, with Finder's prompting, had concluded that Eisenhower might run.[12] A Democratic delegation including such ideologically diverse individuals as Senator Lister Hill of Alabama, Mayor William O'Dwyer of New York City, Jacob Arvey of Illinois, Mayor Hubert Humphrey of Minneapolis, Governor Strom Thurmond of South Carolina, and James Roosevelt of California issued a call for 1,592 convention delegates to caucus to find the "'ablest and strongest man available' to lead the party." "No man in these critical days," it said, "can refuse the call of duty and leadership implicit in the nomination."[13] The only way for Eisenhower to avoid being nominated on the floor, it had become apparent, was a formal statement of withdrawal, which he issued on July 5.[14] The general said once again that he would not identify himself with any political party, "either by accepting nomination from it or by participating in a partisan struggle," adding that "this implies no intention of maintaining silence on any issue of importance to the country on which I may feel qualified to express an opinion."[15] Perhaps it was the last sentence that caused the problem, but it was not until July 8, when the general contacted Roosevelt, Pepper, and Mayor Frank Hague of Jersey City, saying flatly that "no matter in what terms, conditions, or premises a proposal might be couched, I would refuse to accept the nomination," that the agitation finally stopped.[16]

All the pressure, Joe Davies told the general on July 9, was "a great tribute." "You will be President of the United States when the need for you will be far greater and more vital than now." Davies reminisced about a breakfast he had had with Truman and Harry Hopkins on the

White House veranda in August 1945. Truman, he recalled, had said then that "if you would accept, he would relinquish the Presidency and support you in 1948."[17] Eisenhower thanked the former ambassador and said he would "treasure the fine letter."[18]

The general revealed his true feelings about Truman only to his most intimate friends. In later years he would speculate aloud in response to a query from one of them about why the president would consider stepping aside. Truman, he said, "attached an unusual amount of importance to his [own] military career" which "meant more to him than being a judge or being a senator." He thus had "what you might call adulation for people in high military positions." Since Eisenhower had received more public exposure even than Marshall, Truman "probably in his own mind figured that I was the top hero" and recognized "greatness in me clear beyond any reasonable limitations."[19]

But Truman by the summer of 1948 had become suspicious, perhaps because of Eisenhower's delay in making a definitive statement about the presidency. The odds against his own election appeared large. Eisenhower's first statement, said the president, had been "weasel-worded."[20] A poll in late June had projected that the Democrats could defeat Dewey only by nominating Eisenhower; in a Truman-Dewey election, Dewey would win by 5,160,000 votes.[21] The general's decision to withdraw his name from consideration by either party and thus to support Dewey on the GOP ticket, Truman may have reasoned, had established the outcome of the November election and, he feared, his own defeat. Discouraged by the prospect, especially after the effort by a faction of his own party to nominate the general from Abilene, Truman commented to his press secretary that Eisenhower was a "s——a——."[22]

It must have been fascinating to watch Eisenhower, always at or near the center of national attention and cultivating his options. He dodged awkward questions but privately encouraged those who were promoting him. One of his speech writers and later White House assistant, *Time* magazine executive Charles Douglas "C.D." Jackson, in a memorandum entitled "Notes on Ike," later commented on the

Eisenhower appeal. "Irrespective of their actual ages," said Jackson, "some people move 'old'; some move 'young'; Ike [then sixty-three years old] moves 'young.'" This, he said, was "noticeable in the spring of his walk as he enters a room . . . in the flash-like speed in which he moves from sitting to striding in his office in the middle of an interview. . . . His mind has the same spring as his body. . . . He is highly literate, and cultured well beyond innate gentlemanliness. Classical, Biblical, and mythological allusions come tumbling out when he is working with words . . . and in his capacity for unscrambling and fixing an involved paragraph." He has "a low boiling point," but after a "few spurts of steam he recovers quickly and bears no rancor."[23]

After a speech at the Century Club, the prestigious gathering spot for writers, artists, musicians, newspapermen, and professional people in midtown Manhattan—he met Herbert Brownell, New York corporate attorney, chairman of the Republican National Committee, and organizer of Dewey's campaigns. Brownell was impressed by Eisenhower's knowledge of the "actual situation." The politico later confessed he had had "no idea, up to that point [early 1948] that he [Eisenhower] had so much interest in politics" or was so "attractive, vigorous, interesting."[24]

But it was Finder's understanding of Eisenhower's situation, refined by his conversations and correspondence with the general, that was perhaps better than anyone else's.[25] Attracted by the glamour and historical importance of the possibilities, Finder began to push for a possible Eisenhower candidacy almost immediately after publishing the famous letter. He wrote to his parents that Eisenhower's original letter had "placed me in the position of being the unwitting champion of the popular movement to frustrate his [public] decision." Eisenhower's aide, Colonel Michaelis, confirmed this by telling Finder that the general "considers you his confidant and has trust in you. It was no accident that he wrote to you originally."[26] Finder was "confident that he [Eisenhower] has proceeded in the utmost good faith, yet his present [January] stand is at variance with what he intimated privately when he visited Manchester in October [1947]."[27]

Finder had an all-morning meeting with Eisenhower just two days after he stepped down as chief of staff. The general, the publisher wrote in his diary, "has done his best to remove himself from political consideration" and "is not seeking—and does not want—political office." Nevertheless, he "will not refuse the people's will if it is expressed in terms of his nomination by national presidential convention." Eisenhower wished to avoid the political scene but would put that aside "when national security is at stake. That is, I know, the position of Dwight D. Eisenhower."[28]

Finder told Roy Roberts on February 17, 1948, that he had "the general's permission to make public the fact that I had met with him, and that he knew and agreed that it was my privilege to state . . . I was convinced he could be drafted."[29] The New Hampshire publisher told Eisenhower in April that unless specifically requested to do otherwise, he would continue to work for his nomination.[30] "America," he said, "in this hour of great peril, needs you. Your leadership as President is the only way that you can restore confidence." He said he had spoken or been in contact in previous weeks with Franklin D. Roosevelt, Jr., Helen Reid, labor leader David Dubinsky, A. A. Berle (a member of Roosevelt's New Deal brains trust), Walter Davenport, Philip Murray, Leon Henderson, John Cashmore, Senator Olin Johnston, and Joseph Grew, and had addressed a mass rally of the Draft Eisenhower movement in New York. The rally, he told the general, was part of a movement being promoted by "common people" who were paying expenses out of their own pockets. He would, he reiterated, proceed with such activities "unless you specifically tell me otherwise." The American people, he said, were "terrified and intimidated by world developments" but "have faith in you."[31] Eisenhower's standing in the polls (the Gallup poll found that he was the public's first choice, regardless of party affiliation) confirmed this conclusion.[32]

Not only did Eisenhower not stop Finder, his appointment calendar and correspondence reveal that he was encouraging others as well. In February 1948 he explained to Davies that he needed "to decide under what conditions I could actually be of most service," and that events in January had compelled him "to make a far more definite statement on my plans that I originally had intended."[33] He thanked

Burnham and his associates in the Draft Eisenhower League, saying he hoped for an opportunity to meet Burnham personally. He had closed the door to a presidential campaign in 1948, he told the Wall Street executive, "out of deep concern for what I believe best for the country and the Army. Whatever qualities [of his that Burnham desired in a president], I assure you they will be fully available to the nation in my capacity as a private citizen."[34] When Burnham met with Eisenhower in July, he told the general that Dewey owed his nomination to the fact that Eisenhower had withdrawn, and that he remained the choice of millions of younger citizens seeking representation in government. Burnham recommended that Eisenhower aim his speeches at this younger group.[35]

Eisenhower also kept up a cordial and sometimes daily correspondence with columnists. In early July, for example, he received a letter from the political columnist Marquis Childs. After congratulating the general for the way he was handling the political pressure, Childs said he planned to write an article about the "Eisenhower boom" for *Collier's* magazine. Eisenhower responded that he was grateful, admitting that he still had not put to rest all the rumors about his candidacy and that he was curious to know more about them. "If you could ever put together all the pieces," he said, "you could probably get quite an interesting story out of the whole thing."[36]

He also wrote to Harold Stassen, the young, former three-term governor of Minnesota and, since 1946, a candidate for the presidency. Stassen had done well in the Wisconsin, Nebraska, and Pennsylvania primaries, and Eisenhower thanked him for awakening "among our younger people deeper political consciousness and sense of responsibility and your insistence upon a liberal and enlightened approach to the problems of today. . . . You are most admirably equipped to continue the work you have started."[37]

So the nomination went to Dewey. Eisenhower probably judged that he could not have had it because he lacked the support of the professional politicians in the Republican party. Those who were calling for his nomination he considered amateurs. Still, in the words of Stephen Ambrose, "the leading candidates [including both Truman and Dewey] knew that if the general had chose to fight for it, he had an excellent chance of winning."[38]

Perhaps the most important of Eisenhower's behind-the-scenes activities involved Edwin Clark. Of all the individuals who boosted Eisenhower during this period, no one worked harder than this West Point and Harvard Law graduate, New York socialite, and master of wartime logistics to put the partisan political wheels in motion. In the autumn of 1947 Clark had sent his moral, if not financial, support to newspapermen in New England who were engaged in draft-Eisenhower activities. Then, in the spring and early summer of 1948, he began to work with Eisenhower directly.

The son of a small-town druggist who once considered running as a Democrat for the U.S. Senate, Clark was born in Parkersburg, Iowa, in 1902. After graduating from high school, he had received appointment to West Point and was graduated with the class of 1922. In the years that followed—World War I having ended and the army refusing commissions even to West Point graduates—he went to Harvard Law School. He then moved to New York City, clerked in a law firm, married the daughter of a Canadian business promoter, and became part of a society that included, among others, Broadway songwriter Richard Rogers and actor Frederic March. He joined a law firm that specialized in corporate and international law and became a member of the Manhattan Young Republican Club.

After the Wall Street crash in 1929, Clark remained in contact with the GOP through Russell Davenport, then managing editor of *Fortune*. Clark's contact with Davenport was interrupted by World War II. Volunteering for duty in the army reserves, Clark was activated at the rank of major but quickly was promoted to colonel because of expertise he had gained as an agent of the Finnish and Chinese governments in the late 1930s. Indeed, by 1941—drawing in part on his West Point background—he had become one of the nation's leading experts on arms procurement. In early 1942, returning to active duty, he was given command of the Asmara arsenal in Eritrea, a supply depot supporting the British Eighth Army in North Africa. After Allied victories in the Middle East, Clark in January 1944 became deputy to General

Robert Crawford, assistant chief of staff for supply at SHAEF in London. There he helped with preparations for D-day and, in the months that followed, administered the supply effort for the liberation of western Europe.[39]

When the war ended, Clark returned to his civilian occupation as a business consultant in Manhattan. But the wartime excitement and his fascination with Eisenhower would not go away. He offered his services to the general and soon became Eisenhower's attorney and personal agent, drawing upon his contacts and capacity for getting things done. He represented Eisenhower in the ill-fated negotiations with MGM about a documentary film on the war in Europe; helped him publish his memoirs and establish the Columbia Institute on War and Peace Studies; and made arrangements for the bust of Eisenhower that is now on display in duplicate at the United States Military Academy at West Point and at Camberly, the British general staff college.[40]

By 1948, Clark's circle of acquaintances included his neighbor at "Stone's Throw," Clark's home in Aspetuck Corners near the Potatuck River, not far from Westport, Connecticut. James F. Brownlee was a businessman who, during the war, had worked in the Office of Price Administration. Brownlee, it turned out, was a senior partner of J. H. Whitney and Company, a New York venture capital firm. He was also chairman of the board of Minute Maid Company, chairman of the finance committee of the Ford Foundation, and member of an elite national business research group called the Committee for Economic Development (CED). He and Clark fished together in the trout stream at Aspetuck, and they also took trips to the Augusta National Golf Club in Georgia.

In late 1947, Davenport had formed a small group of prominent individuals who called themselves the Republican Advance. They included senators Ralph Flanders, Margaret Chase Smith, Jacob Javits, John Sherman Cooper, Frank Carlson, Clifford Case, and Henry Cabot Lodge, Jr.; governors James H. Duff and Harold Stassen; and, not surprisingly, Kansas City newspaper publisher Roy Roberts. Their aims were, first, to keep the party out of the hands of Taft and the Midwestern conservatives, and, second, to put a liberal Republican back in the White House. Having supported both Willkie and Dewey against Roosevelt in 1940 and 1944, they were, in early 1948, seeking a candidate who could defeat Truman.

During Eisenhower's first year as president of Columbia, Clark and his wife invited him and Mamie for bridge and fishing in Connecticut. The first such visit—it is unclear how many there were—probably occurred in the summer of 1947 when the Eisenhowers went to Aspetuck to look at a house Clark thought they might like to purchase as a residence. Located on twenty-eight acres, it was a two-story, white, colonial clapboard structure, designed by the architect Cameron Clark.[41] The Eisenhowers did not take it but apparently enjoyed their visit. The following year, during another visit, Clark introduced Ike to Brownlee, who quickly agreed with Clark that the general would be an excellent presidential candidate. On the weekend of July 12, 1948, accordingly, Eisenhower and Clark had a "long conversation" about Republican presidential politics. In Clark's words, "this was the first time where clearly General Eisenhower expressed his interest in and the definite possibility of his being such a candidate."[42]

Confirming what he had been saying in his conversations with Robinson, Smith, Finder, Burnham, and others, this meeting was notable nonetheless. Clark had connections, the confidence of Eisenhower (who had asked him to carry out a variety of confidential errands), and independence. Clark recalled that he "became convinced" as a result of this conversation that he "should spend a substantial amount of time surveying, studying, and working toward the goal of nomination for Eisenhower." Having observed the 1948 GOP convention, the two realized that they knew little about the Republican factions, including those of Taft, Dewey, Vandenberg, Stassen, Lodge, and Duff.[43] They agreed that "careful studies" (Clark called them "staff studies") should be made of "the possibility, state by state, of support being organized throughout the country looking toward this goal."[44] Thus, after Dewey's nomination, Davenport and Brownlee formed a small group to develop a contingency plan. (Dewey, after all, had lost in the 1944 election.) They wanted above all to prevent a Taft nomination in 1952 and set out to "analyze the situation for 1952, in the event Dewey was not elected, and to begin some work toward an Eisenhower nomination even during the summer and fall of 1948."[45] Clark obtained the financial support of Brownlee's boss, the wealthy John Hay "Jock" Whitney, and after Dewey's defeat in November he and Davenport swung into action. Clark contributed his own money for the studies, as did Brownlee and Whitney. The list of contributors ultimately included wealthy New Yorkers Major Migel, Robert Woodruff, Louis Wasey, and Roscoe Engels.[46]

As fate would have it, despite Truman's apparently poor chances of even winning his party's nomination, not to mention the election, he won them both. Henry Wallace's lack of close contact with Democratic leaders and his willingness to accept the support of left-wing labor, even Communists, caused disaffection while diminishing right-wing GOP accusations that Truman was soft on communism. The poorly organized Dixiecrat movement gave credence to the view of mainstream liberals that Truman supported a strong civil rights platform. And when Eisenhower refused to be drafted, the Americans for Democratic Action and the Roosevelt brothers decided that Truman was the best candidate they had. Of course, Truman turned out to be much more effective on the campaign hustings than anyone had expected. His criticism of the "do-nothing" Republican Congress for overriding his veto of Taft-Hartley won him the vote of organized labor; and farmers were displeased that the Congress had refused to allow the Commodity Credit Corporation to build more storage bins. Truman made whistle-stop tours through the small-town Midwest, places where they liked his "spunk" and cried, "Give 'em hell, Harry!" He responded, "I never give anybody hell. I just tell the truth on the Republicans and they think it's hell!"[47] Meanwhile the overconfident Dewey was putting audiences to sleep with his platitudes.

Despite the polls and the *Chicago Tribune*'s banner headline proclaiming a Dewey victory on the morning after the election, the final returns were not even close—24.1 million to 21.9 million, with Democrats victorious in both houses of Congress.[48]

After the 1948 convention, Eisenhower had contacted Dewey,

sending friendly greetings. He told the governor he had taken a trip to Colorado where he had discovered that "among people of all walks of life" there was a "deep confidence that you are equipped to seek out solutions to problems of deep concern and worry in this country." He encouraged Dewey to come see him for a "more lengthy account of what I saw and heard."[49] Eisenhower reported to friends that he was "favorably impressed with Dewey," and that the New York governor would "probably be able to defeat Truman without too much difficulty."[50]

Cliff Roberts, who by this time had become one of the general's closest friends—his golf partner, bridge group member, and personal financial adviser and broker—was an acquaintance of Dewey. Roberts spent election evening 1948 with Eisenhower and recalled later that the general voted in his first presidential election that year, for Dewey. When Dewey lost, Roberts recalled, the general "had some misgivings in his own mind about whether he'd made the right decision about staying out of politics."[51] After Dewey's defeat, Eisenhower went to Dapplemere, the governor's farm, for conversations about Berlin, the Communist threat in France and Italy, and the importance of a unified command for the American armed forces. "Russia and inflation," the general told Dewey, were "the concerns of the American people." The governor was delighted by Eisenhower's interest and arranged for the general to receive a special license plate, DDE (the only three-lettered plate in New York).[52]

By December 1948, *Crusade in Europe* was receiving rave reviews in the press. Anyone who doubted Robinson's hopes that the book would stir interest in Eisenhower politically had only to read the general's one-paragraph reference to the presidency, which recounted Truman's offer at Potsdam to help him obtain anything he might desire in the future, including the White House. Although denying such interest now, Eisenhower told his readers, he had taken the offer very seriously.[53] One of the nation's foremost scholars of military strategy and a member of the Council on Foreign Relations Committee on Aid to Europe, Princeton University professor Edward Mead Earle, reviewed the book in the *Atlantic Monthly*. Having "thrice refused the proffered crown [the presidency]," Earle wrote, was "a measure of the man," who in addition to being a "magnificent soldier" was both an "elder statesman and in a sense, a prophet, who is honored both at home and abroad."[54] Doubleday, to Robinson's great satisfaction, arranged for a twenty-six-part, nine-hour television documentary of the book to be produced by Twentieth Century Fox and aired beginning May 5, 1949.[55]

Eisenhower's formal departure from the army, on December 7, 1948, occurred two months after his inaugural as president of Columbia. He took the occasion to calm troubled waters. He wrote MacArthur that he wanted to rebut the cheap columnists who had claimed that "you and I have always been deadly enemies and that [when] I wrote the letter [to Finder] I was also trying to take you out." This, he had told newspapermen recently, was wrong. "I hope you treasured our old friendship as much as I do." He was, he said, saying a "sort of official goodbye," but this did not "imply that I am going to lose a bit of my interest in the Army or in any of my old associates."[56] Eisenhower, it is clear, understood the importance of minimizing the number of one's enemies.

☆ 6 ☆

THE COMMUNIST MENACE

MANY YEARS LATER, Cliff Roberts would summarize the general's views on national security. The only way one could defeat communism was "always to remain strong and wear them down, on the theory that no one could be really happy living under communist rule." The unhappiness "sooner or later would generate enough unrest that communism would gradually turn into some form of democracy. We just had to remain strong and be patient and wait it out. In the meantime [the objective would be] not to let them gain an inch anywhere we could prevent them from making a gain." As for keeping the peace, the only way to avoid another war was to be prepared to hit the other guy harder than he could hit you, and let it [the readiness] be known."[1] This approach was, of course, no different from that of Truman and his foreign policy advisers. But in Eisenhower's view, Truman's way of implementing these policies was deficient.

In the period of increasing international tension following Eisenhower's retirement from active duty, events seemed to challenge the United States to unprecedented responses. After the February 1948 Communist takeover in Czechoslovakia, Congress passed the Marshall Plan for European Economic Recovery. Then the Berlin blockade which began in June 1948 stirred five European nations to form a defensive military alliance, the Brussels Pact, and to seek American military aid. Congress obliged, but only after a long debate. It then authorized American leadership of an expanded defensive alliance that included twelve countries, including the United States and Canada. The resulting North Atlantic Treaty Organization (NATO) became the nation's first peacetime military alliance. This was the situation in January 1949 when Eisenhower, responding to President Truman's request for assistance with the Joint Chiefs of Staff, arrived in Washington. He found the national security establishment in disarray. The precise goals and strategies of the Soviet Union after the outbreak of cold war in 1946 remained an enigma for allied military planners, so they tended to base their recommendations on estimated Soviet capabilities and on "worst-case scenarios." The National Security Act of 1947 had established the National Military Establishment (not yet the Department of Defense) as a loose umbrella under which separate army, navy, and air force secretaries and chiefs of staff operated. A joint chiefs of staff existed, but it had no chairman and no structure to assist the secretary of defense in planning, procurement, and mediating among the services, which vied with one another for congressional appropriations. The onset of the Berlin blockade in early 1948 brought some clarification (the threat now seemed tangible) but no good answers to the security question. The blockade had occurred after the Western powers, as an extension of the ERP, had sought relief for the suffering of Germany and western Europe and had therefore decided to unify their zones in Germany and establish a single currency. Stalin, in response, had sent tanks to cut off ground access routes to Berlin.

Truman had asked Eisenhower to come to Washington and recommend changes that would "energize the whole system," meaning the U.S. defense establishment. His task at the Pentagon was therefore large—indeed, almost impossible when added to his duties at Columbia. He nonetheless undertook work with Pentagon planners and the joint chiefs of staff during the first half of 1949, to develop a strategic concept for American and allied defense. It was arrived at only after a series of meetings in which he experienced firsthand the "inter-service struggle for position, prestige, and power." He later recalled that he practically "blew his top."[2]

The difficulties that he and the planners faced related to what was then called the "new era of warfare." A secret report by the Advanced Study Branch of the Plans and Operations Division of the army general staff (the so-called *superblitz* group he had authorized as chief of staff) appeared on December 16, 1948. Entitled *Patterns of War in the Atomic Warfare Age*, it discussed the implications of a sizable number of atomic bombs and delivery vehicles in possession of both the Soviet Union and the United States. The picture of warfare it portrayed only faintly resembled that of World War II, which had occurred mainly in Europe and Asia, had as its objective the overthrow of enemy governments, and began with surprise attacks. In the next war, said the report, military force could not bring a satisfactory result. Alarmingly, instead of being protected by two oceans as in earlier modern wars, the continental United States would be a battle zone, its strategic air defenses and offensive bombing capacity the initial targets of an enemy air assault. The new, post–World War II era of warfare, it surmised, would begin in 1964, since by that time the Soviet Union would have the atomic bombs—one hundred to two hundred—necessary for "a decisive attack with 15 to 30 Nagasaki-type weapons getting through to their targets."[3] Still, a more rational and limited approach to war, the report surmised, was likely. The unprecedented destructiveness of weapons, the increased role of the popular masses as a result of democratic movements, the desire of weaker nations to remain neutral, and the availability of the United Nations as a diplomatic forum all tended to mitigate against the use of physical violence. Civilian politicians would have greater say, and political, social, and economic strategies would often replace military ones. The Soviet Union would attempt to bring Communist governments into existence in western Europe and force UN recognition of them; to end allied domination of the Near East; and to "exploit" western Europe, Africa, and the Near East. Finally, the Soviets would try to bring the United States and the United Kingdom to accept its concept of world order and to cease hostilities.

Assuming that the United States would never fire the first shot, it would have limited aims. Rather than overthrow the Soviet government, it would try to force it to cease hostilities. The American objective would be a United Nations' settlement without veto, withdrawal from all territories occupied after the outbreak of war, and destruction or neutralization—with allied inspection—of all atomic, biological, and chemical weapons.[4] The United States and its allies thus would need to be able to withstand an initial air offensive and launch a counterstrike to "neutralize the enemy's offensive capabilities" and "develop air supremacy." Western forces would then launch an aerial offensive to reduce the enemy's military capabilities and undertake operations in enemy-occupied territories to encourage indigenous resistance, increasing "military, political, social, and economic pressure until he accepts defeat."[5] Although perhaps less destructive than earlier wars, such a conflict remained horrible to contemplate and, of course, risked escalating out of control.

Eisenhower agreed with this scenario, especially its emphasis on the long-term nature of the political and economic threat from the Soviet Union. But he believed there were major problems in implementing the strategy, and that these problems would become more serious if Soviet actions became more threatening. The United States would have to walk a fine line between military preparedness and excessive defense spending that might impair the "U.S. economy and its fundamental values and institutions."

Eisenhower's thinking was in keeping with the first operating statement of Truman's national security strategy. Embodied in NSC-20/4, which had been written in November 1948 by George Kennan and the policy planning staff of the State Department, it acknowledged that the Soviet Union was capable of overrunning Europe and the Middle East and damaging the United Kingdom in six months, but would be inhibited from initiating any "war involving the United States (unless by miscalculation) by the United States' atomic monopoly and economic potential as well as their own domestic weakness." At the same time, the United States needed to help nations "able to contribute to U.S. security" become economically and politically stable and militarily capable while it sought to "discredit the Soviet Union and communism." The objectives should be (1) to reduce Soviet power and influence to the "point that they no longer are a threat to the peace, independence and stability of the world family of nations;" and (2) to "bring about a basic change in Soviet conduct of international relations."[6]

Unfortunately the congressional appropriations necessary for this global but long-term program were nowhere in sight. Truman's defense budget for fiscal year 1949—after the Communist coup in Czechoslovakia in February and the Berlin blockade in June 1948—increased from $9.8 billion to $13 billion and for fiscal 1950, to $14.4 billion. This despite Defense Secretary Forrestal's insistence that NSC-20/4 required $16.9 billion. The air force, for its part, named General Curtis LeMay commanding general of a newly revitalized Strategic Air Command (SAC). He improved the sources and amount of targeting information and sought more bombers: seventy-five more intercontinental B-36s and ninety more B-29s and B-50s.[7] After listening to the wrangling, Eisenhower accepted LeMay's recommendations over those of the navy (they were seeking another carrier task force) and put his weight behind a budget request totaling $15 billion. But his support was not enough to prevent the administration from cutting it by $2 billion.

Although Eisenhower officially returned to Columbia full-time in late August 1949, his national security activities continued. The first Soviet nuclear test, detected in August 1949—at least five years earlier than expected—brought consternation to the American defense community. The previous July, Truman had authorized production of hundreds of nuclear weapons. While refusing to increase defense budgets, Truman in October approved a joint chiefs proposal for tripling U.S. nuclear production facilities for U-235 (the enriched uranium that had fueled the Hiroshima bomb) and doubling those for production of plutonium (the material of the Nagasaki bomb). The stockpile of nuclear weapons under control of the Atomic Energy Commission would thus increase from fifty in mid-1948 to four hundred by the end of 1950; and Eisenhower, as part of his duties—along with Conant, Isaiah Bowman, Erwin Canham, and John Foster Dulles—now became a presidential adviser on nuclear policy and public information regarding the atomic bomb.[8] It was in these unfortunate circumstances—brought about by Soviet actions and American fiscal constraints—that he joined Bernard Baruch in supporting a "favorable, overwhelming U.S. advantage in the development of atomic weapons" until, as he put it, a "truly effective international control" could be achieved with enforceable international inspection and a standby war mobilization plan, including civilian defense.[9] Eisenhower went on to say, pessimistically, that he was "of the opinion we'll never obtain international control."[10]

The president also established a special committee composed of Acheson, Louis Johnson, and David Lilienthal, chairman of the AEC, to advise him whether or not to develop hydrogen (fusion) weapons. A heated debate occurred between the scientists led by Edward Teller, who favored development, and the general advisory committee to the Atomic Energy Commission led by J. Robert Oppenheimer, who was opposed. The special committee sided with the Teller group, making two recommendations: (1) that the United States produce the hydrogen bomb, and (2) that the secretaries of state and defense "re-examine our objectives in peace and war and . . . our strategic plans" in the light of "the Soviet fission and hydrogen bomb capability."[11] Truman accepted both. The former authorized the AEC to build and test a fusion device; the latter resulted in a study by a State-Defense working group led by Paul Nitze, Kennan's successor as head of the State Department's policy planning staff.

In early November the new secretary of defense, Louis Johnson, handed the president a secret summary of the air force's appraisal of the strategic situation. Signed by Air Force Secretary Stuart Symington and clearly influenced by General LeMay, it recalled that generals Arnold, Spaatz, Eisenhower, and the president's air policy commission had recommended a "minimum peacetime air force necessary for the security of the United States" of seventy groups. The present program, said the summary, would provide only forty-eight, and only twenty-eight of these would be equipped with modern planes. The existing program of funding and procurement, the summary said, would put the United States at its weakest in the air "by 1955, when the Russians can be at their strongest." The most effective Soviet plan for the conduct of a war with the objective of expanding Soviet power to the whole of Eurasia, principally western Europe and the United Kingdom, would be an immediate atomic attack upon its protector (the United States) across the Atlantic Ocean. If this attack destroyed or seriously damaged American military power, "Western Europe would fall almost without a struggle." "The only consideration which could keep the Soviet Union from making this attempt," the report added in stark tones, "is the fear of a retaliatory atomic attack by the air force against the Soviet Union." Both the retaliatory force and the defense force must therefore be in a state of "instant readiness." It called for creation without delay of such deterrent and retaliatory forces.[12]

By December 1949, with Eisenhower's guidance, the joint chiefs adopted an emergency war plan code named OFFTACKLE. It was based on two studies done by the joint chiefs in the late spring of 1949 which reported that a SAC nuclear strike would reduce Soviet industrial capacity by no more than 40 percent and would have little effect on Communist power in the Soviet Union or Soviet capacity to overrun western Europe.[13] OFFTACKLE, though requiring ground and naval forces deployed overseas—in order to blunt any attack and protect air bases—placed "great reliance upon the retarding or crippling effect upon the enemy of a sudden and powerful bombing offensive." It required a "respectable long range strategic bombing force" along with medium bombers, bases, transports, reconnaissance and fighter planes, and four "fleet-type carriers."[14] It stipulated that the U.S. response to a Soviet attack would be "a full scale nuclear strike by SAC using 133 atomic bombs against Soviet urban/industrial targets to disrupt its war-making capacity and to slow the Red Army's advance into Western Europe." The retaliatory attack would be followed by a withdrawal of U.S. and allied forces to Great Britain, North Africa, and the Suez area "while Soviet forces overran the continent. Not until after two years of build-up would the allies, as in World War II, be able to launch any offensive activities to retake Western Europe and defeat the Soviet Union."[15]

The problems of implementation, however, were large. The military component of the strategy, Eisenhower soon saw, was repugnant to the administration and insufficient if deterrence failed. Such repugnance and insufficiency, were they to become known to Stalin, increased the danger that deterrence would fail through miscalculation. The new Defense Department organization that Eisenhower supported (and the president adopted) took effect in 1949 and was a step forward. It allowed the secretary of defense to consider purely military rather than housekeeping or administrative questions because he would have a "principal military assistant" (chairman of the Joint Chiefs of Staff) to oversee and urge a consensus and serve as military adviser to the president.[16] But guidance on the use of nuclear weapons, adopted by the president in May 1948, gave the "decision on employment of nuclear weapons in the event of war" to the president "as he considers a decision to be required." Truman preferred to find an alternative that did not involve "using atomic bombs." Even during the Berlin crisis, he had said, "I don't think we ought to use this thing unless we absolutely have to. . . . It is used to wipe out women and children and unarmed people, and not for military uses." (He did assure his advisers, reluctantly, that he would use the atomic bomb if necessary.)[17]

Meanwhile, unwilling because of his fear of the inflationary effect of a federal deficit to accept Eisenhower's recommendation of a $15 billion defense budget for fiscal 1950, or even a compromise $14 billion, he held it at $13 billion.[18] Thus it was not surprising that in August 1949, Eisenhower decided he had done as much as he could do at the Pentagon. After providing further advice on how to cut the original budget estimate, he announced his intention to return to Columbia.[19] (This occurred after Forrestal suffered a nervous breakdown, had to be hospitalized, and in May committed suicide.)

In the spring of 1950 Nitze's group produced NSC-68, calling for "a massive build-up of defense forces and related measures." The new international situation, it said, called for a new way of thinking about defense spending. Although the document mentioned no precise figures, Nitze estimated that NSC-68 would cost between $40 and $50 billion. While accepting in broad terms the analysis of Soviet objectives contained in NSC-20/4, the new memorandum attributed more aggressive methods to the Soviet Union and advanced by ten years the Soviet air force's ability to deliver a crippling surprise nuclear attack on the United States. "The year of maximum danger" was to be not 1964 but 1954. The report went on to recommend a buildup of both conventional and nuclear forces "to achieve preponderance to both deter war or, if attacked, to go on to win as well as to support other U.S. foreign policy objectives."[20]

The United States, American strategists now said, needed a program "to reduce the power and influence of the Kremlin and the other areas under its control." Rather than merely contain the Soviet Union, the United States needed, in the words of Acheson, "to see to it that freedom of choice rested with us, not the Russians."[21] Just what this "positive program" should be remained unclear except for "timely measures and operations by covert means in the field of economic warfare and political and psychological warfare with a view to fomenting and supporting unrest and revolt in selected strategic satellite countries." Such actions, along with U.S. nuclear superiority and expanded conventional forces—mainly by NATO allies—ultimately "would induce the Soviet Union to capitulate or negotiate an end to the cold war favorable to the West. At present, however, the report considered the realities of power to be unfavorable for negotiation."[22]

Kennan, not surprisingly, protested this analysis. He took issue with its dire view that the Soviet Union desired, in the words of NSC-68, "complete subversion or forcible destruction of the machinery of government and structure of society in the countries of the non-Soviet world and their replacement by an apparatus and structure subservient to and controlled by the Kremlin."[23] The other leading State Department Soviet expert, Charles Bohlen, agreed. Truman, hoping perhaps to reconcile the conflicting views, asked Army Undersecretary Tracy Voorhees to prepare a report about the situation in Europe. When completed, it supported the recommendations of Nitze and NSC-68;

but Truman, perhaps weighing the advice of Kennan and Bohlen, and doubtful that Congress would approve the necessary spending, refused to make NSC-68 the basis for the 1951 defense budget.[24]

When fighting broke out on the Korean peninsula, in June 1950, few observers assumed that Stalin, by giving his nod to Kim Il-sung to attack the South, wanted general war. Bedell Smith had written in early May 1949 that NATO was a kind of insurance policy for European recovery. "Military strength is and will for some time remain the prime factor in retarding the dynamic expansion which seems to be the keynote of Soviet policy."[25] But other observers saw a more ominous meaning of the term "expansion" when applied to the Soviets. Years later, for example, General Clay recalled that the Soviet Union had no expectation of taking over West Germany militarily. Instead it planned to exploit international tensions in other ways. "I think they felt that they were going to be successful with the Communist Party getting into political power in other countries of Western Europe and that this would accomplish over time the same purpose of bringing all Europe under communist political control."[26] Confirming this view was a report in early 1950 from the U.S. military attaché in Moscow. The Soviets, it said, would use their military strength, along with propaganda and the fomenting of internal strife in neighboring countries, to intimidate. "Friendly countries are looking to us for organizational plans and leadership."[27]

It seems clear now, with the availability of material from Soviet archives, that these analyses, despite Soviet adventurism in supporting Kim Il-sung, were substantially correct. An allied airlift of supplies had broken the Berlin blockade in the spring of 1949. But in October, after the Soviet Union tested an atomic bomb, Mao Tse-tung's People's Liberation Army triumphed in China, driving the Nationalists under Chiang Kai-shek onto the island of Taiwan, making the world's most populous nation a Marxist-Leninist dictatorship. In Southeast Asia, communist guerrillas roamed the jungles of Malaya, Indochina, and the Philippines. Finally, on June 25, 1950, the North Korean army, carrying out orders (with the approval of both Stalin and Mao) of its Communist dictator, Kim Il Sung, moved across the northern border of the Republic of Korea at the 38th parallel of latitude and quickly overran its capital, Seoul. To bolster Asian governments and protect American-occupied Japan, Truman appealed to the United Nations for support and sent U.S. military forces into combat.

The United States needed a capacity—one greater than Truman and Congress felt they could afford—to support its allies economically and militarily. And while it is doubtful, in retrospect, that the United States needed an air force of the kind urged by General LeMay, certainly it needed a credible strategic deterrent. Stalin had neither plans nor the immediate ability to attack western Europe or further expand Soviet influence militarily. He had cut his army from 500 combat divisions to 175 under-strength divisions and did not believe, given popular attitudes, world economics, and the need to maintain the Communist party in power, that a successful war was possible for at least twenty years. Still, suspicion was part of his nature. As historians of the Soviet Union have shown, Stalin was responsible for the murder of 30 million of his own people (more than Hitler) whom he considered politically dangerous. He was history's archetypical brutal dictator. As early as April 1947, after Truman's announcement of the containment policy, Stalin had ordered production of ballistic missiles with sufficient range to strike the United States.[28] He considered Washington a threat to his regime because it was trying to rebuild Germany's industrial capacity and interfere in the Soviet-controlled buffer zone in eastern Europe. One could argue that as one of the victors in World War II and the leader of a nation with undisputed postwar national security interests in eastern Europe, especially if economic difficulties continued to plague capitalist economies as they had in the 1930s, the Soviet dictator had no choice.[29] This did not, however, lessen the danger.

Years later, Eisenhower would recall that he believed Soviet miscalculation had caused Kim Il-sung to order his army across the 38th parallel on June 25, 1950. As army chief of staff, he recalled, he had pleaded with Congress not to reduce American troop strength in East Asia. "If we had left a division or two in Korea," he said, "there would never have been a Korean War."[30] Evidence from Soviet archives has now confirmed that Stalin, in giving the green light to North Korea, misjudged U.S. intentions. The Soviet dictator had told his comrades that "the way matters stand now, America is less ready to attack than the U.S.S.R. is to repulse an attack."[31] Stalin apparently was willing, because of his judgment of the correlation of power by the early summer of 1950, to gamble.

For allied strategists the aggression was, quite correctly, a large matter. Bedell Smith had finished his tenure as United States ambassador to the Soviet Union and was about to become director of the Central Intelligence Agency. On June 26, 1950, he wrote to his British friend and former chief of intelligence at SHAEF, British General Kenneth Strong, analyzing the situation. "Without committing a single Soviet soldier, the Soviet Union," he said, had drawn the "United States into what will be a long and expensive military campaign which could well develop into a full-scale war between the U.S. and its [the Soviet Union's] associates and Asia." He referred, ominously, to Chinese Communist forces that "can be employed in Korea, against Formosa, in Indo-China, in Burma, or to invade Tibet." The USSR had put "itself in the favorable position of employing satellite forces in localized action to drain our strength while picking the psychological moment to propose disinterested mediation." The only reason for optimism, Smith felt, was that the war had jarred the American people out of their complacency.[32]

Reacting to the Korean invasion, Eisenhower was ready to return to active duty. He wrote Air Force Secretary Symington on July 31, 1950, that he was "always available on an instant's notice for anything that may be required of me in the present crisis."[33] He traveled to Washington and talked with Generals Collins, Ridgway, and Gruenther. These friends, he would write in his diary, seemed "indecisive, which is natural in view of the indecisiveness of political statements." "We'll have a dozen Koreas soon," he said, "if we don't take a firm stand." The "appeal to force having been made, for God's sake, get ready! Do everything possible under law to get us going. . . . In a fight [our side] can never be too strong."[34] He wrote Secretary of Defense Johnson that he supported universal military service as a means of keeping the nation strong. Short of that, he recommended universal military training and again volunteered his services "on any subject that you might desire to take up with me."[35] He told Harriman, now special assistant to the president for foreign affairs, that he wanted to have a "real chin with you. This country is such a big, splendid, wonderful and always potentially powerful nation that I am convinced the solutions of our internal problems will go a very long way toward achieving our international aims, particularly that of preserving the peace."[36] "Fundamentally Russia does not want war," Eisenhower told General Strong, "yet where a dictator state exists, it is impossible to make any firm calculations." It was important, he said, to stress the "defensive nature of our rearmament" and the long term, when the "growing economic, military, and political powers of Russia will tend to dominate the world."[37] While this estimate proved to be overly pessimistic, the need for defensive rearmament was real. Memories of Tojo, Mussolini, and Hitler had not disappeared.[38]

Relief came, at least temporarily, in September 1950. South Korean and American forces had withdrawn to the so-called Pusan perimeter on the southeastern tip of the Korean peninsula. Then MacArthur's surprise amphibious invasion at Inchon, midway up the west coast near Seoul, flanked the North Korean army, threatening its lines of supply and causing collapse. From September 20 until late November the North Korean army, or what remained of it after General Walton Walker's Eighth Army attacked northward from Pusan, retreated to the borders of Manchuria. Elated, Eisenhower congratulated MacArthur. He wired him that the counteroffensive was "a brilliant example of professional leadership."[39] The Far East commander appeared deeply touched. He replied with his appreciation for the remarks and "warm feeling in his heart" for their "intimate relationship over many hard years." He "had never known," he said, "more savage fighting nor a more determined, tenacious, and able enemy."[40]

With foreign policy again in the headlines, Eisenhower and his fellow university presidents in late September 1950 decided it was their duty to publicize the nature of the Soviet threat and what needed to be done about it. They held a conference on national security at the Waldorf Astoria hotel in New York City. The hosts were James B. Conant, president of Harvard; Colgate W. Darden, president of the University of Virginia; Harold W. Dodds of Princeton, James R. Killian, Jr., of the Massachusetts Institute of Technology; James L. Morrill of the University of Minnesota and the American Council of Education; Harold E. Stassen of the University of Pennsylvania; and Henry Wriston, president of Brown University. Eisenhower was keynote speaker. Honored guests were former president Herbert Hoover and Bernard M. Baruch, head of the War Industries Board in World War I and Eisenhower's longtime friend. The elite of the American financial and media industries also attended. They included a number of individuals who had become friends or supporters of Eisenhower, such as Winthrop Aldrich, Walter Annenberg of the *Philadelphia Inquirer*, Harry Bullis, Ferdinand Eberstadt of Eberstadt and Company, Milton Eisenhower of Pennsylvania State University, Marion B. Folsom of Eastman Kodak, Whitelaw Reid of the *New York Herald Tribune*, Alfred P. Sloan, Jr., of General Motors, and George Whitney of J. P. Morgan and Company.[41]

Eisenhower joined Conant in advocating universal military service (UMS). It would draft all males between a certain age into active military service for a period of two or three years. Congress had defeated universal military training, which, as in Switzerland or Israel, would have provided a less expensive and possibly deterrent military capability in 1948.[42] Given the current emergency, it no longer would suffice.[43] The gathered university presidents voted unanimously for UMS, and Eisenhower passed the results to Defense Secretary George C. Marshall. (Truman's newly appointed defense secretary thanked Eisenhower and his colleagues for the support, but, despite the outbreak of war in Korea, he was doubtful it would pass. At this point, he muttered despairingly, he would settle for UMT.)[44] Soon after the meeting, Roy Roberts, from his vantage point in Kansas City, wrote Eisenhower that "even more than in what Russia may or may not do, . . . the real danger is going to be for the country to slip back into complacency again."[45] The conference at the Waldorf, Eisenhower replied, had expressed its concern about possible "diminishing public interest if our sense of crisis should disappear."[46]

Neither Conant nor Army Undersecretary Tracy Voorhees intended to let this happen. The war in Korea was, in their view, an alarm bell. Conant had written in September 1946 one of the first treatises about the new era of warfare—a classified government document entitled "The Absolute Age." Since 1947 he had been urging universal military service.[47] He had not had much success, noting that in order to obtain funding for Greece and Turkey, Truman had had to frighten Congress (and the American people) by speaking in global terms about communism and the Soviet threat.[48] Passage of the Marshall Plan the following spring had required intense lobbying by a citizens group led by Averell Harriman. In many ways it appeared to Conant, as it did to Voorhees, that the American people after 1945 had lapsed into irresponsible isolationism not unlike that of the 1930s.[49] In the spring of 1950 he had accepted the conventional wisdom that Stalin expected to expand his influence not by war but by subversion and *coups* by Communist parties.[50] Conant wanted preparedness. To prevent the Red Army from overrunning western Europe, he said, the United States must lead a "massive rearmament drive and send a large (million man) contingent of United States ground forces to Western Europe."[51] Preventive war was both impractical and immoral, so the United States needed to increase its military aid to its anti-Soviet allies and develop a national consensus for a policy of long-term and large-scale defense and foreign aid expenditures.[52]

Voorhees, in the words of one historian, became the "enraged public citizen," ready to argue his case to anyone who would listen. At his urging, a number of those in attendance at the Waldorf formed a lobbying organization called the Committee for the Present Danger.[53] The committee brought together individuals who believed the United States faced a crisis not unlike that of 1940 and 1941 after Europe had come under German rule. In October 1950 they saw alarming similarities—a combination of outside threat and domestic complacency. Voorhees, drawing on the research he had done for Truman, elaborated his views in an article for the *New York Times Magazine* entitled "The Need to Prevent Another Korea in Europe."[54] With backing from administration officials; State Department adviser Robert Bowie;

the army's deputy chief of staff for plans and operations, General Alfred Gruenther; and U.S. high commissioner to Germany, John J. McCloy; Voorhees believed this committee of distinguished and influential citizens would "guide the public" in its thinking. Conant, at Voorhees's request, accepted the chairmanship. The committee soon gained the support of Defense Secretary Marshall.[55]

Lobbying by the Committee for the Present Danger, combined with the U.S. commitment to lead the United Nations in stemming the Communist invasion of South Korea, produced the increased spending and military buildup recommended in NSC-68. Nitze's committee now worked with the Joint Chiefs of Staff. With the intervention in Korea in November 1950 of Chinese Communist troops, he began to appear prophetic in his prediction of Soviet boldness. On December 16, 1950, Truman declared a national emergency. Using a variation of NSC-68 as the basis for his declaration, he increased the military force goals presented to Congress for 1952 from 10 divisions, 281 naval vessels, and 58 air force wings to 18 divisions, 397 combat vessels, and 95 air wings. By June 30, 1951, Congress had doubled the number of military personnel on active duty to 3,211,000 and appropriated $49.4 billion for fiscal 1951.[56] Indeed, a National Security Council review that summer of the U.S. buildup determined that NSC-68 had underestimated the Soviet threat, and that the Kremlin would have a stockpile of 200 nuclear weapons by mid-1953, not mid-1954. The resulting sense of crisis prompted Congress in October to authorize defense appropriations for fiscal 1952 totaling $57 billion plus another $4.5 billion for military construction.[57]

Eisenhower's readiness to serve soon found a response from the president. The large problem for U.S. cold war strategy was the defense of western Europe. The passage of the Marshall Plan had required cooperation and initiative on the part of the European nations in pooling their needs to develop a plan for the use of American economic assistance. The security concern of the five most important nations—Britain, France, Belgium, the Netherlands, and Luxembourg—had initially been a resurgent Germany, and the stated purpose of their joining together in the 1948 Brussels Pact for joint defense planning was to defend against that possibility. But by 1949 it was clear that the potential enemy was instead the Soviet Union. It had also become evident that the European alliance needed to expand to include both other European countries and the United States.[58] Consequently, when the North Atlantic Treaty was signed on April 4, 1949, its members included, in addition to the Brussels Pact signatories, Denmark, Iceland, Italy, Norway, Portugal, Canada, and the United States. Most observers believed NATO to be a logical extension of the Truman Doctrine and Marshall Plan, with the important political purposes of, in the words of one observer, keeping "the Soviets out, the Americans in, and the Germans down."[59] The Senate ratified the treaty on July 21, 1949, and Truman immediately asked Congress for $1.5 billion for European military aid. By 1951 it was clear to most observers that German participation, something that American leadership alone could bring about, would be essential to NATO's military mission of preventing a Red Army attack or of stopping it at the Rhine.

In mid-September 1950, Eisenhower had received a letter from General Gruenther. "The name of Eisenhower was figuring very prominently, as a candidate for U.S. supreme commander at NATO," it said. "One chap said the selection of Ike for this position is the only way to prevent World War III."[60] Harry Truman found himself with an urgent need to instill confidence both at home and in Europe in his approach to international security, one that involved American participation in a peacetime military alliance to guarantee the security of western Europe but at the same time elicited the full participation of all European members, including possibility a revitalized West Germany. Eisenhower, the beaming symbol of victory in Europe in World War II (and an individual versed in the intricacies of contingency planning for war in the nuclear age) was the obvious choice as NATO supreme commander. No one, absolutely no one else came close to having Eisenhower's qualifications for the job. Truman's request that he become NATO supreme commander reached the general the following month, when he and Mamie were returning from a speaking engagement in the Midwest. Their train had stopped temporarily at a siding in Bucyrus, Ohio.[61] The general walked back down the tracks to a freight station, the location of the nearest telephone, with his aide, Schulz. Ike told the president that his own feelings had nothing to do with it. If the nation needed him, he, of course, would do it.[62] NATO, unlike the UN, he told Hazlett the following month, is "not plagued by the vetoes of hostile groups." It was simply trying "to work out a way that free countries may band together to protect themselves. . . . I rather look upon this effort as the last remaining chance for the survival of Western civilization."[63]

By mid-November, Eisenhower was organizing his new command, the Supreme Headquarters Allied Powers in Europe (SHAPE). Fortunately he did not have to start from scratch. Western Union headquarters at Fontainebleau, established two years earlier by Field Marshal Montgomery, provided a framework.[64] But he had much to do to set up the new command, so he called upon his friends and close associates to help him. They included Edwin Clark, Colonel Paul T. "Pete" Carroll, Strong (in Great Britain), Gruenther, Churchill, Marshall, and his study group at the Council on Foreign Relations.[65]

Before departing for a tour of NATO countries in early January, Eisenhower in conversations with Truman and Harriman summarized what he saw as his mission—and the obstacles he would need to overcome. It was stirring rhetoric rather than his typical terse, carefully worded weighing of the need for preparedness against the requirements of domestic economic stability. The struggle against "Soviet imperialism," he said now, "will continue until either we or the Soviets are destroyed or [until] the other side has recognized the hopelessness of attempting to conquer the free world through force and will seek, with us, a reasonable and practical basis for living together in the world (this they will never do except to gain time)." Western Europe, he said, was "the keystone of the defensive arch we are trying to build up . . . the United States is the foundation." The objective in Europe was "confidence, the will to fight." The United States, he said, should build its military strength and, after informing public opinion on the "critical nature" of the problem, bolster western Europe through a "drastic increase in our material help" in order to create there "a respectable munitions industry." This, he said, would begin "restoration of the traditional counterbalance to Russian ambition." The United States had agreed to assume national responsibility for command at a time when it was "badly extended in the East" and had "no opportunity of sending promptly into Europe sizeable military units to support the psychological effect that our diplomats (and staffs) anticipate as a result of naming me to command."[66] In letters to his friends, Eisenhower called for greater education in the United States about the importance of western Europe and the need for unity, priorities, and universal military service. A "free form of government," he said, "is the political expression of an abiding faith by a race in Superior Power, in a God."[67]

☆ 7 ☆

THE POLITICS
OF NATIONAL
SECURITY

AFTER THE 1948 PRESIDENTIAL ELECTION, Eisenhower was moving ever closer to partisan Republican politics. When conversations with visitors turned to one of the topics that he felt most strongly about, such as "the expanse of government bureaucracy or the drift toward statism," he told Hazlett, he became sidetracked.[1] Indeed, by the time he left for his NATO command he was participating in a variety of efforts by some of the nation's most influential individuals and organizations to promote him as a candidate in 1952.

His untiring devotion to duty and his efforts to remain viable as a candidate for high office contributed to a serious illness and his efforts to conceal it from the public. The almost frantic pace of his existence, including Herculean efforts to establish harmony among the nation's military services, a four-pack-a-day cigarette habit, volatile blood pressure, and hectic commuting between New York City and Washington combined on March 21, 1949, to cause what may have been a heart attack—at least that is what his cardiologist, Dr. Thomas Mattingly, later considered it to have been. At the time, General Howard Snyder, his personal physician (and Eisenhower later in his diary), called it a digestive upset. Eisenhower was able to reach the telephone from his hotel bed in Washington, D.C. But instead of contacting Walter Reed army hospital, as one might expect, he called Snyder in New York, who flew down to see him. Eisenhower recalled that Snyder "treated me as though I were at the edge of the precipice and teetering a bit. For days, my head was not off the pillow. The doctors transferred me to Key West, Florida, and I remained on the sick list, forbidden solid food and cigarettes. During most of that time I was so ill that I missed neither."[2] The doctor canceled all his appointments, including a reception at the White House for his wartime associate and friend, Winston Churchill, and on Snyder's advice, Eisenhower gave up smoking (he quit "cold turkey"). After two months of recuperation at President Truman's vacation White House at Key West and at Augusta National Golf Course, he returned to his duties at Columbia University and the Pentagon.[3]

For years historians, unaware of the possible seriousness of this illness, interpreted the episode as the digestive tract indisposition that Eisenhower and Snyder claimed it was at the time, and an excuse for a much-needed retreat from the stress of work. Basing their assertions on a study done by Eisenhower's former cardiologist, Dr. Thomas Mattingly, several historians have suggested that Eisenhower's indisposition in 1949 was a heart attack. A more recent study by the historian Clarence Lasby has raised questions about Mattingly's account, and electrocardiograms apparently reveal no heart damage. Certainly Snyder did not diagnose him as having had a heart attack or treat him for one in the days and weeks that followed. He called it a gastrointestinal illness. Whatever the truth of this debate—and Cliff Roberts was probably correct when he said that in Eisenhower's case "there seems to have been a connection between stomach upsets and heart strain"—Eisenhower knew he was very sick.[4]

Bill Robinson, meanwhile, stoked the political fires. With almost missionary fervor in the months after the general returned to Columbia, Robinson recruited corporate officials and journalists who might be interested in either the university or an Eisenhower candidacy.[5] One of the latter, David Lawrence, editor of *U.S. News and World Report*, interviewed Eisenhower and received what was essentially a reiteration of the general's private conversations with Finder. "Broad laws of strategy," said Eisenhower, and the "broad laws of life" both involve "cooperation and surprise, concentration and maneuver." The important thing is to have a "viewpoint that is broad enough."[6] Their conversation ranged over the various issues of public policy, from labor-management relations and federal economic intervention and regulation, to the Soviet Union, and, finally, to the presidency. Eisenhower admitted privately to the editor that while he had "never sought and will not seek political office," he would respond "to a call of duty." "I certainly would like to be a useful citizen to my country, and that means readiness to serve whenever I can be of help."[7]

After an address by Eisenhower at the Columbia University high school forum, Robinson told him that what he had said with "such elegant simplicity is the most important public statement that has been made by anybody in this country in many years."[8] The American people know what they are against, he wrote Eisenhower. "What we desperately lack is an honored and respected voice which will define and explain the soundness and high moral value in our doctrine and creed, on the positive side."[9]

Eisenhower's stature and beaming countenance in the company of others had other political advantages as well. Although he rarely, if ever, asked for money himself, fund-raising occurred easily after an appearance by the war hero, whether it involved a speech, a visit, or simply an appointment. L. F. "Mc" McCollum was forty-eight years old and had no party affiliation, but because he was president of Continental Oil Corporation and a leader of the younger men in the Texas oil industry, Burnham contacted him and arranged an hour's visit with Ike.[10] Afterward the oilman revealed his high regard for Eisenhower's "aims for both Columbia and the country." He was, he said, "willing to work [to raise money]," and knew "ten men who would give a million dollars."[11]

An Eisenhower diary entry of July 7, 1949, provides a glimpse of one of his preoccupations at the time. The previous day Governor Dewey—who was pondering whether to run for reelection as governor of New York—had visited 60 Morningside Heights, staying for almost two hours. The two men discussed Dewey's conviction that "all middle-class citizens of education have a common belief that tendencies toward centralization and paternalism must be halted and reversed," but that "no one who voices these views can be elected." Eisenhower agreed with the governor, citing the futile efforts of Hoover, Landon, and Willkie. The Republican party, said Dewey, needed to "look around for someone of great popularity and who has not frittered away his political assets by taking positive stands against national planning." Eisenhower, he said, was such an individual. The general was flattered but replied that "he did *not* believe that anything can ever convince me that I have a *duty* to seek political office." ("Even as I said this," he noted in his diary, "I knew that to *him* I meant—'why surely, provided I ever become convinced I can win.'" Dewey, he noted, "is a rather persuasive talker. . . . God—how I wish that both parties had the courage to go out for militant advocacy to the middle' of the road.") Dewey then outlined a means by which Eisenhower might gracefully enter the partisan political arena—by declaring his GOP affiliation, running for and being elected governor of New York, and, finally, accepting the nomination for the presidency—all without saying much "as to my specific views." Eisenhower wrote that Dewey refused "to accept a final answer of 'no' on the governor business. . . . I am to let him know in the fall."[12]

To get a more systematic sense of how he was viewed by the public, Eisenhower accepted an offer from one of the resources at his disposal, the sociologist Robert K. Merton at the Columbia University Bureau of Applied Social Research. In July 1949 the bureau performed an analysis and summary of the twenty thousand political letters, postcards, and telegrams the general had received during the spring of 1948. Such an analysis was unprecedented, a twenty-seven-page summary with 160 pages of supporting information—arrived on Eisenhower's desk in September.[13] According to the report, Truman was viewed as sincere but lacking in competence. Dewey was competent but lacked sincerity. Eisenhower, however, possessed the "virtues of each and the inadequacies of neither."[14] Eisenhower, the summary reported, was perceived as a nonmilitaristic military man who had "earned through action the right to speak in the name of national unity."[15] Two of every three letters revealed concern about the international situation; the more worried the correspondents were, the more likely they were to mention his personal qualities.[16] Eighty-nine percent pleaded with him to run for president. Of the 9 percent who opposed a candidacy, almost three-quarters did so, interestingly, because they feared that his contact with politicians would "mar his otherwise unimpeachable position in the eyes of the American public." He was, they said, neither self-seeking nor a "tool" of special interests. His sincerity and warmth were his most appealing qualities. The kind of human being they felt him to be was more important than his achievements. He elicited feelings of affection, loyalty, and security.[17]

Eisenhower quickly placed the analysis under lock and key, much to the dismay of its authors. Merton and especially his assistant, Joan D. Goldhamer, had hoped for scholarly publication, but the report remained secret until after Eisenhower's death.[18] (Goldhamer suspected that keeping it from public view protected Eisenhower's image "as a selfless leader, concerned only with the public good," a "precious asset, most certainly if Eisenhower intended to become a candidate for president.")[19]

Invitations for speeches continued to arrive. Eisenhower accepted some of them as a means of floating trial balloons. In one such address, in Denver, he urged the nation's politicians to avoid extremes of left and right and move to the "middle of the road." Robinson sent him copies of the *Herald Tribune*'s coverage and wrote on September 6, 1949, "Your thesis that the middle constituted the only 'truly creative area' and that only here was the preservation of freedom possible, were telling points."[20]

Politics was the subject of a notable conversation in late September 1949. Eisenhower had turned down an invitation from President Truman (via their mutual friend, George Allen) to be a contestant for the 1949 Democratic nomination in the New York election to pick Senator Wagner's successor.[21] Robinson—who, of course, had much larger ambitions for the general than this—began to collaborate with GOP strategist Clarence Budington Kelland to create "opportunities to win the personal friendship of party leaders in a private way." "If this were done," said Kelland, "it would be easy to bring about spontaneous movements by certain valuable groups, acting independently to demand a draft. These things do not happen of themselves."[22] Perhaps such machinations prompted Henry Luce's wife, the Republican congresswoman Clare Boothe Luce, to stop by for a visit with Eisenhower. She bemoaned increasing federal subsidies, paternalism, the weakening of community responsibility and individual rights, federal power, loss of industrial leadership, and the worsening of the economy, and encouraged Eisenhower to continue to speak out on such issues. Mrs. Luce wrote to thank him. Their conversation, she said, had "lifted my heart about the nation greatly."[23] Eisenhower replied that he was "mighty glad that you were concerned enough, and thoughtful enough, to bring me the help of your ideas."[24]

"I may not be able, eventually," he confided to his diary after Luce's visit, "to resist the demands that could be placed on me to enter politics." Before the 1948 conventions, he recalled, the GOP leadership had favored Dewey and the grass roots had put pressure on him (Eisenhower) to run. In the Democratic party the situation had been the opposite. The bosses, "except for HST and his personal crowd," favored Eisenhower and the grass roots did not. But by mid-1949, he noted, the situation in the two parties had reversed. Numerous GOP leaders and many local Democrats now urged him to run. "If I ever, in the future, decide affirmatively on this point," he hastened to add, "it will be because I've become *over*-sold by friends! Well—nothing to do now but continue to fight for what I believe in—which is decentralization of both responsibility and authority in government."[25]

The various promptings that he "was to be a political figure in 1952," he said, had included: that the GOP had no leader with a following and therefore no one else could be built up to a position of leadership by 1952; that reelection of the Democrats would bring "socialization"; that "the people trust me"; that he could be nominated and elected; and, finally, that he could save the nation. He admitted that he could not "say to anyone that I would *not* do my best to perform a duty." But he could not, he said, "conjure up any picture of emergency, disaster or danger that would point irrevocably to *me* as the sole savior of the United States."[26]

Dewey came to Morningside Heights a second time on November 18, 1949, this time as a guest of Eisenhower for a luncheon to commemorate the completion of a Columbia University study of medical care in New York. Again Eisenhower refused Dewey's entreaties that he run for governor. This time, however, Eisenhower recorded the names of people who had talked politics with him in the past weeks. They included, in addition to Dewey and Clare Boothe Luce, Allan B. Kine of the Farm Bureau; David R. Calhoun, president of the Union Trust Company of St. Louis; Bedell Smith (who had talked with a group of industrialists); Lucius Clay (after talking with former Secretary of State James F. Byrnes); and Houston oilman Roy Cullen. Those who had offered help included Alton (Pete) Jones, Bill Burnham, and, of course, Bill Robinson.[27]

It seems evident that Eisenhower was in the midst of asking himself what constituted duty. Civic duty and the two-party system, he said in early 1950, "normally" requires that an individual participate in party activities. But his situation was not normal. As the former wartime European supreme commander, he would "never lose my direct and intimate interest in the legitimate aspirations and welfare" of the veterans of World War II, "both Democrats and Republicans." As a professional soldier, he would like to continue "to be of some help from time to time" to the nation regardless of the party in power. As president of Columbia, he represented students, faculty, trustees, alumni, and supporters. "My joining a specific party would certainly antagonize some." Finally, returning to the Finder letter, he worried that "many people considered a soldier's entry into politics an effort to overturn the concept of civil power as master over the military." Still, he fretted over the apparent decline in the importance of constitutional government, sound money, reasonable support for competitive enterprise, economy in public expenditures, states' rights, and equality before the law. Returning to what was now a refrain, he lamented that the day's politicians lacked the courage to take the "middle road and to face these issues." One newspaper that had espoused such principles was the *New York Sun*—it had to fold "because of unreasonable demands by labor leaders." And, of course, people kept coming to volunteer their services for "when I have decided I have responsibilities in the political field." These included Russell Sprague, a member of the Republican National Committee from New York; Herbert Brownell, the former GOP national chairman and Dewey's campaign manager; Sam Pryor, vice president of Pan American Airways; Arthur Gardner, a former tank corps officer and now assistant secretary of the treasury; Russ Forgan, a Chicago investment broker; and Wes MacAfee, president of the Union Electric Company of New Jersey.[28]

And if duty required that he enter the partisan political arena, how should he proceed? Cliff Roberts and Bill Robinson, his two closest friends and advisers, disagreed with Dewey's plan but also among themselves. Roberts argued that Eisenhower should support liberal members of the GOP in the 1950 election. If he did not, Taft might be the only notable Republican victory. This would assure the Ohio senator's nomination in 1952 and his defeat by Truman. If, on the other hand, Eisenhower did campaign and his candidates were successful, he might receive a Republican draft for the 1952 nomination, "even against your wishes." Robinson disagreed, believing that Eisenhower should remain aloof and "husband his resources" until the Republicans called upon him to "lead independent voters to their side."[29]

Without ever coming to a public decision in these matters, Eisenhower's actions provided answers. He had long since come to accept that virtually everything he said was newsworthy. Indeed, the only way he could avoid politics was to remain silent and thereby relinquish his duty as a citizen in behalf of policies he favored. This he had no intention of doing. His Gabriel Silver Lecture on March 23, 1950, mildly criticizing American defense policy, asserted that the United States had disarmed "to the point that its safety could be threatened." Five days after the speech appeared in the *New York Times*, Eisenhower found himself testifying at a hearing of the Military Subcommittee of the Senate Appropriations Committee about what he had meant.[30] He explained that he had helped to plan force levels represented in the

Defense Department's budget for 1950 and had generally agreed with the low budget, some $14 billion—which the president had then cut to $13 billion. But security in the postwar era, he said, involved much more than military spending. Although the United States was being threatened to some degree, there was no immediate crisis. Defense was a long-term proposition and combined economic, industrial, moral, intellectual, scientific, and, perhaps most of all, political strength—"a readiness among us to work earnestly and selflessly for a common cause."[31] "No absolute security," he said, could be "obtained through maintenance of armaments; I still believe that, as of today, our greatest chance for avoiding war is reasonable readiness for it. Moreover, I believe that without military force to back up moral integrity, intellectual honesty, and economic strength, our determined efforts to establish a peaceful world cannot succeed." He also had argued, he said, for a different distribution of resources. Certain areas of the military budget were too sparsely funded. They included garrisons at principal airfields in Alaska; plans to maintain forty-eight regular and twelve National Guard air force groups; anti-submarine forces; a program for modernizing the army's tanks, anti-aircraft, and vehicular programs; planning for industrial mobilization; a vigorous, incessant, and adequately supported effort for universal military training; and, finally, enhanced logistical transport for land, sea, and air.[32]

After the outbreak of the Korean War, pressures on Eisenhower to enter politics intensified. J. Earl Shaefer, a friend from Wichita, wrote to warn him that Defense Department officials were seeking to blame him (Eisenhower) for American unpreparedness in Korea.[33] Eisenhower responded angrily, referring to the points he had made at the congressional hearing.[34] His former boss, former Army Secretary Royall, reported to him a conversation with Republican National Chairman Guy Gabrielson. The two of them, he said, had gone through a list of possible presidential candidates and determined that all except Eisenhower were either unsuited or impractical. In response to a question about Ike's availability, Royall said he had told Gabrielson that Eisenhower would enter the race if the party offered the nomination without any effort on the general's part.[35] Douglas Southall Freeman sent reminders. In the autumn of 1946, he recalled, the general had told him that he "could not and would not run unless a situation developed in which you would be the man to whom the country would turn." "The time is near at hand," he said. "America is in the gravest dangers."[36] Eisenhower replied that he had not forgotten, and that the historian's words had "made a deeper and more lasting impression on me than anything else I have yet heard on the subject."[37] News of MacArthur's Inchon landing on September 15 and resulting enemy withdrawal brought a respite from political entreaties, but on October 13, Dewey telephoned that "if questioned he is going to announce his hope that" Eisenhower "would accept a Republican draft in 1952." Eisenhower replied, "No comment."[38]

The war in Korea brought yet another prominent Republican to see Eisenhower. Senator Henry Cabot Lodge, Jr., had admired the general ever since they had first met in North Africa in 1943.[39] By early June 1950, before the outbreak of war, Lodge, as junior U.S. senator from Massachusetts, had spoken about the security of the Western world in terms almost identical to those of Eisenhower. Now, after the North Korean army invaded the south, Lodge said he believed the weakness—not merely military but also political, economic, and spiritual—of the Western world made it vulnerable to being overwhelmed. Militarily, he asserted, the West was "totally inadequate to deter a Soviet aggressive act." As the leading and most prosperous nation in the Western bloc, the United States should continue to provide economic assistance but also should assist in developing a military strategy with a multinational framework and allied command structure (with a supreme commander). This, Lodge believed, should include Germany and a troop buildup to thirty divisions.[40] He and Eisenhower talked and discovered they were on congenial turf. In the weeks that followed his visit, Lodge stated publicly his conviction that Eisenhower should run for the presidency.

Eisenhower reiterated Lodge's themes in the months that followed the outbreak of war in Korea. In a speech for an American Legion groundbreaking ceremony in Denver on August 19, he bemoaned the wages of unpreparedness. "Unless there is intelligent, comprehensive, and ceaseless preparation in advance, we will always find ourselves woefully unready in emergency to meet aggression." An important reason for reasonable preparedness, he said, was its effectiveness in preserving peace. As things stood now, Americans, though "living up to the finest traditions of the American fighting man," were "outnumbered and fighting in Korea under indescribable difficulties."[41]

Robinson, meanwhile, in a letter to Freeman Gosden, writer and producer of the "Amos 'n' Andy" radio and television show, pointed out that the situation in Korea affected American strategy and its linchpin, Europe. The Europeans, he said, had become fatalistic. They had been expecting Russian aggression somewhere, and the United States had not. Eisenhower, he told Gosden, would be "ready for duty when the time and circumstances (meaning a real call from the American people) were appropriate."[42]

It was at about this time that Burnham told Eisenhower that Secretary of Defense Louis Johnson (replaced in August by George Marshall) was feuding with Secretary of State Dean Acheson, and that the joint chiefs had little respect for their civilian superior. The country "always looks for a military leader in time of danger," Burnham pointed out, and "there are only two today—you, and in a lesser degree, General Bradley." Burnham reported that the military would welcome Eisenhower's return to Washington and that the political leadership was "afraid of your power and popularity with the people."[43]

The political wheels that Eisenhower had set privately in motion in the early spring and summer of 1948 also continued to roll. As Eisenhower's agent, Ed Clark, along with Robinson and Burnham, had brought various people to Columbia University to meet the hero from Abilene. On his own, Clark also began seeking an individual of national political stature to lead an Eisenhower-for-President movement and, keeping the general informed about what was happening, made trips to key states.[44] Republican National Chairman Gabrielson, asked Clark's group—now called the Republican Progressive Movement (with the catchy acronym RPM) and including such congressmen and senators as Henry Cabot Lodge, Jr., Irving Ives, Christian Herter, Clifford Case, and Jacob Javits—to "draft something positive in respect to Republican principles." They complied. Clark sent a draft to Eisenhower in January 1950; and on February 9—mainstream Republican leaders having issued a policy statement—Clark told Eisenhower that the RPM hoped to have sufficient following by autumn "to cause selection of liberal Republicans in the primaries in each state for officers ranging from dog catcher to senator." The RPM planned to appeal to independent voters and younger elements of the party.[45]

Clark and Brownlee, meanwhile, invited Eisenhower to become a trustee of the Committee for Economic Development (CED), whose board members included such prominent individuals as W. Walter Williams, chairman of Continental Can; Marion B. Folsom, chairman of the CED research and policy committee; and Philip D. Reed, chairman of General Electric. Eisenhower declined. He supported their work, he told them, but was too busy.[46] In fact, he was probably not yet ready to associate himself publicly with their positions on the issues.

The CED's approach to Eisenhower was not surprising, and its interest in him was important politically. Its chairman was none other than Eisenhower's friend, Paul G. Hoffman, an individual whose convictions and activities in the months that followed did much to bring him the Republican presidential nomination. A Los Angeles automobile salesman who became a regional distributor of Studebaker cars in southern California, Hoffman had risen from director of the near-bankrupt South Bend, Indiana, automobile corporation in 1930 to become one of the nation's most influential citizens. With Studebaker sales plummeting because of the Great Depression, Hoffman took over as president of the company. With the help of Wall Street attorney Maurice "Tex" Moore (the husband of Henry Luce's sister Elizabeth), he drafted a reorganization plan, and in succeeding years Hoffman and Luce became friends, the publisher traveling to South Bend to write an article about the young corporate president and his automobile company. Fortune magazine touted Hoffman for his managerial skills in its very first issue in 1930, and in 1942 Hoffman became national chairman for Luce's favorite charity, United China Relief.

After the war, in 1946, not surprisingly, *Life* carried a ten-page article about Hoffman and Studebaker.[47]

With Luce's assistance, Hoffman came to represent enlightened business practices. He believed corporate executives must be citizens and contributors, and in 1939–1940 he initiated discussions about such things with University of Chicago president Robert M. Hutchins. Hoffman recommended that the University sponsor a forum that would bring together scholars, businessmen, and representatives of organized labor to seek solutions to current economic problems and, more broadly, to study the historical reasons for the collapse of free societies. Hutchins and his assistant, William Benton, soon agreed to sponsor the American Policy Commission (APC) to carry out these activities. The members of the first APC were Henry Luce, Marshall Field, Ralph Flanders, Beardsly Ruml, Thomas B. McCabe, R. D. Deupree, and Ray Rubicam.[48] In 1942, with U.S. involvement in World War II, the secretary of commerce established a business advisory committee and encouraged Hoffman and his colleagues, in addition to their other duties, to sponsor research and issue reports for the government. Accordingly, the APC enlarged its board to eighteen members (who also served on the Department of Commerce advisory committee), changed its name to the Committee for Economic Development (CED), and established two divisions—research and field. The former studied and wrote reports on the effect of wartime decisions on the postwar economy; the latter provided assistance to industry. By 1946 the CED had 75,000 members (organized by Federal Reserve region); Hoffman was chairman, spokesman, and the focus of publicity.[49]

With the end of the war the CED found itself involved in politics. It concerned itself with how to ensure economic freedom and provide incentives to productivity while keeping a satisfactory level of employment, and supported some elements of the New Deal, such as the minimum wage, unemployment compensation, workers' pensions, public works to compensate for local unemployment, all government measures—including the Bretton Woods monetary agreements—to expand international trade, and the Employment Act of 1946.[50] Not surprisingly, these positions put the CED at loggerheads with Senator Taft, who desired most of all to return to free-market mechanisms. For him, the International Monetary Fund—that part of the Bretton Woods arrangements designed to spark postwar international development—was "pouring money down a rathole."

As CED chairman, Hoffman operated on the principle that any attempt by the United States to fight communism by itself would merely increase its possibility of becoming a garrison or corporatist state. For him, international generosity was part of enlightened self-interest.[51] In late 1947, Hoffman became a member of a nineteen-member committee on foreign aid which, under the direction of Averell Harriman, lobbied for the Marshall Plan.[52] By that time he also had joined representatives of the National Association of Manufacturers and the United States Chamber of Commerce to form the Committee on International Economic Policy, whose chairman was Winthrop Aldrich.[53] It therefore made sense that Senator Arthur Vandenberg, the former isolationist but now committed internationalist GOP chairman of the Senate Foreign Relations Committee, supported Hoffman's appointment in 1948 as administrator of the European Recovery Program.[54] With the outbreak of war in Korea, interestingly, Hoffman also became a member of the Committee for the Present Danger.[55] (On November 7, 1950, the European Recovery Program well on its way, Hoffman accepted the invitation of Henry Ford II to become president of the Ford Foundation. He brought with him as legal counsel his longtime friend and associate, "Tex" Moore.)

On November 30, 1950, Lodge again met with Eisenhower. Several days earlier, several hundred thousand troops of the Chinese People's Liberation Army had appeared on the Korean side of the Yalu River, surprising and splitting MacArthur's armies and sending them into retreat. The senator from Massachusetts and Eisenhower now covered topics ranging from German rearmament to universal military service, but the situation in Korea was paramount. Three and a half divisions in South Korea in June 1950, Eisenhower reiterated, would have been a 50 percent increase and "would have made all the difference." As things were now, he "was very much troubled." As for his appointment as SACEUR, Eisenhower said it would be, in large measure, a question of "rebuilding the morale of the French." Only half in jest, he invited Lodge (recalling that the senator had served as his liaison with French commanders) to take a six months' leave from his Senate duties and accompany him to Paris, "to provide leadership for the French." Lodge, flattered by the idea, hesitated, but Eisenhower went on, enjoying the conversation. "People say I have a wonderful chance of being President," said Eisenhower. "If Europe collapses and we are isolated in the world, it would mean that I would be President of a police state. The Presidency would not be very attractive," he said, "with all the rest of the world as slaves."[56]

Robinson now found himself fending off entreaties from individuals who wanted Eisenhower to declare, if not his candidacy, at least his party affiliation. He told Ralph Moores of Portland, Oregon, that Eisenhower would prefer to remain as president of Columbia University, but "it is possible he would be moved by overwhelming public demand."[57] In another letter Robinson alluded to a practical difficulty with an Eisenhower declaration of affiliation—the fact that the GOP was the minority party. A candidate, he said, could not be elected on the registered Republican vote alone. He must be able to attract "independent and unaffiliated votes."[58]

By this time, and apparently unbeknownst to Robinson, Clark had met with Governor James Duff of Pennsylvania, who was running for U.S. senator and would be elected in November. An excellent speaker, Duff, at Clark's request, agreed to lead a draft-Eisenhower movement.[59] In October and November of 1950 the two men were meeting frequently to discuss strategy. They advised Eisenhower to continue as he was doing and remain publicly aloof from Dewey, who also was working to promote an Eisenhower candidacy.[60] In late November 1950, a few days before his conversation with Lodge, Eisenhower had met with Clark, Duff, and John G. Bennett, a politician from Rochester, New York, whom Helen Reid had recommended. Russell Davenport had planned to attend but was stranded by a transportation failure of some sort and wrote a letter afterward. The meeting was, he told Eisenhower, the "fruit of almost two years of very humble and painstaking work on the part of Eddie, John, and myself." The next step, he said, was "to begin to get fairly concrete about policies" and "better acquainted, in an informal way, with your thinking."[61]

Clark, Bennett, Duff, and Davenport met with Eisenhower for one last time on December 27, just three days before he left for his NATO assignment.[62] By this time Clark and Burnham agreed that they should remain in the United States. Burnham, having headed the National Draft Eisenhower League in 1948, was "too hot" to have on the NATO staff, "where all political implications should be avoided." It would be better, he said, for him to be in the United States where "whatever needed to be said or whatever needed to be done could be accomplished without [the appearance of] your knowledge." Clark, rather than become Eisenhower's NATO logistics chief—a possibility they discussed—would work in the political field, making trips back and forth to SHAPE as Eisenhower's private liaison with Duff and the politicos.[63]

Thus it was clear that by the time Eisenhower departed for his new military command, he was deeply involved with individuals and organizations who yearned for his presidential candidacy. He was giving them such encouragement that it is difficult to characterize his role as anything other than participation in a quiet conspiracy.

☆ **8** ☆

NATO COMMAND

EISENHOWER'S NEW MISSION came at a time when the atomic bomb, now in possession of both the United States and the Soviet Union, had created the unprecedented possibility that a war could bring destruction of sufficient magnitude to cause the deaths of hundreds of thousands, probably millions of noncombatants. His new job was to create an allied military command in Europe that included West Germany. (It would be admitted to NATO membership in 1955, but in 1950 this was far from certain.) Eisenhower knew he would need the forces of this new ally to stop any attack by the Soviets. A challenge of almost unimaginable difficulty, the alliance's cumbersome administrative structure increased the chances for failure.

President Truman had designated Eisenhower Supreme Allied Commander in Europe (SACEUR), and he thus served at the pleasure of the American commander-in-chief. But he received his authority from a joint resolution of all twelve member governments of NATO. At the top of the ladder of authority was the supreme policy-making body, the North Atlantic Council (NAC), made up of the foreign ministers of the NATO countries. It met periodically in a variety of locations and appointed so-called council deputies who met in continuous session in London. A defense committee of the member defense ministers, and a military committee of the member military chiefs of staff, reported to the council. The SACEUR reported to the standing group, which in turn reported to the military committee.[1] The success of Eisenhower's mission depended on his ability both to inspire and to maintain lines of communication with all those above and below him and the authorities, including Congress, at home — persuading them all to support what he proposed.[2]

After taking an indefinite leave from his duties at Columbia and arriving in Paris, in January 1951 Eisenhower traveled by air to visit the ten NATO European capitals and Ottawa, Canada.[3] He wanted to introduce himself to the heads of state and council members, and to get a sense of the cooperation he could expect. When he returned to Washington at the end of January, he was the man of the hour. President Truman greeted him at the airport. At a cabinet meeting the next day, he laid out his contingency plan — the basis for requests for troops and weapons that would, he hoped, promote the political unity necessary to build confidence and deter a Soviet military attack that he doubted was near at hand. The "only reason the 350 million people of Western Europe," with tremendous industrial capacity and "a highly skilled and educated population," had to fear "190 million backward people [of the Soviet Union]," he said, was the unity the Russians forced on their people "at the point of a bayonet." His job, he declared, was to bring about genuine unity in the defense of Western Europe. If he could do that, "most of the danger would end." The biggest hindrance to this was not the appeal of communism but "neutralism."[4]

To the cabinet secretaries, generals, and admirals gathered in the cabinet room of the White House, Eisenhower described Europe as a bottle. Its base was Russia and the neck western Europe; "stretching down to the end of the bottle" was Spain. On either side of this neck to the north and south "are bodies of water," the Baltic and the Mediterranean, respectively, "that we control with land on the far side of the water which is good for air bases." In the Mediterranean he would provide arms to Turkey (not yet in NATO) and Yugoslavia (since 1948 no longer part of the Soviet bloc). In the event of Soviet aggression, he would apply air and sea power in converging fashion toward eastern Europe while relying on solid land forces in the west. If the Russians sought to move ahead in the center (western Europe), he would hit them on both flanks, putting them in a vicelike trap.[5]

Eisenhower wanted the United States to mobilize materiel "as if

we were actually at war." He called for "rapid conversion of the American economy so that we can get the equipment to these people [in
Europe]."[6] The combined NATO army, he said, ought to be "50 to 60
divisions, not including Germany . . . just as rapidly as possible."[7] "I
don't know how fast Charlie Wilson [Director of Defense Mobiliza-
tion] is producing tanks," he said, "but I know it's not fast enough."[8]
Responding to the charge being made by Senator Taft that such a
force might provoke the Soviet Union to attack, he said that fifty divisions (approximately 850,000 troops) on the Rhine could not possibly
attack Russia, "and Russia knew it." By the time such an army reached
the borders of Russia, it would be "too feeble to do anything at all."
Given the advantage of the defense over the offense, this force nevertheless would be sufficient, assuming adequate air and naval support,
to resist a Soviet attack.[9] The key, he said, was to "get this spiral of
strength going up in Europe. Right now it's going down."[10]

His next task, on February 12, was to address a joint meeting of
Congress. Without "aggressive or any belligerent intent in a world in
which the power of military might is still too much respected," he said,
"we are going to build for ourselves a secure wall of peace and security." The alternative would be "to stand alone and isolated in a world
dominated by communism." An independent, cooperating, economically resurgent western Europe, with the help of American troops and
materiel, soon would be able to defend itself.[11] But Eisenhower urged
moderation. The aim, after all, was to preserve "a way of life." Political, religious, and economic freedom in the United States could be
jeopardized by too large an undertaking to defend them. "We must remain solvent as we attempt a solution to this great problem of security,
else we have lost the battle from within that we are trying to win from
without." The American burden, he believed, would involve military
readiness and economic support for free governments for more than
twenty years.[12]

Responding to questions about the possibility of his presidential
candidacy, he told the legislators that he "had no end to serve, as I
know you have no end to serve, except the good of the United
States."[13] His painstaking, thoughtful, and comprehensive approach;

forthright and gracious manner; sonorous voice; and magnetic intensity—a kind of electricity that followed him wherever he went—were enormously persuasive. Edward J. Bermingham of Chicago—a member of the Columbia University fund-raising group and of the Republican National Committee—had his ear to the ground, so to speak. He reported to Eisenhower that the country as a whole considered his tour "a national triumph—now you can let the chips fall where they may."[14]

But Eisenhower had reason to be pessimistic. Perhaps better than anyone else, he knew that his mission depended upon the support of the American people and their representatives in Congress, their willingness to turn away from the criticisms and blandishments of the neoisolationists. The 1950 congressional elections had revealed the confusion and unhappiness of the American public. The victors that year had been conservative and right-wing Republicans. In Indiana, for instance, Senator Homer E. Capehart—a rotund, cigar-smoking, former jukebox manufacturer—was elected to a second term. (He ultimately would serve three.) A Midwestern conservative, he combined red-baiting with nationalistic sentiment (he had voted against the Marshall Plan). Later he would trim his sails and become one of Eisenhower's supporters as chairman of the Senate Banking Committee. In 1950, however, he spoke favorably of Taft and won reelection by more than 103,000 votes despite a strong Democratic opponent.[15]

Senator Taft, the man pundits had labeled "Mr. Republican" because of his prominent position in the Senate and his past appearances as a candidate for the GOP presidential nomination, also won reelection, a victory even larger than Capehart's. He defeated four-term state auditor Joseph T. Ferguson by the second largest plurality to that time (431,184) in the history of Ohio senatorial elections. Carrying eighty-four of the eighty-eight Ohio counties, Taft had what one historian called "the most impressive triumph of any Republican senator in 1950."[16] The Communist "menace"—specifically, revelations of Soviet atomic espionage in the United States which had been taken up by the Republican demagogue from Wisconsin, Senator Joseph R. McCarthy—was a major factor. The accusations had become alarming because of the Soviet atomic bomb, the outbreak of the Korean War, and the possibility by this time of Chinese intervention in Korea. The cost of living in the United States, because of increased military spending and wage pressure from organized labor, had risen.[17] With these issues as ammunition, the regular Republican organization in Ohio launched voter registration drives in politically active middle-class wards.[18] After his triumph in Ohio, Taft looked forward hopefully to the 1952 presidential nomination. After Dewey's defeat in 1944 and 1948, he believed it was his turn.

Eisenhower was dismayed. Senator Arthur Vandenberg, the ranking Republican and former chairman of the Senate Foreign Relations Committee, the individual whose resolution in 1948 had prepared the way for U.S. ratification of NATO, was now dead of cancer. The party thus looked to Taft for guidance in foreign affairs.[19] The new SACEUR sensed what historians later discovered, that the Ohio senator was uninformed and naive about strategic matters. Taft's statements about NATO after his reelection in the late autumn included the follow: "'The thing about Europe,' he asked, 'is can you defend it? If Russia has the atomic bomb, can't they knock the devil out of Europe?'" He did not know the answer to these questions, he admitted, but said he advocated "re-examining" American foreign policy." Then, revealing no comprehension of the importance of western European confidence and unity, he suggested that a large land force was of "dubious value." Defending American interests, he insisted, "rests far more on an all-powerful air force."[20] Taft's biographer, James T. Patterson, later concluded that the senator "knew relatively little about foreign affairs and had scorned the Pentagon and State Department over the years." He thus "leaped into the fray of foreign policy in 1951," according to Patterson, "without finding time to brief himself."[21]

One must assume that Taft, whose wife had recently been invalided by a stroke, for whatever reason failed to comprehend the extent of the problems the nation faced. Certainly he had a very different view of how to address them.[22] In any event, he misjudged the popular atmosphere of carping and ideological accusation. He assumed mistakenly that most voters believed McCarthy's partisan attacks and thought the Truman administration was following both faulty foreign policy and "socialist principles."[23]

Probably at the suggestion of Ed Clark, Eisenhower decided to seek personally the senator's commitment to American participation in European collective security. In the days before his return to Europe in early February 1951, having completed his visit to Washington, he arranged a private meeting with the Senate minority leader.[24] It took place secretly early one evening in an office in the Pentagon arranged for Eisenhower's use. If he could get a commitment from Taft, Eisenhower told certain members of his staff, he would remove himself from consideration as a presidential candidate. In the course of the conversation, however, Taft refused the entreaty. Unknowingly, he thereby ensured a formidable and, as it would turn out, insurmountable challenge to his quest for the presidency.[25]

Departing for Paris in mid-February 1951, Ike and Mamie traveled in civilized fashion, aboard the Cunard liner *Queen Elizabeth*, the world's largest passenger vessel. At a farewell dinner the evening before, Bill Robinson had gathered Eisenhower's friends, and they gave the general a leather briefcase as a going-away present. He told Robinson that he did "not see how you could occupy a more advantageous position than you already do for potential assistance to me and to the beliefs that you and I hold in common." Nevertheless, he added knowingly, "it is wonderful to know that you are ready at any moment to take on any new chore."[26]

Mamie was not happy to leave New York. She tended to settle in wherever she and her husband found themselves. And she and Ike had purchased a farm—a retirement location—in a bucolic setting near Gettysburg, Pennsylvania, virtually on the site of Pickett's charge, where Union grapeshot and rifle fire in 1863 had put an end to Robert E. Lee's hopes of taking the war to the North and marked a turning point of the Civil War. The Eisenhowers had hoped to settle there after their Columbia duties were over. It was a way also to be close to John, now an instructor at West Point. His wife, Barbara, on March 31, 1948, had given birth to the Eisenhower's first grandchild, a son, David. Mamie adored the child and enjoyed afternoon drives up the

Hudson River to visit him. Now, suddenly, these pleasures were over.[27] Still, as an army wife she had learned to be flexible. She justified this latest move by saying, patriotically, that it was "something we have to do for our children and our grandchildren, so we might as well do it with all our hearts and souls."[28]

Arriving in Paris by train from Cherbourg on the Normandy coast—a location with momentous memories for the former supreme commander of the D-day invasion just seven years earlier—the Eisenhowers moved temporarily to a six-room suite at the Trianon Palace Hotel while workmen renovated the white, fourteen-room mansion with Tuscan columns, called Villa St. Pierre, in the suburb of Rocquencourt, thirty minutes' drive from downtown Paris.[29] The newly appointed SACEUR scribbled a note to himself: "We must remember that we are building defenses against the possibility of an emergency which will never be of our making. The tactical incidents of cold war and localized shooting wars must not be allowed to weaken our resolution promptly to attain respectable strength."[30] It is possible to understand Eisenhower's perception of the Soviet threat—and therefore his definition of "respectable strength"—from reading his notes of February 22, 1951, on that subject. Rear Admiral Leslie Clark Stevens had recently returned from duty as American naval attaché at the U.S. embassy in Moscow. Working now as consultant to the Joint Chiefs of Staff in the Office of Policy Coordination of the Central Intelligence Agency, he had given an address at the National War College classified "Top Secret." It was entitled "A National Strategy for the Soviet Union." Averell Harriman, the president's assistant for national security affairs, had obtained a mimeographed copy of the talk and scribbled on it: "This is most interesting reading. I'm sure you will agree," and passed it to Eisenhower.

The general read it thoroughly, underlining and annotating it. The United States, Stevens asserted, had overestimated Soviet capabilities and intentions, and their willingness to use war as an instrument of national policy. The prevailing military wisdom (influenced by Pentagon contingency plans and prudent "worst case" analyses as incorporated in NSC-68) seemed to be that the Soviets sought world domination and, given an opportunity—which could come as a result of achieving nuclear capability—would move aggressively to gain their objective. But Stevens saw a far different Soviet Union, one still largely prostrate from World War II but in the hands of a leadership that used hostility to the West as a means of retaining power. These leaders, he said, perceived their country to be weak in the short term but strong in the long term. They believed their Marxist-Leninist predictions of the superiority of their system and that it would prevail. This would happen, in their view, however, not because of actions they would take to bring the downfall of the West but rather because capitalism was prone to economic depressions that made it vulnerable to takeover by militarists. In other words, they probably foresaw a replay of the events that led in the 1930s to European fascism.

The Soviet threat to the United States and its allies, Stevens said, was thus twofold—and, interestingly, in the power of the allies to control. The first source of the threat was excessive Western defense spending; the second was complacency and isolationism. The first assumed that the U.S. government, anxious not to be caught off guard, would exaggerate estimates of Soviet capabilities and intentions and return to an excessive military buildup and government controls that would damage both civil liberties and the economy. The second assumed that the Soviet leaders, deciding the time was not yet right for expanding their political influence, would employ a conciliatory strategy to produce a perception in the West that military preparedness no longer was necessary. This would increase relative Soviet strength through intimidation and subversion, as in eastern Europe, or through their capacity to influence proxy wars, such as those in Korea and Indochina. "What would happen to the North Atlantic Treaty," he asked, "when the common catalyst of fear of the Russians was removed?" Such a strategy, said Stevens (one is reminded here of the concerns of the CPD) "would be more effective than war over an equivalent time in disarming us and destroying our alliances."[31]

Eisenhower, like Stevens, discounted the air force's view that "the only thing keeping the Soviet Union from initiating global war . . . is the damage they would receive from air bombardment—specifically, the atomic bomb." This was, he scribbled in the margin of the Stevens speech, "short-cut thinking."[32] Eisenhower noted that he "had preached for five years" the view that the "national strategy of the Soviet Union . . . does not contemplate any global war of her own choosing under the conditions that now obtain in the world and which would continue to obtain as long as the West continues to demonstrate that the basic Communist philosophy is false."[33] And he "thoroughly believed" Stevens's assertion that the Soviet leadership would use not just military means but also an "understanding of enemy [Western] weaknesses and conflicts. . . . in the fields of politics, ideology, and economics" and "cunning, deception and force to take maximum advantage of them."[34] "It seems probable," Stevens wrote, that "for many, many years we shall be confronted with much the same sort of dangerous, uneasy world in which we now live." Eisenhower noted his agreement—"the very foundation of logical policy today"—and wrote to Stevens, complimenting his work.[35] The Stevens speech, he said, had "few if any equals in current military and political writings for its readability and splendid logic of its arguments." He made it "required reading at once" for SHAPE staff members.[36]

In the weeks that followed, Eisenhower moved forward on the political side of his undertaking as well as the military. Indeed, as he had shown by his private meeting with Taft, the former was more crucial to him. General Alfred Gruenther, his chief of staff (and later his successor as SACEUR), later recalled that Eisenhower had to "inspire a somewhat apathetic civilization in Europe, as well as in the United States," and be a sort of "combination Billy Sunday and military genius." He was, needless to say, "heavily involved in political matters."[37] Support both at home and in Europe, Eisenhower knew, was a *sine qua non*; dedication and enthusiasm had to precede tanks, aircraft, troops, and industrial supplies. He established a NATO congressional liaison office and placed in charge the man with more experience than anyone else at military lobbying, General Jerry Persons, the army's contact with Congress during World War II.[38] But Eisenhower remained his own best advocate. Brown University president Henry Wriston once exclaimed that he had "never heard any public figure give as good an exposition of his general outlook as Eisenhower."[39] One notable instance of this occurred on Labor Day, 1950, when Eisenhower gave the opening radio address for a special cause that was being led by Lucius Clay and funded by the CIA, called the Crusade for Freedom. In the six weeks that followed the speech, 15.5 million Americans joined the Crusade and contributed $1.3 million to Radio Free Europe for the purpose of broadcasting messages of truth and democracy to countries behind the Iron Curtain. This type of leadership, said Clay, referring to Eisenhower's magnetism, "making full use of our native salesmanship," would enable the United States to "avoid full-scale war."[40] Robinson meanwhile corresponded with the supreme commander and worked with Helen Reid to see to it that the *Herald Tribune* countered efforts by the Hearst papers and the *Chicago Tribune* to portray Eisenhower as an instrument of the Truman administration's foreign and domestic policies. The administration, Robinson said, had taken until 1950 to wake up to the warnings that Eisenhower had asserted in 1947. For his part, Eisenhower wrote Bermingham, protesting rumors that his new command meant that he was "joining the administration." He was "only performing a military duty." He had opposed in an "extreme degree," he said, some of the foreign and domestic policies "of the past years." He wanted Bermingham's help to achieve "that unity of basic purpose that we must have if this effort is ever to enjoy any success." Military tasks, he observed—echoing what he had often said at Columbia University—were not like "constructive" educational ones, "to create and develop." They instead were necessary evils, "to protect or defend."[41]

In order to rally support, Eisenhower warned that the Soviet Union combined traditional Russian imperialistic designs with the physical resources of Asia and eastern Europe, working toward the Communist objective of world revolution and "domination of all the earth." The Soviet Red Army, after all, had beaten back the *Wehrmacht* on the eastern front during World War II and had liberated eastern Germany. The United States, he told the Republican committeeman, must be ready to meet threats of aggression and internal subversion, first of all by remaining economically strong—proving wrong the Communist

claims that capitalism is "weak, inefficient, and unfair." The importance of western Europe became evident, he said, pointing to the
value of the European colonial possessions, when one contemplated
the "staggering" increase in Soviet military might if the people and resources of that region and its spheres in Africa—including the Belgian
Congo (radioactive cobalt), the Middle East (petroleum), and the
Suez Canal (lines of shipping)—came under Communist control.
The possibility that these resources, including materials for the atomic
bomb, would no longer be available to the United States, he said, kept
him awake at night and had caused him to return to military service
rather than do as he preferred, which was to devote his remaining
years to Columbia University.[42]

At home, the Columbia trustees and Eisenhower's friends and supporters of the American Assembly became a kind of NATO support
system. They included W. Alton "Pete" Jones, Ellis Slater, David
Rockefeller, Jock Whitney, and Robert Woodruff. Pledges to the Assembly, accordingly, continued to pour in, and by November 1950 to-
taled $536,000.[43] (The first session of the Assembly, on May 21, 1951,
addressed the theme "United States Relations with Western Europe."
It also provided a forum for a debate between Taft and, in support of
U.S. policy, Democratic senator Paul Douglas of Illinois.)[44] Meanwhile the officers of the Committee for Economic Development—
Reed, Brownlee, and Clarence Francis, chief executive officer of
General Foods Corporation—met with Columbia School of Business
dean Phil Young to discuss the possibility of a merger of the CED and
the American Assembly. They agreed, ultimately, that the two organizations should work in tandem instead of merging, the CED basing its
actions at least in part on the deliberations of the Assembly.[45]

On the military side, Eisenhower had first of all to mesh the new
European defense force with American contingency planning and
preparations, including planning by the U.S. air force. That service
had responded to the outbreak of war in Korea by requesting 140 combat wings for fiscal 1954. Air force chief of staff, General Hoyt Vandenberg, observed that the Strategic Air Command had three missions:
"to destroy Soviet war-making industry, to neutralize its atomic deliv-

ery capacity, and to delay a Soviet advance into Western Europe." By early autumn 1950, Truman had approved expansion of the air force to 143 wings (including 17 troop carrier wings and 57 for SAC).[46] Eisenhower accepted this in planning his ground force.

U.S. planning called for a European ground defense by troops from the NATO European members. As Eisenhower put it, the United States would supply the rifles, the European allies the men for a NATO army.[47] As the historian of NATO, Lawrence Kaplan, has pointed out, the Korean War made possible what heretofore had been out of the question. Before the North Korean aggression, the European nations, and especially France, had found the idea of German participation in a European military alliance abhorrent. Memories of German aggression were simply too strong. The Korean War changed this. Now it was clear that military action by Soviet-sponsored proxy states was possible. In Kaplan's words, "the specter of 60,000 East German paramilitary troops backed by 27 Soviet divisions in the eastern zone, demanded more than increased military aid. The crisis demanded the reorganization of the alliance."[48] By the time he left Europe in May 1952, Eisenhower, drawing upon his enormous prestige among the former World War II allies, had accomplished this reorganization. He won concessions from France, in return for U.S. troops and command, that allowed the incorporation of German troops into NATO forces and in May 1952 the signing of a treaty creating a European Defense Community. The French National Assembly later voted down this treaty, but by 1955, with restrictions on German production of nuclear weapons and a requirement that German troops would be commanded wholly by the alliance, the Federal Republic of Germany became the fifteenth member of NATO, after Greece and Turkey.[49]

The military buildup was not, however, easily accomplished. In December 1950 the NAC, besides creating an integrated defense force and the post of SACEUR, established force goals for 1954 at 49½ ready divisions (excluding German forces) with an increase to 95⅓ within 90 days of the outbreak of war. Germany would be expected to rearm and participate in the future. Since the European nations had no desire to allow their countries to be overrun as proposed by the American OFF-

TACKLE plan, Eisenhower planned to hold a line at the Rhine river—despite the fact that the American joint chiefs refused to deviate from the OFFTACKLE withdrawal concept. Truman asked Congress on July 26, 1951, in addition to $1 billion already approved, for $3.5 billion for supplemental assistance to alleviate huge European shortages in artillery, tanks, half-tracks, and aircraft.[50]

Eisenhower soon saw that the major obstacle to these force goals was a lack of urgency, both at home and abroad. Harriman, Eisenhower's designated contact at the White House, reported that Congress was intent upon "side tracking" UMT and universal military service and cutting funding for the Voice of America.[51] The allies had conflicting interests in Africa, the Middle East, Korea, and Southeast Asia.[52] Britain faced loss of its oil fields in Iran because of a nationalist revolution; and France was reticent not only because of its historical experience of three German invasions but because of its possible loss of Indochina to a revolution led by the Communist Viet Minh guerillas of Ho Chi Minh.[53]

In any event, the force levels could not be met. By mid-1951, declines in industrial output and rising trade and balance-of-payments deficits were plaguing the European economies. Nor could the United States meet its goals for military assistance shipments. In September 1951 the NAC established a Temporary Council Committee of Averell Harriman, Jean Monnet of France, and Edwin Plowden of Great Britain to determine more feasible goals. Their recommendations at the Lisbon conference the following February reduced the original force goals, set a quota of 12 West German divisions, and adjusted overall levels to 41⅔ ready divisions, increased to 89⅔ by thirty days after the outbreak of war.[54]

These NATO difficulties reflected in part the politics of American defense planning. U.S. defense commitments in both Asia and Europe, according to the Joint Chiefs of Staff fiscal 1952 budget, required 21 army divisions, 3 marine divisions, 408 major combat vessels, 143 air force wings, and total personnel of 3.9 million. But with the decline of Truman's popularity as the Korean War stalemated and federal budget deficits reached $10 billion for 1952 and $12 billion for 1953, the president approved the force levels but not the appropriations request of $108 billion. Then, in December 1951, Truman delayed the buildup, holding spending to $44 billion in 1952 and $60 billion in 1953 and pushing back the target date when the United States could meet the Soviet threat from 1954 to 1956. Congress then cut $2 billion more from the budget, mainly from the army, and reduced the $5.3 billion requested by Truman for aid to Europe to $4.2 billion.[55]

This cost-cutting enhanced the importance of nuclear weapons as a part of the Western defense force. There was no question but that nuclear weapons would be available for use in the event of a Soviet attack on western Europe. As early as 1948, Eisenhower and his successor as army chief of staff, General Omar Bradley, recognized that the European allies would never accept a contingency plan that entailed an American withdrawal from the continent. By October of that year the Atomic Energy Commission, as noted earlier, had told the joint chiefs that it would be able to deliver four hundred Nagasaki-type plutonium bombs by January 1951. This was much faster than anticipated. U.S. planners could now develop contingency plans with an eye to having as many such bombs as they considered necessary.[56] In early 1949, as acting chairman of the Joint Chiefs of Staff, Eisenhower had ordered the preparation of plans that included the bombing of targets that would retard a Soviet advance, as well as strategic bombing of industrial areas.[57] On March 10, 1949, at a time when the U.S. nuclear arsenal numbered perhaps fifty large strategic weapons, General Kenneth Nichols, head of the Armed Forces Special Weapons Project, sought Eisenhower's support for a nuclear production program for thousands, rather than hundreds, of weapons. The following October 19, Truman, after the Soviet atomic explosion and on the recommendation of the National Security Council, approved the request.[58] As SACEUR, Eisenhower now had somehow to integrate these weapons into NATO strategy, without threatening the Soviet Union or making it appear to either the allies or the American public that nuclear weapons would render ground force levels unnecessary. If this was to occur, a key element was that the SACEUR have "all necessary authority in the planning and control of atomic operations in his area."[59]

The allies needed to understand the importance of atomic weapons, be willing to accept their use in the event of war, and allow U.S. nuclear forces to be based on their soil. (It was not until December 1954, with Eisenhower as president, that NATO force planning was sufficiently advanced that his replacement as SACEUR could assume that nuclear weapons would be used to meet a Soviet attack.)[60]

By December 1951, Eisenhower, with Lodge's assistance in the Senate, had brought movement toward a NATO army with German components and six American divisions. Harriman reported that while the original target for 1954 was unattainable, funds authorized by participating governments should make it possible to reach total force requirements by 1956, with a "substantial level" of deterrence by 1952.[61] Eisenhower's name, Harriman had reported to the president on November 21, remained "the symbol of united effort in Europe." Truman replied that his faith in Eisenhower "has never wavered nor ever will. He is the man for the job" and he has all the "dynamic qualities of the true leader." But Eisenhower knew that his mission was still far from accomplished.[62]

Douglas MacArthur and Eisenhower on May 10, 1946, after Ike's arrival at Tokyo's Atsugi Airfield. (U.S. ARMY SIGNAL CORPS PHOTO)

With the football team while president at Columbia University.
(EISENHOWER LIBRARY)

From left, Eisenhower, Mamie, Cliff Roberts, an unidentified woman,
William Robinson, and George Allen in April 1948 in Augusta, Georgia.
(EISENHOWER LIBRARY)

From left, Dick Garlington, John Hay "Jock" Whitney, Cliff Roberts, William Robinson, Bobby Jones, Ellis "Slats" Slater, Robert "Colonel" Jones, Eisenhower, and Phil Reed at the Augusta National Golf Club, circa 1949–1950. (ELLAN ROBINSON REYNES)

Eisenhower with Mamie and Thomas E. Dewey on May 6, 1952, in New York City. (CORBIS-BETTMAN)

From left, James Duff, Henry Cabot Lodge, Jr., Eisenhower, and Paul
Hoffman on June 3, 1952, in Washington, D.C. (CORBIS-BETTMAN)

In July 1952 Eisenhower arrives at the Republican National Convention in Chicago. (AP/WIDE WORLD)

Eisenhower with Senator Robert A. Taft at the Republican National
Convention in Chicago. (CORBIS-BETTMAN)

☆ 9 ☆

POLITICAL FIRES

BY EARLY 1951, Leonard Finder had redoubled his efforts. He wrote Dewey on January 27, 1951, that he had been seeing Eisenhower periodically, most recently "a few weeks ago." Finder held three convictions, he told the governor: one, that Eisenhower's election as president was essential to end "the present reign of confusion and uncertainty"; two, that of all the possible candidates, Eisenhower "most holds the public's confidence and so offers the greatest assurance of a successful candidacy"; and, three, that in his opinion Eisenhower "definitely will accept a genuine Republican draft."[1] Dewey replied that he "wholly agreed" with the first two points and hoped Finder was right on the third. "The events of the next year," he said, "will serve only to strengthen the convictions we jointly share."[2] Finder then wrote Eisenhower of the "declining public confidence in the Truman administration"; the isolationism of Hoover, Taft, and Senator Kenneth Wherry of Nebraska; and the public demands for Eisenhower's "national leadership" that continued "to smolder, waiting only for the right time to burst into open flames."[3]

No sooner had he arrived in France than Eisenhower discovered he needed help with his political activities. He asked Burnham to join him in Paris.[4] The Wall Street banker-turned-politico's title at SHAPE was economic adviser, but his job was to assist with visits of congressmen and other VIPs. Burnham also corresponded with McCollum, Young, Duff, Stassen, Jock Whitney, George Whitney, Watson, Robinson, and reporters for *Life, Time,* and the *Christian Science Monitor.*[5]

Still, the supreme commander worried that these political activities might get out of hand. On March 10 he warned Clark, who as previously arranged was traveling back and forth between Paris and New York, that "any effort to generate or further excite the political speculation about me is bound to react unfavorably on this job." He threatened to remove himself from consideration if he sensed a danger to "the great objective of western security."[6]

It was at this point that Lucius Clay, who according to Kevin McCann felt that Eisenhower was "the one man who could restore the pride and dignity to government," became the catalyst.[7] He and his wife had been friends of Ike and Mamie since the two officers had served together under MacArthur in the Philippines in the 1930s. During World War II, Clay, by then a lieutenant general in the corps of engineers, had been assistant to James F. Byrnes, then director of war mobilization. (Byrnes's office was in the White House, and his job was of such importance that pundits had called him the assistant president.) In the closing weeks of the war, Clay had gone to SHAEF to work on logistics with Colonel Edwin Clark and General Robert Crawford, and was there at the time of the German surrender on May 8, 1945. When Eisenhower became army chief of staff, Clay replaced him as military governor of the U.S. zone of Germany.[8]

Eisenhower's supporters in the spring and summer of 1951 faced a fast-moving and confusing situation. Foremost was the Truman–MacArthur controversy. General MacArthur would not stifle his disagreement with the president after the Chinese intervention and forced retreat of UN forces in Korea. Truman, with UN consent, had ordered his commander to send forces across the 38th parallel in pursuit of the retreating North Korean army following the brilliant Inchon landing in September 1950. MacArthur soon occupied Pyongyang, the North Korean capital, and moved his forces up to the Manchurian border along the Yalu River, this despite warnings by the People's Republic of China not to go that far. In November 1950 the Chinese began sending troops across the frozen river at night, some 300,000 of them filtering into the mountains. Their attack near the end of the month surprised the UN troops, forcing them into a bloody, midwinter retreat to a line south of Seoul. Truman, over Mac-Arthur's repeated objections, now returned to his earlier strategy of Europe first, and in Korea from rollback to merely containing Communist expansion. MacArthur was adamant and expressed his dissatisfaction with the new strategy directly to members of Congress. He wanted to use nuclear weapons if necessary and, short of that, to send B-29 bombers across the Yalu River. After repeated warnings, on April 12, 1951, Truman fired him. This, along with a new domestic Red Scare, brought a public outpouring—not for a president who was upholding strategic prudence in a nuclear age and the constitutional principle of civilian supremacy, but for MacArthur, hero of the Pacific war and, more recently, architect of the Inchon landing. Truman's public opinion ratings plummeted to 23 percent, the lowest of any president since such polling began.

MacArthur's actions involved more than mere insubordination. In MacArthur and Eisenhower, Truman had under his command the two most successful wartime theater commanders of the twentieth century. Close acquaintances themselves, they nonetheless represented distinct ways of thinking about both the military in a democracy and cold war strategy. MacArthur had had a remarkable career, graduating number one in his class at West Point, serving in the 42nd "Rainbow" division during World War I, and becoming army chief of staff at the age of fifty.[9] While he was aware of the constitutional restraints on military men, he was willing to criticize the President of the United States in public. He had done this in the Philippines in the 1930s and now, with the United Nations reversals in Korea, was doing so again. Having already tried unsuccessfully for the GOP presidential nomination in 1948, it was no secret that he had the same objective in 1952. His reception by the American people was thus of considerable interest. Truman might be able to prevail politically, but what if MacArthur, while not gaining the Republican nomination himself, influenced the partisan debate to such an extent that Taft became the popular choice for president?

MacArthur's homecoming after his dismissal (he had been in the Far East since the mid-1930s) resembled that of a Roman proconsul returning from the imperial wars. In New York City a ticker-tape parade brought out an estimated seven million people to welcome him. To a joint session of Congress he made a melodramatic speech, concluding with a quote from an old army ballad: "old soldiers never die, they just fade away." At Milwaukee, his birthplace, half the population turned out to greet him.[10] (It was not clear at the time, but at this point his star then began to fade. Only 27,000 went to the Cotton Bowl to hear him in Dallas, and congressional hearings upheld the administration's strategy in Korea and the Far East, not MacArthur's. MacArthur soon revealed himself as an egotist who put his own reputation and pre-nuclear modes of thought ahead of prudence and even truth. He disagreed publicly not only with the president but also with Secretary of Defense Marshall and chairman of the Joint Chiefs of Staff, General Omar Bradley.)

On March 23, Ed Bermingham wrote Eisenhower that "Washington can best be described as depressing. . . . General Fellers (a MacArthur aide) is presumed to be supplying Messers Taft and Hoover material for their discourses."[11] The following month Robinson wrote that MacArthur's influence had damaged Truman and Acheson, causing the public to mistrust any position they might take, "an unfortunate and unfair liability for both their Asian and European policies." He and Cliff Roberts, he said, agreed that "even the appearance of your taking part in the political controversy would damage your effectiveness in Europe and dilute your influence for good at home."[12] It is important here to note that on January 5, 1954, Senator Taft had delivered a ten-thousand-word speech on the Senate floor, in the words of his biographer "his most comprehensive address on foreign policy, and the most widely noted in the press." It was his contribution to what reporters by then called "The Great Debate" over American foreign policy. Taft argued that while the Soviets did not want war, Truman nevertheless was sending Eisenhower to Europe to create a European army and "covertly planning" to include 300,000 American combat troops and twice that many support troops. It was important to honor one's commitments, Taft acknowledged, but he believed that such forces would both strain the American economy and cause Europeans to depend upon the United States rather than themselves. Instead of trying to match Soviet forces on the ground where they were strongest, which he considered provocative, Taft advised a buildup of U.S. air and naval forces. Finally, he charged that such commitment of American forces in peacetime without prior approval by Congress was unconstitutional.[13]

The liberal Dewey faction of the GOP now spied an opening, though a small one. The public began to see that MacArthur had overreached.[14] Clay wrote Eisenhower on April 13 that he had been talking with "our friend" (their code name for Dewey), and that the two of them had come to a decision. Since the "Taft forces are definitely aligned with MacArthur, their official strategy is to maneuver you into taking a position on the MacArthur issue, thus aligning you with the President." Clay recommended silence.[15] Eisenhower replied that he would "maintain silence in every language known to man" because controversy would "impede our effort to strengthen Europe."[16] Still, Roberts reported glumly on April 18, "Truman had succeeded in making a popular hero out of MacArthur—something the general was never able to do for himself." Roberts was "a little worried because MacArthur has now, probably without knowing it, become the standard bearer for all those people who think our Far Eastern policy, beginning with Yalta, has been wrong."[17]

Finder was less pessimistic. He told Eisenhower that the Hearst publications and the *Chicago Tribune* were exaggerating MacArthur's public approval rating. There were at least as many papers—such as the *New York Times, New York Herald Tribune,* and *Chicago Sun Times*—that were inclined to criticize. But he was distressed that "important Republicans encouraged General MacArthur to pursue his own inclinations rather than to accept the soldier's discipline of obeying his government's policies." The controversy, he said, dramatized the fact that MacArthur "has become a symbol of the people's underlying lack of faith and fears. . . . They cheered the man but repudiated his views and did not observe their own inconsistency." The more MacArthur waned as a symbol, he said, "the more the Republicans suffer for the conduct of some of their members." Finder said he had spoken with Governor Sherman Adams of New Hampshire who had determined that the GOP "can win [in 1952] only if you [Eisenhower] are drafted as candidate." The polls continued to show Ike as the choice of the majority of Americans.[18]

Eisenhower's decision to remain mute was, of course, the correct one politically. Truman, needed as much political support as he could get and confided to Harriman that Eisenhower was "on top of the situation."[19] The president wrote Eisenhower to explain that he was "sorry to have to reach a parting of the way with the big man in Asia but he asked for it, and I had to give it to him. You are doing a wonderful job and anything I can do to make it easier I'll certainly be glad to do."[20] As opposed to MacArthur, who looked to widen the Korean War in order to win it, Eisenhower thought the most the United States could hope for would be for the Communists "to quit pushing there."[21] (But he had no intention of antagonizing the Far Eastern general. The following month he wrote him cordially, explaining how much he had "truly valued" MacArthur's friendship and appreciated the fact that his senior had "never, even accidentally, uttered a word" that might make plausible the statements of sensation-seeking journalists that the two of them were "mortal enemies." His respect as a fellow West Point graduate and comrade in arms, Eisenhower implied, remained intact. MacArthur reciprocated his "warm esteem and cordial regard" which, he said, are "well known and understood by everyone.")[22]

Aware of both the decline in Truman's public opinion ratings and the growing activity in the Taft camp, the Eisenhower-for-President group in New York City decided in May 1951—as it turned out, prematurely—that it was time for more active engagement by their candidate. During the height of the Truman–MacArthur controversy in April, Eisenhower had sought the advice and support of Henry Luce. He invited the publisher to SHAPE, telling him that he would derive "personal pleasure" and "profit from hearing your views and reactions to numerous ideas and suggestions."[23] Luce was delighted but said he could not come at once. Instead he sent one of his people, Max Ways.[24] Now Dewey, Duff, Harry Darby (GOP national committeeman from Kansas), and Harold Talbot (of Chrysler, and former campaign finance chairman for Willkie and Dewey) asked Clay to contact Eisenhower.

The situation was enormously delicate. The first problem, of course, was the legal one. Army Regulations, Article 600-10, 18 stipulated that "members of the regular army, while on active duty, may accept nomination for public office, provided such nomination is tendered without direct or indirect activity or solicitation on their part." The second problem was political. Any sense that Eisenhower was using his new position merely as a stepping-stone to higher office could create a suspicion that he had ulterior motives. Thus Clay, in his correspondence with the supreme commander, used a crude encryption system as protection in case a piece of correspondence fell into the wrong hands. It allowed him to refer to individual members of the group using a misleading letter from the alphabet or secret code name (e.g., "Our friend").[25]

"It is time to move now, and this can be done without direct commitment from you," Clay wrote on May 18. "Please let me know quickly that you do not object."[26] Dewey, meanwhile, asked the New York GOP chairman to endorse Eisenhower, thereby pledging all the state's convention delegates to him.[27]

But Eisenhower was not ready. He was "surprised," he told Clay, "that any of the individuals you mention should feel the need for any comment on my part." He said he had already told Milton and Robinson, both of whom had asked, that he would not admit a party sympathy or affiliation or "seek anything" unless "a larger duty compels me to do so." For communications security reasons, he had asked Milton to send any messages to him through Robinson (yet another emissary), who would be visiting him in Paris from time to time.[28] He now recommended to Clay that Dewey and Duff ("Our friend" and "A," respectively) reach some kind of understanding "from the standpoint of advancing the policies in public affairs for which they both seem to be working." A recent conversation he had had with Winthrop Aldrich (allegedly in Paris for a game of golf), he said, had conveyed the sentiment that he should "keep still, both publicly and privately." Unless Dewey and Duff "visualize a situation that would obviously represent a higher call to duty than does even my present job," he could not imagine them asking for his assistance.[29]

If the politicos were discouraged, they soon took heart. A Gallup poll published on June 8 showed that Democrats favored Eisenhower over Truman by 43 percent to 18 percent; Republicans favored him over Taft by 38 percent to 22 percent; and all those polled favored him over MacArthur by 51 percent to 27 percent.[30] A week later Clay wrote that Dewey was going ahead on his own to talk with Duff and those whom he trusts. "I believe things will begin to evolve slowly, quietly, but surely. I will keep you posted in ways which you will understand."[31]

Finder reported that MacArthur's popularity was fading, with only a fraction of the expected crowds now attending his speeches. The famous general, he said, was blocked by the unanimity of the joint chiefs, his own "intemperate comments against Mr. Truman," and a "demagogic" approach. The publisher reiterated his concern about new international tensions resulting from lack of leadership, extreme political viewpoints, and the failure of the United States "to expound a clear attitude." (Finder was concerned about Taft. Eisenhower alone, he declared, could save the country from the despondency that would follow a Truman election or isolationism.[32] He urged Eisenhower, when he "let it be known he would not refuse the nomination," to indicate his party preference.)[33] But Robinson, who was in Paris from June 29 through July 8, recorded in his diary that Eisenhower was resolved to "do nothing to attempt to obtain the Republican nomination." The *Herald Tribune* executive supported the decision, counseling him to make no "commitment to anybody about anything political," that "no matter what he did he would be nominated by the Republicans at their convention and would be elected."[34]

Henry Cabot Lodge arrived on July 16. The general had an upset stomach and told his staff he could see Lodge only briefly. They met at 9 a.m. and, as usual when the two were together, Eisenhower relaxed, began to talk, and soon disregarded his schedule. They had lunch together and talked for another hour. Eisenhower repeated his criticism of the handling of the Korean War, recalling that when the war broke out, he had urged "all-out mobilization, so we could develop great military strength, and regain the initiative, put pressure on the Soviet Union—and organize the peace." As it was, the United States had all the expenditures and drawbacks of a heavy military program without the advantages of "regained initiative which strength would give."[35] Eisenhower asked about political platforms (Lodge had been chairman of the resolutions committee at the Republican convention of 1948). He expressed his fear, however, that partisan politics would destroy his usefulness at NATO.

Lodge reminded him of their previous conversation. The senator's view then had been that "neutralist and defeatist influences in the Republican party might get so strong that it would be your duty to enter politics in order to prevent one of our two great parties from adopting a course which could lead to national suicide." Such arguments were, he claimed, "a great deal more persuasive now." If Eisenhower did decide to enter politics, he would need to let this be known "quietly, without necessarily being quoted, not later than January, and you will have to be back in the United States by March or April." Eisenhower's response was lighthearted but only half sarcastic. "I am glad I have got until January."[36]

When the conversation ended, interestingly, Lodge was satisfied that Eisenhower would run for the nomination. He noted in his diary that Eisenhower "will think that his duty is to prevent the Taft victory from taking place, and I do not foresee much trouble in the word going out privately in January." The senator's only fear was that the general would be unwilling to return until after the convention—"and if we at home can pull off that trick (of getting him nominated without his being there), it will be remarkable."[37]

By August the team had swung into action. Robinson wrote Cliff Roberts, predicting that Eisenhower would refuse to seek the Republican nomination but would express his willingness to accept it. The general, he said, "stood ready to accept any call to duty providing it comes from the hearts and minds of my fellow citizens, clearly and unmistakably."[38] Roberts, this time himself in Paris with Ike, asked Robinson on August 27 to try to obtain copies of recent editorials in the *Washington Post* and a Boston newspaper. The first had argued that the Republicans should stop debating the pros and cons of an Eisenhower candidacy and "go ahead and nominate the general." The second had asserted that Eisenhower's Republican sympathies were evident in the content of his speeches. Roberts suggested that if, after Robinson read the Boston editorial, he found it "not well done, why don't you do the job?"[39] Robinson replied, enclosing the *Post* article by Russ Wiggins. He admitted that he had urged Wiggins to "do the piece just about the way it came out." As for the Boston piece, it was "an excellent one from all accounts. It should be published in the November *Reader's Digest* and should do an awful lot of good. . . . The pace of events with respect to General Ike is just about as it should be. There is, of course, the constant danger that it may run too fast to the point where the acceleration would require some kind of premature comment from the General. At the moment thought [sic] it is all right."[40]

The elements of an Eisenhower-for-President organization seemed to be falling into place. Milton reported that Harold Talbott wanted to head an Eisenhower-for-President finance committee, that most large and small businessmen would contribute, and that the New York and Kansas delegations to the GOP convention would work to prevent a Taft nomination.[41] Dewey and Duff, who had experienced some friction, now had a "satisfactory working relationship."[42] Harold Stassen admitted that his candidacy was merely to keep Taft at bay and the nomination available to Eisenhower. Winthrop Aldrich, who disliked Talbott, was also prepared to raise money.[43] Perhaps most noteworthy, Clay on August 22 wrote Eisenhower that Byrnes ("Our friend from South Carolina"), now governor of that state, was organizing Southern Democrats for Eisenhower. Byrnes believed that an Eisenhower victory was possible in as many as nine states; he was "confident more than ever that our only hope for unity and for a bi-partisan foreign policy rests in you." Clay thus recommended that Eisenhower plan "the early part of next year" to request release from active military duty and the designation of a successor as supreme allied commander in Europe. No matter how badly Eisenhower might be needed in Europe, said Clay, "you are needed even more here, and perhaps if you do not return nothing accomplished there would have any real permanency.[44]

September brought more letters. By this time Edgar Eisenhower had put everything in perspective, suggesting that his younger brother not take into "his confidence any goddam political person of any kind, stripe, character, color, creed, race, religious inclination or otherwise. I don't trust any of them."[45] Perhaps buttressed by this filial logic, Eisenhower answered most inquiring letters by saying merely that because of his "present position" he must refrain from commenting on "current political questions." This was not easy to do. Douglas Southall Freeman sought another confirmation of a conversation they had had in 1946. "In absolute confidence," he asked whether Eisenhower recalled telling him that "no individual could decline a call to service if recognized leaders of the nation, regardless of party, told him a situation had arisen in which he was the only man who could save the country from ruin?" Eisenhower affirmed that Freeman's "recollection of our conversation my office in the winter of that year coincides exactly with my own."[46]

After receiving another letter from Finder, the general asked the newspaper publisher not to come see him in Paris.[47] Finder understood but said that "the tempo of political activity and interest," with Eisenhower at "the center of the heightened attention," was rapidly accelerating. Senator Baldwin of Connecticut, he said, had announced his support of an Eisenhower candidacy, and Senator Styles Bridges of New Hampshire had begun to waffle, "denying he is necessarily committed to Taft." Finder referred to the scene from Plutarch's *Lives* in which Numa Pompilius "at the urging of his fellow citizens" reluctantly agreed to be King of Rome. Eisenhower replied that Pompilius was apparently both "wiser and, when it came to his readiness to sacrifice himself, nobler than the average."[48] He told the New Hampshire publisher that he would put a volume of Plutarch on his bedside table "for occasional reading when I get a chance."[49]

☆ 10 ☆

THE
DUFF
LETTER

PROBABLY NO ONE except Mamie and perhaps Milton knew Eisenhower's thinking in the autumn of 1951 as well as Cliff Roberts. Many years later, in an oral history interview, Roberts summarized the general's attitude toward the possibility of a presidential candidacy. "He did not want the job," Roberts said. "Of that I am as certain as I am of the fact that I am alive today. He'd had all the honors and more than he could ever have hoped to achieve as a youngster, and he wanted to do a number of things in the years that were left to him. And he wanted to enjoy life a bit. He most assuredly did not want to be President of the United States. Now there again, that does not mean he wasn't willing to do it, if a set of circumstances presented themselves that made it clear to him that that was his duty and obligation."[1] Those circumstances began to apply in mid-October 1951.

On October 14—his sixty-first birthday, as it turned out, and two days before Taft officially announced his candidacy—believing that the nation's destiny was at stake, he wrote a secret letter to a handful of supporters. Eisenhower assured them that he was a Republican and, if nominated, would resign from the army and return home to campaign for the presidency. Eisenhower's former assistant, William Bragg Ewald, Jr., published the letter, addressed to Senator James Duff of

Pennsylvania, in the *New York Times Magazine* in 1993, after discovering it in a private holding of Edwin Clark's papers. Its three pages, in Ike's handwriting, illuminate his clandestine preconvention activity.[2]

For Eisenhower the problem boiled down to Senator Taft. "That was the compelling reason for his decision," Roberts later remarked. "He would literally do anything on earth that he thought would be best for his country. It didn't make any difference whether it was an unpleasant thing to do, or whether it was profitable, and so on."[3] While Eisenhower admired "a good many of his fine qualities, he did not think Taft had the capacity to be a top-flight President of the United States" and "objected very strongly to Taft's isolationist views. He didn't think Taft understood or appreciated the world role that the United States was obligated to carry on." Taft didn't have "any enthusiasm for the leadership role that it was necessary for our country to play." "All of us," Roberts recalled, repeatedly told the general that "he was the only one that had a chance of beating Taft. See, Taft had so many delegates already wrapped up in his hip pocket that nobody could take them away from him."[4]

But how to proceed? Eisenhower wanted to be sure he controlled the rapidly unfolding events. He desired to foster the perception that instead of seeking the office, it was seeking him. A public declaration of intention to run might cause the European allies or NATO's opponents in Congress to question his motives. At SHAPE his dedication to the task had to be beyond question. As one of Eisenhower's aides, Brigadier General J. H. Michaelis, put it, the fact that Eisenhower was able to organize a headquarters with eight nations represented in its troop division was a sign of "his organizational genius." Eisenhower, he said, "had managed to inculcate within each and every officer within his staff a sense of urgency and an intense desire to make the experiment succeed."[5] Any movement into the partisan sphere would violate his assertion that military men had no business running for high elected office. Eisenhower thus inserted in all letters responding to urgings that he run, the following passage: "The job I am on requires the support of the vast body of Americans. Those Americans have the right to believe that their agent is serving all of them and is not seeking to advance the fortunes of any one group as compared to another. For me to admit, while in this post, or to imply a partisan political loyalty would properly be resented by thinking Americans and would be doing a disservice to our country."[6]

On September 7, Leonard Finder again took the initiative. He reported that MacArthur had given a speech in Cleveland supporting Taft. In New Hampshire a delegation pledged to Eisenhower was being organized, and a separate national group led by Senator Henry Cabot Lodge supported Eisenhower. Finder said his goal was to keep hope from dying and Republican delegates from Taft. He told Eisenhower he was preparing an article "setting forth the reasons for my belief why, despite your genuine distaste for political involvement, you will accept the Republican nomination if it is offered." He said he would send a copy to Schulz. If it came back with request for changes or even cancellation, he would know that Schulz was speaking for his boss. Some days later Finder received it back without notations. Schulz, in his transmittal letter, said he was returning the article "as requested." "General Eisenhower," he said, "has made it a practice never to comment on such articles, and consequently doesn't even read them."[7] Finder thereupon sold his piece to Collier's magazine. It appeared in the November 3 issue.[8]

Meanwhile, at the White House, Truman's press secretary overheard the president refer to MacArthur, Eisenhower, and the presidency and made note in his diary. Truman, he said, doubted Eisenhower would become a candidate. He liked Eisenhower "as a man and a soldier," but education for a military career did not equip one for the presidency, which required accomplishing things by persuasion rather than by giving orders. Truman nevertheless believed Eisenhower might become a candidate if MacArthur were to run. "Eisenhower," said Truman, "hates MacArthur as much as anyone."[9]

MacArthur's activities could both arouse public alarm about generals in politics and strengthen a Taft candidacy. Clay reported on September 29 that "recent polls indicate a surprising increase in popularity of MacArthur in certain sections, among them being New Hampshire. I think this comes about only from his immediate activities and from his political speeches, which have been very good. However, to be in sight is to be in mind, and he is definitely in sight."[10] On October 19, Lodge would receive an unsigned letter—possibly from Dewey, Clay, or perhaps Voorhees—about MacArthur's attack on the Atlantic Pact the previous day at the national convention of the American Legion. Unfortunately, said the author, "Senator Taft was taking the same stance."[11] These views Tracy Voorhees characterized as talking about "too much rearmament [in Europe] when the real danger is too little." Such talk, along with stalemate in Congress and the "ineptitude of the present administration," said Voorhees, meant that Eisenhower needed the "power and influence of the Presidency [in his hands]" to "cement the free world, make it strong and keep it free."[12]

The MacArthur factor clearly had become more serious. Eisenhower's supporters, Dewey and Duff, as they spoke around the country, were discovering areas of Eisenhower weakness. Dewey considered the situation under control in Oregon, but Washington state was "pretty well set for Taft." In New York, with a major convention delegation, he noted little progress. The governor blamed Senator Harry Darby of Kansas for the difficulties and began collaborating with Duff to get Senator Frank Carlson of Kansas to take over preconvention activities.[13] But Lodge, with Clay and John Cowles, blocked this.

Clay also was discouraged. Stassen, he reported, had stated publicly that he was not committed to Eisenhower. The Minnesota governor believed "a vacuum" had been created and that he had no choice but to move into it. Taft's people, meanwhile, had been trying to woo Winthrop Aldrich. Clay told Eisenhower that two separate sources had advised that Truman would not run "if you run," but would run if Taft were the nominee and "would beat Taft to a frazzle." This, he said, would bring a "minimum of four more years of bad government and could mean the downfall in this country of the two-party system." The question of leadership, he told Eisenhower, "cannot be solved satisfactorily unless you lend a hand."[14]

By this time Eisenhower, it seems clear, was beginning to enjoy the maneuvering. But he was proceeding with caution. The code system that he and Clay were using was a good idea, he admitted, since "if any single letter should go astray and should be read by outsiders, misinterpretations could be made." "You and I," he assured his colleague, "think so much alike on so many problems connected with public service, and you are so detached from partisan affairs . . . that I think it would do me good just to have a long talk with you."[15] He would not indicate a choice for his campaign chief because such action could be interpreted as "a voluntary entry into the political field . . . disastrous to this job and, therefore, damaging to our country." "Having said this," he quickly continued, "I do not mind commenting upon the special items in your letter." He assured Clay that Stassen had promised him to be his "loyal and sincere lieutenant" when it became "completely clear" that the general was available. As for the leadership quandary, he suggested that Darby, Carlson, and Roberts act as the "Kansas Committee." He assured Clay that he never would disregard the advice of Dewey because he had "implicit confidence in his sincerity and in his good faith," adding, wistfully, "Wouldn't it be nice if we could just forget all this kind of thing."[16]

Despite the caution and disclaimers, and much to Clay's satisfaction, Eisenhower's words left little doubt that he was a participant in partisan politics. The events of the first two weeks of October thereupon brought unforeseen and, as it turned out, irresistible pressure to act. Robert P. Burroughs, president of a Manchester, New Hampshire, pension fund company, a prominent Republican in the state, had visited SHAPE in August. On October 1 he wrote Eisenhower that while the support for him was "less than before General MacArthur returned to this country," it was "still great enough to indicate that at the present time you would be bound to stand very high in a general poll." He urged Eisenhower to let the New Hampshire presidential preference poll in March "help you to make up your mind." The only question for state Republicans, he said, referring to the now-famous Finder letter of 1948, was whether "we can count on your not saying to the New Hampshire secretary of state that you will not permit your name to be listed on the ballot." Burroughs said he would promise, if Eisenhower would give such assurances, "if that is your desire," not to show the letter to anyone else or quote directly from it. He said he would be meeting in the next four or five weeks with Congressman Norris Cotton, Governor Sherman Adams, and other individuals interested in an Eisenhower candidacy.[17]

Within the next week, Bermingham forwarded a sharp letter from Senator Karl Mundt of South Dakota. The senator regretted that Eisenhower was "still disinclined to make known his political affinity. I presume that being so far away from the scene of activity, he does not realize how fast things are shaping up delegate-wise for the next Republican convention" or the importance of a "strong, clear-eyed, consistent American government." The success or failure of NATO, Mundt said, "is eventually going to be determined entirely apart from anything he can do in far-off Europe. . . . The final outcome will rest almost entirely with the kind of national leadership we have in the White House during the next four years."[18] At a meeting of Republican governors, Bermingham reported, Dewey had told the state leaders that "Truman would not run and [would] put no obstacle in the way of General Eisenhower."[19]

Still, Eisenhower was not ready. He thanked Burroughs, telling him that he dared do nothing to "harm his own effectiveness an American commander in Europe and hinder us from accomplishing our aims in the quickest possible time." He said he would "take no action . . . in regard to matters of a political nature."[20] He told Bermingham he agreed with Mundt's opinion "that the success of NATO is largely going to be determined in Washington." His position nevertheless demanded of him "complete devotion to the interests of the entire country."[21]

Eisenhower left no doubt about his stance in a letter to his old friend Aksel Nielson, president of the Title Guaranty Company of Denver. Nielson, who had no idea of the secret relationship with Duff but who had a good sense of the growing political urgency, had suggested that Eisenhower invite Governor Dan Thornton of Colorado and Senator Duff to Paris to tell about their work lining up governors who were "ready to go to work for you, if and when you want it."[22] Eisenhower replied that both Thornton and Duff "are friends of mine and, if they are over here, of course I would be delighted to talk with them." He added, however, that "if I would get pushed into the position that I now have to make a public statement concerning these matters, the only thing I could do would be to make a negative statement of complete repudiation."[23]

So much for the public posture. The work of Clark and Duff had meanwhile reached a critical stage. Duff, now the freshman senator from Pennsylvania, had been speaking throughout the United States since February 1951, urging a liberal (meaning internationalist) presidential candidate and European unity, and of course commending Eisenhower's fine performance at NATO. He gave a Lincoln Day dinner address in Boston and another in Houston. He spoke at the Michigan GOP state convention in Detroit on February 17; delivered a nationally broadcast speech from Washington, D.C., on February 25; and spoke in various locations in the East, Midwest, and Rocky Mountain states through June. At each location he sought from local liberal Republicans a commitment to an Eisenhower candidacy.[24] But too many Republican professional politicians, Duff and Clark concluded, remained "solidly in Taft's camp." Particularly worrisome was the fact that these regulars constituted an organized opposition. Through the spring and early summer of 1951, they had been telling reporters that Eisenhower was "not a politician and an unknown quantity as a Republican and, anyway, probably would never be a candidate." Many local leaders, Duff had discovered, were reluctant to back a candidate who, in Clark's words, "at a late date would turn out to be not a candidate at all." "What real knowledge," they kept asking Duff, "did he have that Eisenhower would accept the nomination?"[25]

Clark, meanwhile, was traveling back and forth across the Atlantic between Paris and New York. By September he and Duff had concluded that "unless an immediate aggressive campaign is made against them," Dewey's waning influence and the control by party regulars of the machinery for selecting convention delegates in the various states would allow the Taft forces to squash an Eisenhower draft.[26] They needed unqualified assurance, they concluded, that Eisenhower would be a candidate "on the Republican ticket and only on the Republican ticket." Only this, they determined, would provide state officials the assurance they needed that the "fight was on and it was on to the finish."[27]

This conclusion had come out of conversations the two men had been having in regular meetings with Russell Davenport (the three had begun to call themselves "the team"). Davenport drafted a "progress report," which he sent to Duff on October 5. It asserted that since the Taft people had begun lining up delegates, the time had arrived to find a leader of the Eisenhower forces, someone to "call the signals, put people in their places," and encourage appropriate action.[28] This leader, someone who could not be labeled a Dewey man, would have to be accepted by the organization as an Eisenhower leader without any public announcement by the general to that effect. The report proposed that Duff be this so-called "team captain," and that Eisenhower give him "direct personal assurance of his intentions" so that he "could say to his political associates that he was satisfied that when the draft movement has reached a proper level, Eisenhower would be forthcoming." In lieu of an announced candidacy, the information would be spread to friends of the movement by, for example, leaking "the lowdown" to Henry Luce and his news editors "on a confidential basis, not as a news story." A report of Duff's selection as the official leader, for example, could be sent to the editors of *Look*, the *Des Moines Register*, *Newsweek*, and the *New York Herald Tribune*.[29]

Davenport's purpose was to create conditions for the overthrow of the Republican Old Guard. The difference between the present conditions and those that had brought the ill-fated draft in 1940 of Wendell Willkie, said Davenport, would be the knowledge by those involved that "if Eisenhower can be nominated, he will be elected."[30] "The possibility of success this time is increased by the eagerness of the public for a change of administrations and its worry about the world situation."[31] The first issue to be raised by the Eisenhower forces was thus the moral one—political chicanery and demagogy, and the desire for a leader who could distinguish good from evil. As for the second, Eisenhower should state his "much clearer view [than Taft's] of the nation's foreign aims and policies." He should advocate turning federal social programs over to local private initiative following the "associative principle" of voluntary cooperation as a means of controlling taxes and avoiding high costs and red tape in a time of expanding defense budgets.[32]

The first phase of a four-phase strategy, the report went on, was now over, with many Eisenhower volunteers in place throughout the country. The second phase, beginning immediately, would be the "rapid welding together of a national organization, including by January 1, the integration of the team with active organizations and leaders in twenty states." The third phase would begin when Eisenhower "takes some kind of action." Before then he should always answer questions about his availability and party affiliation by saying "he is not seeking the presidency, and that he is not a candidate." He would affirm, however, that he considered the office of the president to be "the highest honor that the American people have it in their power to bestow and no man can treat the subject lightly." Eisenhower should say he did not understand "why he should be spoken of in that connection, but if it becomes clear to him that the people want him, he will of course give the matter serious consideration."[33] An announcement of Eisenhower's retirement and indication of his availability should come sometime after Christmas. An interview with a reporter in which the general would say he "is and always has been a Republican" would come shortly thereafter. If during this period, said Davenport, Eisenhower announced his availability, it would both shake the Taft forces and speed the expansion of the draft-Eisenhower organization. In any event, Duff would emerge as the leader.

The fourth and final phase would begin with Eisenhower's permanent return to the United States and acknowledgment of the efforts in his behalf by Duff and others. He would set up an office in New York to take care of his private affairs and begin to meet with convention delegates.

Duff read the report and accepted its plan. He had misgivings about his designation as leader but indicated he was willing to do whatever was necessary.[34] In a memorandum of his own, the senator from Pennsylvania was less sanguine. Taft, he said, appealed neither to independents nor to the Southern states. A grassroots demand for a "new face" and a "new attitude" could be exploited by prompt, well-organized action. In Duff's opinion, an Eisenhower candidacy would carry the traditionally Democratic states of Virginia, North Carolina, Florida, Texas, and probably South Carolina along with the Northern industrial states of New York, Pennsylvania, and Massachusetts. Duff was nevertheless convinced that without immediate "positive aggressive organization and action," Taft would sew up the national convention. Taft's support among Republican regulars, and procedures for selecting delegates, he said, "almost necessarily eliminates the possibility of a draft [of Eisenhower] either before or at the convention."[35] The general needed quickly to give his private but "definite and unqualified assurance" to a small group of people "that he will be a candidate on the Republican ticket and only on the Republican ticket."[36] Duff also saw an immediate need to establish an organization and identify those in command. Above all, the general needed to "commit himself unqualifiedly to a campaign, come what may." "The preservation of the two-party system and the future and security of the nation," Duff wrote in conclusion, required a leader "of the type of the general."[37]

Clark's trip to Paris on Friday, October 12, 1951, thus had a momentous purpose. Arriving in Paris early the next morning, he checked in at his hotel, the Raphael, and then went to SHAPE headquarters at Rocquencourt for lunch. He told the supreme commander that Duff needed a memorandum or letter, something in writing, and explained why. After discussing the situation, Eisenhower and Clark went to Villa-St. Pierre, where Mamie had arranged a dinner for their house guest, their good friend and prominent Democrat, and the U.S. ambassador to Luxembourg, Pearl Mesta. (To complicate matters, Mamie was planning a birthday party for Ike scheduled for the next day.)[38] The general asked Mamie to make a place at the table for Clark. After dinner, as was the custom, the women departed to play canasta and the men went to another room. It did not take long, Clark recalled, for Eisenhower to accede to the desires of his political advisers. Unfortunately, such a letter, needing careful wording, would take time to draft; so they decided to wait until morning.

Early the next day, Clark and the supreme commander met to compose, edit, and rewrite the letter. In its final form, in Eisenhower's handwriting, it ran to three pages. It was addressed "Dear Jim" [to Senator Duff] and was marked "personal and secret." Clark promised Eisenhower he would carry it to New York where he would let Duff read it and then put it in a secure place. By the time the two men had finished their work it was afternoon, and thirty to forty officers, including Gruenther, were waiting in the dining room to "surprise" their commander on his birthday. Ike joined them, leaving Schulz to make a pencil copy of the letter for Eisenhower's personal reference.[39] Clark thereupon returned to New York where, conscious of the magnitude of his responsibility, he explained to Brownlee, his Aspetuck neighbor, what had occurred, and agreed to rent a safe deposit box in which to deposit the letter. The two then took the letter to Duff. At a dinner attended by Clark, Brownlee, Jock Whitney, and Nelson Rockefeller, Duff, referring to the letter, announced his plan to intensify his efforts for Eisenhower.[40]

The letter, which Eisenhower could have disavowed were it necessary for some reason to do so (he was already in violation of Army Regulations) removed him inexorably from the political sidelines. Only the influence of people in whom he had "great confidence," said the letter, had caused him to entertain "the thought of political office." He adhered to the Republican party and to liberal Republican principles. He would say or do nothing to hinder the performance of his duty at SHAPE or that would "react adversely on American support of the free world's effort to establish collective security." But, he added, "any American would have to regard nomination for the Presidency, by the political party to which he adheres, as constituting a duty to his country that would transcend any other duty." He reiterated (ingenuously) that he would say or do nothing to gain a nomination and would "maintain complete silence to any questions posed to me." If, despite these conditions, he should "nevertheless be nominated by the Republicans, I would resign my commission and assume aggressive leadership of the party, working, of course, through the established organization." His respect and friendship for Duff, he said, required that he "enter no objection of any kind to your pursuing whatever course (consistent with what I have said) you may deem proper in organizing like-minded people." This letter, he said in conclusion, was for the senator's personal assurance and not for general use, because as supreme allied commander he must "remain absolutely aloof from partisan politics." It was thus that—with the assistance of Dewey, Clay, Bermingham, Clark, Duff, and Davenport—Eisenhower moved toward candidacy for the 1952 GOP presidential nomination.[41]

☆ 11 ☆

ORGANIZING
THE CAMPAIGN

EISENHOWER KNEW that partisan politics—especially since Taft and
the GOP were reluctant to support collective security—were tied to
his mission at NATO. But becoming a candidate for public office
while serving as NATO commander was another matter altogether.
Despite the awkwardness of the situation, in the thirty days from mid-
October to mid-November Eisenhower advised and encouraged his
"team" in New York and Washington as they set up an organization to
promote his candidacy.

The Eisenhower supporters, of course, had no way of knowing
how difficult a course Taft would encounter. Luce and his people
threw Taft's campaign off stride almost at its inception. The day after
Eisenhower wrote his letter to Duff, on October 15, 1951, an article appeared in *Life* magazine with a picture of Taft, Dewey, and Vandenberg. It referred to the recently published diaries of the late secretary
of defense, James Forrestal. According to the diaries, President Truman had received a letter immediately after the 1948 election from, of
all people, Taft. It congratulated the president on his victory and said
"that neither he nor his wife were particularly disappointed with the
result."[1] This was, in turned out, a fabrication by Forrestal (upon hearing the allegation, Truman sent the letter, which contained no such
passage, to Taft, who promptly forwarded it to Dewey). The episode

demonstrated that Forrestal was capable of underhanded tactics. Luce and his editors, for their part, were just reporting the story.[2]

Taft nevertheless had the advantage, and the battle was just beginning. By the time he announced his candidacy on October 16, 1951, his cousin, David Ingalls had traveled thirty thousand miles and visited Republican leaders in twenty-eight states. His fund-raisers had secured more than $1 million from prominent businessmen. Colonel Robert McCormick's *Chicago Tribune* had come out for Taft.[3] The candidate had given speeches in the Dakotas, Iowa, and Nebraska. After the announcement, beginning October 23 he spoke in South Dakota, Pittsburgh, Cincinnati, Knoxville, Providence, Chicago, Birmingham, Biloxi, New Orleans, Kansas City, and Tulsa, and appeared to reporters as "relaxed, even genial." By the end of his tour he had given twelve major speeches, appeared twice on television, and held seven press conferences in five days.[4] Despite this flurry of activity, according to public opinion polls his appeal to independents remained low. In January 1952 a Roper poll revealed that even his hometown, Cincinnati—which had voted overwhelmingly for him in 1950—now favored Eisenhower 43 percent to 39 percent.[5]

Prudently, the Eisenhower forces took little comfort. The campaign for the nomination had begun in earnest when Taft declared his candidacy. He hoped that his early announcement, his stature as a previous candidate, and his Midwestern conservative credentials (the eastern, liberal Dewey having now been twice defeated in the general election) would persuade Eisenhower to stay out of the race.[6] If Eisenhower nonetheless came in, Taft knew that none of his effort would make any difference if he could not gain the commitment of 604 delegates before the 1952 national convention.[7] State primary elections would begin in New Hampshire and Minnesota in March, then move to Wisconsin, Illinois, New Jersey, Nebraska, Pennsylvania, Massachusetts, and Missouri in April, then on to Ohio, West Virginia, North Dakota, Wyoming, Oregon, Rhode Island, Vermont, and across the nation.[8]

But if Taft felt uncertain, at least he was campaigning. The Eisenhower forces, on the other hand, knew that they had just begun to get organized, and rather awkwardly at that. Indeed, in September, the month before the general wrote his secret letter to Duff, Dewey had invited Clay to his apartment in the Roosevelt Hotel in New York City for a one-on-one discussion. At a second meeting—one that included former New York GOP national committeeman Russell Sprague; former secretary of the New York GOP and administrative assistant to Senator John Foster Dulles, Thomas Stephens; and Brownell—Clay said he knew that Eisenhower would run only if he sensed a strong public demand and had an effective organization, including financial support.[9] Lodge, who felt not enough was being done, soon called a meeting in Senator Frank Carlson's office in Washington. Those present, including Dewey, Duff, and Senator Irving Ives of New York, decided to establish an Eisenhower-for-President campaign office in Washington, with Stephens in charge.[10]

The press soon got wind of these activities, and Milton Eisenhower found himself in an embarrassment that inadvertently fueled the Eisenhower movement. On September 20 he wrote Robinson of a difficulty he had had with a *Newsweek* correspondent after a conversation with Senator Hugh Scott of Pennsylvania. Milton had told Scott confidentially that he opposed his brother's entering politics. He knew that Ike was "violently opposed to engaging in partisan politics," something that his present assignment precluded in any event. In response to questions from Scott, Milton had acknowledged that he (Milton) was a Republican, as were his brothers Arthur, Edgar, and Earl. A *Newsweek* article in early September to his chagrin reported that he "was telling Republican leaders the General is a Republican." Another story then appeared—relying on Milton's alleged assurance—that Dewey, Duff, Carlson, and others were preparing a Republican draft-Eisenhower movement. After reading it, Duff called Milton for confirmation, but Milton refused. The ultimate embarrassment occurred when, on the Sunday night before September 20, columnist Drew Pearson reported over the radio that the general was a Republican "and would respond favorably to a draft by the Republican party." When a reporter from the Associated Press called Milton about this, he replied emphatically that he "had made no such statement, was not authorized to make a statement, and will not make a statement." Milton then wrote Ike and, through Carlson and Duff, contacted Scott, who apologized and assured Eisenhower's supporters that "there would be no more difficulty."[11] This was no doubt also part of the impetus behind Clark's trip to Paris on Eisenhower's sixty-first birthday to seek assurances.

Isolated from the furor, the supreme commander remained quiet, carrying out his work at SHAPE, awaiting the appropriate time for more forthright action. Two letters, one from Clay on October 16 and the other from Milton, four days later, conveyed that such a time was approaching. Clay reminded Eisenhower that because of his retirement from Continental Can, he could come to SHAPE at any time and was "at your service." Dewey and Aldrich, he said, wanted him to "go over at once . . . before Senator Carlson does." Since "you are the only person who can pull our people together," he had "made up his mind to work in my humble way for your nomination regardless of whether or not you want it."[12]

Milton also was concerned. "Letters, telegrams, long distance calls, and personal callers," he said, kept coming in. Republicans who were opposed to Taft, the only active Republican candidate, and knew "they can't stop Taft with nobody," were saying the party must draft Eisenhower. Dewey had had to say on the television program "Meet the Press" that no one had a commitment from Ike but that "everyone was simply going on the firm belief that you would do your duty . . . and that you [would] become a candidate." However irritating or distracting this might be, said Milton, "your position in this country and in the world makes this sort of thing inevitable." Bill Robinson, he reported, was prepared to set up a campaign issues research agency at the *Herald Tribune*, ostensibly to obtain material for editorial use but of course to be of assistance to the campaign. The two of them, Milton and Robinson, were ready, also with Ike's consent, to bring together a "few of your closest and most trusted friends, weigh all the evidence in the present situation, and tell you [their] honest conclusions." They worried that Duff, Carlson, Darby, and Dewey were pressing too hard for a statement, and that a public announcement at this date might be both premature and negative in its effect, damaging to the general's mission.[13]

As if on signal, on October 19, Eisenhower wrote to Robinson. His concern was another, related, matter—the "curious allegation" in the United States that he was "one of those responsible for the dissipation of American military strength immediately following the cessation of hostilities in 1945." He defended his record, listing his recommendations for universal military service, his efforts to resist the discharge of two-year men, and his attempts to obtain passage of UMT. All this, he said, showed "how soon people forget the actual events of history and succumb to the effects of unwarranted and baseless statement."[14] (Robinson, meanwhile, wrote his daughter that he was certain Eisenhower's "sense of duty and passionate patriotism can ultimately find satisfaction only in the fulfillment of his destiny—a destiny which has never been more clearly marked in any man's life.")[15] Not coincidentally, on October 25 the New York Herald Tribune ran a front-page editorial announcing that it would work for Eisenhower's Republican nomination and election to the presidency.[16] "At rare intervals in the life of a free people the man and the occasion meet," it said, "the opportunity for service that falls to a great party is matched by the appearance of a leader, wise and tested, capable of giving reality to what masses of men and women have dreamed. . . . We believe Dwight D. Eisenhower is the man. He cannot, by the nature of his immediate position, respond to political appeals from this country. Perhaps for the same reason, he cannot as yet determine in his own heart what is right for him to do. Yet those who have confidence in the man . . . see in the drawing to a close of his present assignment in Europe the occasion for a new call to effort and to service."[17] Robinson wrote Eisenhower the next day, explaining that "everyone here" felt the "necessity for fortifying the enthusiasm, the faith and hope of the more enlightened Republicans and independents who are depressed at the prospect of a Taft nomination." As a result of the editorial, which had gone out on all the radio networks and news service wires, he reported,

the uncertainty that had given Taft an advantage "has now been substantially dissipated."[18]

A letter from Phil Young at Columbia University, however, relayed
a continuing urgency. "The general furor," he told Eisenhower, "had
reached a peak over here during the last few days." He referred to stray
rumors that "you might come back to report as your first year of operation draws to a close." There was, he said, "a real undercurrent of desire . . . for you to accept a Presidential nomination; and I believe that
this undercurrent is not just stimulated by our political friends who
have axes to grind." "Thinking friends," he said, hoped that when
Eisenhower found "some kind of punctuation point in [his] job,"
which they hoped would occur sometime that spring, "you would at
that time be relieved of your present assignment."[19]

Eisenhower already planned to return in early November, but not
to campaign. He had NATO business to conduct in Washington. He
also arranged to meet those most directly concerned with his political
future. "If I fail to meet you," he told Milton, "I shall write you a long
letter after I return here because there have been a few small developments of which I think you are unaware."[20] (He no doubt was referring
to his letter to Duff.) The general also sent Milton a copy of a longer
letter to Robinson which informed the newspaper executive that he,
Eisenhower, and Milton had been so "very close . . . for many years"
that "in many respects, we think exactly alike." The letter to Robinson
said that he was "highly complimented, and I mean highly" by the
Herald Tribune editorial. Its purpose, he said, seems to have been "to
give encouragement to a great underlying sentiment that might be
called truly grass roots, but definitely inarticulate." The response to
such editorials, he said—betraying his strategy—would be important
because he would "get tangled up in any kind of political activity"
only if "forced to do so as the result of a genuine and deep conviction
expressed by a very large segment of our people. . . . There has been
no fundamental change in my thinking over the last several years. . . .
I have always been ready to respond instantly to anything I saw as a
clear duty. On the other hand, you both [Robinson and Milton] have

known my complete lack of desire or ambition for any kind of political career." He was "now assigned," he reiterated, "to the most delicate military task of my career; the need for singleness of purpose in serving the national interests is probably greater than ever before." He nevertheless expressed his "delight that you, with the support of Pete [W. Alton Jones] and Cliff [Roberts], are undertaking the study and analysis of some of our major questions of the day. You are really establishing a junior 'American Assembly.' All of us will unquestionably profit from the result."[21] It was an interesting allusion, perhaps implying that the Columbia University forum had had a larger purpose than revealed at the time.

By this time the war in Korea was a national preoccupation and of course a continuing distraction from Eisenhower's European strategy. Charles E. Wilson, former president of General Motors and head of the Office of Defense Mobilization, sent the NATO supreme commander a speech he had given on October 10 at the Society for the Advancement of Management in Dallas. Entitled "The Camel's Nose Is Under the Tent," it argued that the overriding problems confronting the nation were the possibilities of a third world war or of losing "our type of free society in the process of preparing for war." This latter risk, in Wilson's view and in that of many of his fellow corporate executives, was the more pressing concern. The Korean War, he noted, was being used to justify more and more government restrictions and controls, "more and more state planning." For example, the war was taking less than 10 percent of the nation's steel production, but the government was, "contrary to the recommendations of the steel industry itself," rationing all of it. When the government took control, he said, problems were "usually magnified and made much more difficult."[22]

Eisenhower replied effusively. Wilson, he said, was fighting "against the dangerous theory that bureaucratic control can solve our country's industrial, economic and financial problems." Being a soldier did not mean that one's thinking was "distorted to the extent that he believes in arms and arms alone as the basis of peace abroad and freedom at home. . . . Permanent maintenance of a crushing weight of military power would eventually produce dictatorship." As for preparedness, he referred to the War Department in the 1920s where he worked with a congressional committee investigating the best way to mobilize the American economy for any future world war. "If we will only put our industrial brains to the task of devising an efficient plan for emergency mobilization, we will," he said, "save billions if ever we again face the tragedy of war. I hope that you and General Motors will keep plugging away at this vital problem."[23]

The official purpose of Eisenhower's trip home the first week of November 1951 was to smooth the way toward a NATO army. SHAPE, he said, was receiving insufficient numbers of tanks for the six U.S. armored divisions he was preparing, and too little information about the development of tactical nuclear weapons. As soon as he arrived in Washington on November 5, the press was unrelenting, driving Ike almost to distraction.[24] After a short visit with the president and a morning at the Pentagon, he attended a White House luncheon and at 3:15 p.m. met with the National Security Council in the cabinet room. Truman asked the gathered officials for their "complete and earnest cooperation" as to the "allocation of weapons and equipment to NATO."

But even in such official circumstances, partisan politics reared their head. The president joked in front of the gathered officials that he had not brought Eisenhower back earlier because of the "Great Debate"—referring to the clash in the Senate and the press about U.S. troops for NATO. Ike retorted, laughingly, and alluded to the press speculation about his own presidential ambitions. "Another 'Great Debate,'" he said, "was going on now." Truman replied that he was "not interested in that. . . . You can see anybody you want to and do anything you want to while you are here."[25] Returning to the subject at hand, Eisenhower observed that the Pentagon had promised NATO 2,708 tanks but had delivered only 2,148. Defense Department officials responded, referring to the difficulties they faced because of the drain on resources of the war in Korea."[26] Eisenhower then insisted on the need to increase production of coal and modern military equipment in the European countries, to free them of dependence on the United States.[27] Robert Lovett, who recently had replaced Marshall as secretary of defense, responded that Congress hated to provide funding to build aircraft factories in Europe and "cuts it to hell."[28] Concluding, Eisenhower thanked the officials for their help in progress toward a European defense force which, he said, emphasizing a key ingredient, was "the only way to get the Germans in."[29]

It was after leaving Washington—with his plane parked on the tarmac at La Guardia Airport in New York City—that he met with Clay, Bill Robinson, Cliff Roberts, and Milton. There he reaffirmed both his commitment to NATO and his willingness to accept a GOP draft—if it came without his overt participation. Robinson, elated, wrote Eisenhower in the days that followed that he was "thrilled and heartened," and that Milton now seemed "completely reconciled to the inevitability of the draft . . . and we share . . . the feeling that your well being, your satisfactions for the future, might not be ill-served in leading the nation to a higher plateau of moral responsibility and unity of purpose." The trip home, he told Eisenhower, "enhanced your already solid prestige with the public. I could only have wished that some of the press queries had been directed toward NATO."[30]

Eisenhower mused to Hazlett at what he was reading about himself. The Communist press called him a fascist war monger; American isolationists, for their part, said he was a friend of Stalin or of the "internationalist do-gooders of the world." One columnist charged that he was "too fearful ever to attempt to fill a political office," while another asserted that he was, "with Machiavellian cunning, pulling every possible string to become President of the United States." His own view, he said, was that "a man cannot desert a duty, but it would seem that he could lay down one in order to pick up a heavier and more responsible burden. So far as personal desire or ambition is concerned, there will never be any change for me. I could not be more negative."[31] "Every passing day," he told Robinson, "confirms and hardens my dislike of all political activity as a personal participant." Not only would he be "giving up friends, recreation, and activity of my own choice . . . there is [in partisan politics] discernible very little desire to service [sic] the public; often the inspiration seems merely to gain opportunity to exploit the public." He was not sure, he said, where he was headed, "but one thing is certain—feeling as I do—if ever I get into this business, I am going to start swinging from the hips and I am going to keep swinging until completely counted out. One great thing of doing a job where you feel it is not of your own choice, one doesn't have to placate or appease anybody."[32]

On November 8, Eisenhower accepted Milton's suggestion for the creation of a personal advisory committee. Cliff Roberts, besides being an investment banker at Reynolds and Company on Wall Street (and Eisenhower's financial adviser), was cofounder and chairman of the executive committee of the Augusta National Golf Club. As such, he was at the hub of a network that included some of the nation's most influential businessmen. Since Ike and Mamie considered him "practically as one of the family," it was not surprising that Eisenhower asked him to suggest the names of individuals who would be "completely independent of whatever political group might organize itself around the idea of forcing me into the political picture." Their task, he said, would be to "take a hard-headed look at the propriety, decency, and desirability of any proposition that might affect me personally."[33]

Two days later, Duff, Clay, and Brownell met with Dewey in his suite in the Roosevelt Hotel. After much debate, they selected Lodge as chairman of a campaign organization that subsumed the Kansas activities of Darby and Carlson and then set up an Eisenhower-for-President finance committee under Harold Talbott and a Citizens-for-Eisenhower movement under the leadership of Paul Hoffman. Under Hoffman's direction, the Ford Foundation had been creating programs to assist individuals and groups resisting or fleeing communism in central and eastern Europe. (Disillusioned with what he called Taft's "pedantic arrogance," the former president of Studebaker had begun to urge that Eisenhower seek the GOP presidential nomination.)[34] Dewey, they all agreed, would continue to work secretly; Brownell would plot strategy and contact delegates; Clay would be liaison with SHAPE.[35]

The following week Roberts offered Ike a list of men who, he said, were free of ambition and, except for Milton, acquainted with one another. The group, when it finally came together, included corporate

chief executives from the board at Augusta National Golf Course—
Louis B. Maytag, founder of the washing machine company; Robert
T. Jones, Jr., former golf professional and lawyer from Atlanta; B. F.
Peek, chairman of the board of Deere and Company; Alton "Pete"
Jones, head of Cities Service Oil; Philip D. Reed; E. D. Slater, president of Frankfort Distilleries; Barry T. Leithead, president of Cluett,
Peabody and Company; and Douglas Black—plus Milton Eisenhower
and Bill Robinson. As a kind of monitoring committee, this group
would keep tabs on the other Eisenhower-for-President organizations
around the country and discourage the circulation of information that
was "incorrect" or "in bad taste." Perhaps most important, considering
the prominence of these men in corporate America, they would also
provide what Roberts called "other services"—fund raising. With the
addition, on Eisenhower's suggestion, of Clay, Jock Whitney, and Calhoun, this group soon swung into action.[36]

Assisted by Clark, Eisenhower also moved on other fronts. He told
Duff of two individuals whose participation in strategy planning he
considered essential. They were Hoffman and his colleague at the
Ford Foundation (and Luce's brother-in-law), Maurice Moore. The
two had come to Paris, and while there, Eisenhower recruited them.
He told them about the secret letter to Duff and asked that they, upon
their return to the United States, talk freely with the senator from
Pennsylvania.[37] Hoffman was ready, writing Eisenhower on November
15 that he and Moore had concluded on their trip home from Paris
that "only one move made sense": the initiation of a draft-Eisenhower
movement "of such intensity that the . . . extent of support for you in
the Republican Party ranks could be quickly determined." Edwin
Clark, he said, had told them that "a grand coalition was underway,"
and Hoffman had told Clark and Duff that he and Moore were ready
to help. "Clark," Hoffman added, had "handled the situation developed recently with consummate skill, his only motivation being to get
into the White House the man the world needs."[38]

Eisenhower then received good news from Bermingham. The national committeeman from Illinois had worried about another GOP
defeat if the eastern wing again nominated a candidate. His worries

were over, he said, and he no longer needed to disassociate himself from the eastern Republicans. Duff and the others had "dug me out," and he was "very pleased" that things were falling into their proper places. The New York investment banker Clarence Dillon, he said, was happy; and Lodge and Fred Gurley, president of the Atchison, Topeka, and Santa Fe Railroad, were coming to meet with him in Chicago.[39]

Henry Luce, meanwhile, had found out about Eisenhower's Pentagon meeting with Taft the previous January. This was not surprising, considering the fact that the magazine publisher's network of acquaintances included Dewey, Brownell, Clay, Watson, Aldrich, and Lodge. (Lodge interestingly, had worked for *Time* briefly in the 1920s and had written articles for *Fortune*.) And, of course, Luce's wife, Congresswoman Clare Boothe Luce, also was immersed in the Washington scene. Working behind the scenes, Luce had much to say about his magazines' editorial policy.[40] Taft, perhaps attempting to woo Luce away from Eisenhower, by this time had adopted the publisher's Asia-first strategy, and also belatedly supported sending some divisions to Europe—four, not six. Unfortunately for the Ohio senator, Luce had made his decision. *Time* published an article criticizing both Taft's insistence that Truman dispatch no more troops without congressional approval, and his opposition to sending money to help the Europeans rearm. Upholding Eisenhower's program instead, *Time* urged the sending of six combat divisions.[41]

With the establishment of Eisenhower-for-President headquarters at the Hotel Commodore in New York, *Time-Life* editors—including C. D. Jackson and Edward K. Thompson, managing editor of *Life*—began to visit SHAPE to make plans for a political campaign. Thompson felt at home, having served at SHAEF as an intelligence officer.[42]

A strategist of proven brilliance, Eisenhower knew, of course, that the possibility of failure increased in direct proportion to a campaign's complexity. His activities now were becoming complex indeed, and he had to intervene to keep them under control. The process of finding a leader for the campaign organization—someone who could overcome philosophical and sectional distrust and personal animosities and move the campaign vigorously—was a case in point. Duff had been the obvious choice, but Dewey had preferred Barak Mattingly from Missouri. Duff, Darby, and Stassen's people considered Mattingly too obviously a Dewey man. Eisenhower, during his trip home, had tried to resolve the impasse, no doubt mentioning Lodge as a possibility. Upon his return to Paris he had received the text of a newspaper column by *New York Times* columnist Arthur Krock, identifying Lodge as the newly selected Eisenhower-for-President campaign leader.

Eisenhower was almost apoplectic. The only person who could have revealed the information, he feared, was Ed Clark. He tried to reach Clark hurriedly by telephone, and when unsuccessful he drafted a letter reviewing their arrangement (and in the process revealing it to future historians as well). "You and I have several times agreed that your role in any development that might come about would be a sphinx-like one, so that you could constantly act as a trusted messenger. It seems to me terribly important that there remain to me one old friend who can trot back and forth to my headquarters without arousing undue notice. The importance of this point," he said, revealing the strain of his continuing effort to separate himself mentally from his actions, "would not be so great if I wanted a political office, if I were openly and directly dealing with a group organized to promote such a purpose."[43] By the time Eisenhower completed the letter, Schulz had reached Clark by telephone. What he discovered calmed the general. Clark told him that "Harry [Darby] and Red [Duff] agreed on a certain man . . . Massachusetts cabbie [Lodge] and that this had brought about 'complete harmony.'" "That name has now leaked," Clark explained, "and is in most of the morning newspapers."[44] A letter soon arrived from Clay, who reported that Duff had leaked the information but that everything is working "all to the good, and a really effective organization is certain to develop quickly." Dewey, he said, had "really driven through the final decision." A research staff was now at work, and "we know you will make no comment until and unless you return here."[45] Perhaps to signal Clark and the others how delicate the situation remained, Eisenhower sent Clark the letter anyway, including as a postscript that his concerns were now resolved.

In retrospect it is clear that events were moving more favorably than Eisenhower or his organization knew at the time. Stassen's campaign manager, Bernard Shanley, on November 14 met with Alfred P. Sloan, chairman of the board of General Motors. When Shanley explained that his purpose was to enlist the support of Sloan and other leading businessmen in behalf of Eisenhower or Stassen, Sloan—who also had met with the Taft people—interrupted to ask where Shanley had gotten the impression the top businessmen in the country thought Taft could be elected. Sloan said he thought he knew all the "top businessmen," and they all favored Eisenhower. He said he was one of the largest contributors to the Republican party and would give generously to an Eisenhower-Stassen coalition.[46]

This news may not have reached the Eisenhower forces, who had no intention in any event of reducing their effort. As Duff explained on November 19, Taft still had "the inside track with the considerable majority of the professionals." These partisans, he said, were engaged in a campaign of smear and suggestion against Eisenhower, implying, most damagingly, that the general would not run. Many delegates were therefore afraid to "put their necks out politically for fear they won't have a candidate." The positive information they had was that Eisenhower dominated the public opinion polls. The latest Gallup poll, for example, gave him twice as many votes as any single candidate, "more than Taft and MacArthur combined and more than Taft and Truman combined."[47]

The Eisenhower forces therefore set out on two missions, first to establish a solid national organization, and second to prevent Taft from consolidating his position in the South. As for the first, Lodge—discovering that he was the one individual acceptable to all the leaders—readily accepted the campaign chairmanship, which was announced to the public in a press conference on November 16.[48] A flurry of correspondence ensued between Lodge and Dewey, with the latter as political coach. He told the campaign chairman to read

Eisenhower's book, *Crusade in Europe*, and his many speeches to see his "complete mastery of world affairs, which is so essential for our national survival." Dewey agreed to release his staff assistant, Gabe Hauge, to do research for the campaign.[49]

Duff, attending to the other priority, was traveling in the South, visiting Texas, Louisiana, Georgia, and North Carolina. He was optimistic but in a letter to Eisenhower warned of complacency, saying that the pro-Taft GOP Old Guard's motto in both state and national elections was "rule or ruin." The key to success, he said, would be timing. "Too soon will deprive us of surprise. Too late will give them too great an opportunity for build-up and consolidation."[50] On November 23, Dewey sent Lodge the latest Gallup poll of a "trial heat" in thirteen Southern states. Eisenhower defeated Truman by 54 percent to 36 percent (10 percent undecided); Warren defeated Truman by 43 percent to 40 percent (17 percent undecided); and Truman defeated Taft 48 percent to 35 percent (17 percent undecided). He recommended that these statistics be "hammered and hammered and hammered by mail and personal interview . . . in those thirteen states."[51] Duff's efforts, clearly, had yielded results. Before sending his letter, Duff added a postscript that Lodge was "in complete agreement" with what Duff had written but believed it was "vitally necessary" that "a public announcement [of Eisenhower's candidacy] be made . . . before the end of January."[52]

On December 3, Lodge reported that the committee had opened an official Eisenhower-for-President headquarters in Topeka, Kansas, with a branch office at the Shoreham Hotel in Washington. The New York City office at the Commodore would direct operations. Stephens had accepted the position of executive officer, and Jock Whitney and Harold Talbott had taken over "financing of the campaign which insures that adequate funds will be raised in a way as to create no obligation at all." Roy Roberts had agreed to select a Kansas newspaperman to take charge of public relations. The strategy group now included — in addition to Duff, Dewey, and Brownell — Mattingly, Hugh Scott, Mason Sears, and Maxwell Rabb.

Lodge by this time had established personal contacts in eight states, stimulated activity in three others, and initiated a research project to develop positions for Eisenhower on "all the big issues of the day." He was arranging for an Eisenhower convention headquarters in Chicago and had held press conferences in Chicago and Washington. He praised Duff, who he said, "has made and is continuing to make an immense and highly successful effort." He urged the general to accept an invitation by Republican National Committee chairman Gabrielson to attend a meeting of GOP officials from eleven Western states, to be held in San Francisco January 17, 18, and 19. "People want to know what you think from your own lips. . . . Senator Taft is beginning to be praised for his willingness to 'get out and discuss the issue.'"[53]

Cliff Roberts's group also was taking shape. It now included, at Eisenhower's request, McCollum, Young, and Nielson. The only qualifications for membership, Eisenhower repeated, were "personal friendship, reliability, and keen judgment." It was undesirable that they "all should think alike politically, especially about me and the possibility that I might get into the political business." The "sole reason for this group," he said, was "to help keep me informed and advised." And the whole business would have to be kept confidential. "You would have to do it as your idea and merely on the basis of helping out a friend who hasn't time to think of a lot of these things himself and in response to my referring the occasional questions to you for your conclusions."[54]

In early December good news arrived at SHAPE from Texas. Winthrop Aldrich, returning from a week's tour of the state, sent the supreme commander the results of a poll taken by the publisher of a chain of seventy-five newspapers in the state. It showed a three-to-one margin of support for Eisenhower as the 1952 Republican candidate for president.[55] About this time, Eisenhower decided to ask Kevin McCann to take leave from his presidency of Defiance College in Ohio and join him in Paris to handle political activity.[56]

☆ 12 ☆

REPUBLICAN
AFFILIATION

THE END OF 1951 and the beginning of 1952 provided a crucial moment in Eisenhower's political life. In January 1952 he declared that he was a Republican, and for practical purposes, despite his unwillingness to announce this publicly, he became a candidate for the presidential nomination.

It all began easily enough. In early December, Hoffman told him that he alone had the capacity to redeem the Republican party, change the atmosphere "from fear and hate to good will and confidence," and "start the world down the road to peace."[1] Burnham, who after handling partisan political matters at SHAPE for several months had returned to New York City, sent a letter. The great wealth in the United States, he said, contrasted with the "dirt and poverty" of France. "Large new cars clutter the road—particularly Cadillacs. New homes are going up still, at a fast rate. The stores are crowded. . . . The rich, of course, are grumbling about taxes, but I suspect that the average guy in spite of rising prices is better off than he has ever been." He reported conversations with Robinson, Young, McCollum, Cameron Thomson (president of the Northwest Bancorporation), Harry Bullis (president of General Mills), Young, and Lodge. All of them, he said, had been optimistic, the latter three believing that if he received the GOP nomination he could carry Texas, the Dakotas, Iowa, Nebraska, and Minnesota.[2]

Eisenhower was fixed on his job. Cliff Roberts would recall that the general was concerned with the long-term needs of western Europe. He wanted "to get all these countries and put them together and make one nation that would be substantially the size and the same total resources of the United States." He had an "unusual grasp of the benefits that would accrue."[3] Such an outcome was, he believed, a vital American interest. "American leaders," Eisenhower told his brother Edgar, needed to inform their fellow countrymen of the "essentials of the American system and the dangers that can threaten them." The United States was powerful but not economically independent. "We must annually import great quantities of raw materials or our whole industrial system will begin to dry up and great political changes would necessarily ensue." The United States needed good relations with the countries that are the sources of its production. It had to "make sure that, in those areas, there are governments and populations that desire to trade with us. If those areas should be occupied by enemies of ours, the conditions requisite to trade would not exist." Turning to politics, he said, the average political leader was interested merely in obtaining power. As for himself, he said, "there can be no political duty . . . before there is something substantial in the way of a public mandate."[4]

The possibility of this now seemed suddenly to wane. Within the week came letters from Clay and Burnham, each carrying bad news. Clay reported friction in the organization. Clark, he said, had inspired Duff and Jock Whitney to exclude him [Clay] from strategy meetings. "Both Burnham and I," he said, "feel Clark to be unreliable; in fact dangerous." There were other problems as well. Duff "was full of ego and determined to be the 'anointed,'" this despite the fact that he could not deliver his state's vote and kept "spreading the word that Dewey's name is poison." Dewey "is irritated and has expressed doubts about Duff." Clay recommended that Eisenhower not send Duff any more messages. Stassen, he said, was "an enigma—not one of your group trusts him fully." The finance chairmanship still was not settled because Lodge had decided Talbot should not serve in that position. (Philadelphia banker and former assistant secretary of war Howard

Peterson would replace him in that post.) Lodge, he said, was making progress but was not a strong man and tended to be dominated by Duff.[5]

Burnham agreed. Lodge, he said, needed "a little more steel in the backbone." As for the difficulties perceived by Clay, Burnham had discussed them with Lodge and believed they would be "ironed out." The problem, he said, was Clark's "representations that he has the ear of DDE" which were "terribly disturbing to Cabot, Lucius Clay, Bill Robinson, and myself." He hoped, therefore, that "any further visits from him can be avoided."[6]

At about that time a letter arrived from Robert P. Burroughs. Doubts had surfaced in New Hampshire about Eisenhower's party affiliation. A Democrat from Littleton had announced his intention to obtain one hundred signatures on a petition identifying Eisenhower as a Democrat. Burroughs hoped that Eisenhower would make a public declaration of party affiliation and intention to resign from the army in the "very near future, hopefully before the delegate filing deadline on February 9."[7]

Eisenhower now decided the wheels were moving too fast. Cliff Roberts and Robinson were planning a December 23 trip to Paris. Before their departure they expected to gather the "gang" in New York to consider all the angles and offer advice. Their intent, Cliff told the general, was to provide the "satisfaction and assurance that comes from the willingness of trusted friends to supply counsel."[8] Eisenhower was pleased, writing Roberts that this was exactly what he had in mind, that he was looking forward to their visit, but that a crisis had arisen. He was referring to the letter from Lodge urging him to attend the conference in San Francisco. There was, he said, a conviction that he needed to make a statement of political intent or render the whole effort hopeless. "As you know," he said, "I simply am not going to do any such thing. To my mind, it would be a dereliction of duty—almost a violation of my oath of office." He had no duty, he said, "to seek a nomination." He added that Roberts had his permission to discuss this with any member of the advisory groups.[9]

On December 12, Eisenhower conveyed this same message to

Lodge. His words were stark. If a mere assurance that he would not repudiate the efforts of supporters was no longer sufficient, "the program in which you and your close political associates are now engaged should, logically, be abandoned." Current responsibilities, Eisenhower said, made "pre-convention activity impossible for me."[10] That his meaning not be mistaken, he wrote Clay in a similar vein. If this rendered the "whole project an impossible one," he said, "I will be free of a lot of extra-curricular anxiety and worry." He then turned to the issue of Clark. He had told Clark in unmistakable terms only a few days ago, he said, that he would repudiate completely any impression Clark might give that he "was a 'spokesman' for me." He added, ruefully, that two people he was sure "would never offend in this way were Bill Burnham and Ed Clark."[11]

Fortunately for everyone, this trouble seemed to recede as quickly as it had arisen. A letter from Clay explained that he continued to be excluded from strategy sessions and distrusted Clark, and now Burnham too.[12] But Clay also enclosed a long memorandum from Dewey, which brought Eisenhower some relief. It took issue with the proposition that the general needed to become active to win the nomination. Indeed, the New York governor questioned whether a public announcement was necessary. He pointed out that at the last three conventions, the man out in front in December had been defeated. Now, he said, half the delegates were in the Eisenhower camp with another 25 percent undecided. Taft's main advantage was his momentary domination of the headlines. Since New Hampshire petitioners were required by law to swear an oath to the party allegiance of their candidate, Dewey suggested that another individual, possibly Milton, answer a letter of inquiry from the governor of New Hampshire as to the general's party affiliation. This could be followed by Eisenhower's public reply that he had fulfilled his NATO mission and, after a farewell tour of the allied countries, would return home to retire from all military titles and duties—all this without formal announcement of a candidacy. "Everyone," said Dewey, "is hysterically insisting on an announcement. I insist with equal vigor that the one thing the American people want most is the one thing they cannot get."[13]

In the same mail (and before the campaign chairman could have received Eisenhower's letter of protest) was another letter from Lodge, this one exuberant. The elements of a great convention victory, he said, were in place. He had talked with Hoffman and Luce ("who had said he would print all the news about the campaign just as fast as we develop it" and "would come out for Eisenhower as soon as he comes out for himself"). Lodge reported that he had established an organization that would allow those "who want to support you publicly to make their support known." He no longer believed it necessary for Eisenhower to appear in San Francisco.[14] His earlier request had been based upon a misunderstanding of the general's schedule.[15]

Things were back on track. The supreme commander wrote Clay two days later, making clear his attitude toward his candidacy. He said that he instinctively found himself "largely in agreement with it [the Dewey memorandum]." He added that he already had admitted in conversations with Dewey and Duff that his "family ties, voting record, and convictions" aligned him "fairly closely with what I call the progressive branch of the Republican party." He hesitated, nevertheless, "to be a party to engineering a statement, the purpose of which would be to help clarify a partisan political position." It made him uneasy "to contemplate such a thing" because of the danger it could pose to NATO.[16]

A visit by Harold Stassen also brought reassurance. The former Minnesota governor again pledged his loyalty—this time in writing— and outlined his strategy, which was to be in contact with the general to "discuss personally any phase of the developments with you if your circumstances change so that you wish to talk with me." He planned an all-out campaign—not as a standard-bearer or stalking horse— against Taft in the Wisconsin and perhaps in the Illinois and Ohio primaries. His aim was to keep the Ohio senator on the run. At the same time he would put forward a program of issues—inflation, honesty in government, mutual respect among socioeconomic groups, and "an effective, affirmative dynamic foreign policy"—congenial to Eisenhower and ready in the event he decided to enter the race.[17]

George Sloan, a director and member of the finance committee of United States Steel (and former president of the Cotton Textile Institute), having just returned from meetings with Southern business and civic leaders in New Orleans, also reported favorably. The individuals he had met, he said, were anti–New Deal Democrats from Mississippi, Alabama, and Louisiana who were "without exception . . . counting on Eisenhower as the Republican candidate" and "ready to go all out for Dwight Eisenhower." Senator Taft had spoken there some weeks earlier, he reported, and "had not made much of an impression."[18]

Still, with Christmas approaching and soon thereafter the New Hampshire filing deadline, Eisenhower's situation was increasingly awkward. He had not accomplished his assignment at NATO, but everyone, save his very closest advisers, seemed to need a public declaration of his candidacy. Indeed, on December 19 he received a handwritten note on White House stationery. Aware of the pressures on the general about the 1952 election, President Truman apparently still hoped that Eisenhower would run as a Democrat or not at all. "As I told you in 1948 and at our luncheon in 1951," he said, "do what you think best for the country. My own position is in the balance. If I do what I want to do, I'll go back to Missouri and maybe run for the Senate. If you decide to finish the European job (and I don't know who else can), I must keep the isolationists out of the White House. I wish you would let me know what you intend to do. It will be between us and no one else. I have the utmost confidence in your judgment and patriotism. My best to you and Mrs. Ike for a happy holiday season."[19] If Eisenhower accepted the commander-in-chief's first suggestion and declared his candidacy, he would be putting his NATO mission at risk and contradicting what he had been saying (though, of course, not what he had been doing) about his participation in partisan political · activity. And since Truman really was hoping that he would declare as a Democrat, he would be disappointing the president, with all the potential risks of that. If he decided to remain out of the race, he would be terminating all the activities in his behalf—including those of Duff,

Clay, Dewey, Lodge, and Hoffman—and any chance of attaining the presidency (and thereby ensuring personally what he believed to be the national interest). Choosing either path, he no doubt concluded, opened him to criticism.

Eisenhower now found himself smoothing ruffled feathers in his organization. On December 21, Clay told him that the substance of Eisenhower's harsh letter of December 12 had not been consistent with what they had agreed during their conversation in Washington in November. Since Eisenhower no longer was happy with the way things were unfolding and apparently suspected that people were misrepresenting him, Clay would "withdraw from further activities with the 'pros.'"[20] Eisenhower, startled, responded immediately. Clay, he said to his old friend, was the "personality in the United States who was best acquainted with me and my methods, who had a good knowledge of Europe and the European problem, and who also had a wide acquaintanceship with people of substance at home." Of all his friends, he said, you are "best qualified to act as intermediary between me and the 'pros,' since direct communication between us could obviously be embarrassing."[21]

The supreme commander then wrote to Lodge. "Your letter," he said, "assures me that you clearly understand the position I shall maintain." Clay's "accuracy in interpretation is so great and his personal loyalty so complete, that nothing he could ever say about me could be contrary to his belief as to what I would want him to say. . . . Clay retains my complete confidence and friendship. This I cannot overstate."[22] Clay, the four-star general who had faced down the Soviets during the Berlin blockade, was, Lodge now knew, the candidate's personal liaison. If Clark had any misgivings with the turn of events (and there is no evidence that he did), he also could take satisfaction. His usefulness—as was probably inevitable given the stature of the individuals involved and the momentous nature of their endeavor—had faded. He wrote Eisenhower a New Year's note indicating the pride he took in their friendship and his willingness to serve in 1952 as he had in 1951.[23] Eisenhower replied immediately, noting that he shared "the value you place upon our friendship."[24] Clark's loyalty to Eisenhower, even as he moved to the sidelines, continued. In later years he would occasionally take on tasks for the man whom he had helped become president.[25]

Eisenhower now heard from New Hampshire governor Sherman Adams. The general's go-between with the state's Republicans was none other than Cliff Roberts, who was a friend of Frank Sulloway, GOP national committeeman from New Hampshire. (When Sulloway had a question he would ask Roberts, and the latter would then query Eisenhower and get an answer without telling the general that he was asking for somebody else.) Sulloway had asked whether the general was in the race, and Roberts had replied only that "the more people who do come out for him, the more likely . . . he'll come up with a favorable decision."[26] The Adams letter, however, signaled a need for something more definite. The New Hampshire "committee for promotion of Dwight D. Eisenhower for President," it said, needed to know by January 1, if possible, an answer to the question, "to which political party does General Eisenhower belong?" New Hampshire law, it said, required that the names of individuals to be voted on in the primary election "shall be printed solely on petition of New Hampshire voters of the same party as the prospective candidates."[27]

With the help of Roberts and Robinson, both of whom by this time had arrived in Paris for the holidays, Eisenhower began to frame his announcement. His two friends had brought the consensus of "the gang" that "the time had arrived when, if he still entertained any idea of refusing to be a candidate, that he must say that under no circumstances would he run." The gang now included among its members Roberts's cronies from Augusta National: A. F. McCollum of Continental Oil; Louis B. Maytag; Robinson; Albert Bradley, new chairman of General Motors; Pete Jones; Bob Jones; and Douglas Black. They had met in Manhattan at Roberts's suite in the Parklane Hotel. "There was not a single one of us," Roberts recalled, who "did not hope that he [Ike] might become a candidate."[28] Various politicians at home, Roberts and Robinson now told the reluctant candidate, needed to de-

clare themselves, and they did not desire to run the risk of political suicide by declaring for the general if he did not plan to run. By saying
"no" now, Eisenhower would free them to declare for Taft.[29]

On January 1 the general answered Truman's letter, denying his
partisan political activities. Despite his desire for a life of reflection,
writing, and farming, he wrote, circumstances had caused him to follow a "conviction of duty," another military duty in a foreign country,
this time as SACEUR. He did not, he said, "feel that I have a duty to
seek a political nomination, in spite of the fact that many have urged
to the contrary. Because of this belief I shall not do so." Such activity,
he said, would interfere with his present important task by encouraging partisan thinking and would at the same time violate Army Regulations. He then inserted the device he had resorted to since January
1948: "Any group of American citizens has a right to fight, politically,
for any set of principles in which its members believe and to attempt
to draft a leader to head the fight." He added that his "policy of complete abstention will be meticulously observed by me unless and until
extraordinary circumstances would place a mandate upon me that, by
common consent, would be deemed a duty of transcendent importance."[30]

No record has been found of Truman's reaction, but it is difficult
to imagine that the president, after reading it, considered Eisenhower
anything other than a candidate. The president had accused him in
1948 of using weasel words; he cannot have had much question now.

The die having been cast, Eisenhower thereupon dictated a letter
to be sent over Lodge's signature to Adams. "During 1948, 1949, and
1950," it said, "while he [Eisenhower] was serving as president of Columbia University, we several times discussed with him subjects of
political and economic importance to the nation. During these discussions, he specifically informed us that his voting record was that of a
Republican. At the same time, he stated that he had no intention
whatsoever of seeking any public office and expressed only an ambition to do his duty as he saw fit." Since army regulations prohibited the
general from undertaking "political activity that could be interpreted
as the seeking of a nomination . . . we are relating to you the facts that

establish the foundation on which we are working to produce a clear-cut call to duty without participation on his part."[31] "The signers of the Republican petition," it said, "are completely secure in their signed sworn statement that General Eisenhower is a member of their party."[32]

Why, one might ask, did Eisenhower and his advisers continue to be coy? Clearly, the most important consideration at this point for Eisenhower was his sense of mission. The objectives of security and peace for the free world gave meaning to everything he did, including both organizing SHAPE and moving toward a presidential nomination. This attitude is confirmed in Bill Robinson's notes on the deliberations that he and Cliff Roberts conducted with the general at Christmas, 1951. They were purely strategic and concluded, first, that Eisenhower should not *seek* the nomination, meaning that he should make no speeches or statements on partisan politics and not *personally* reveal his party affiliation; and, second, that he should remain in Europe until his mission there was completed or until his nomination seemed likely. This probably would not occur until June 1. "His feeling midway between aversion and reluctance is 100 percent real and not a pose," Robinson wrote. This "has proven to be a great political advantage which must be exploited and not regretted . . . a major element in the public demand for him. . . . General Eisenhower is much more devoted to the success of his mission in Europe than he is intrigued by the idea of being President. (The failure of the defense of Western Europe would neutralize or vitiate his greatest glory—victory in World War II)." The political reality was, said his advisers, that "his success in Europe is essential to efforts of his campaign managers. His failure there would leave them with a candidate in temporary bankruptcy. However, his power and influence there is a virtual guarantee of success (barring a Russian attack) by June. By that time, even though his task was not completed, he would be completely available for the nomination, providing continued public preference and delegate strength indicated a clear call to duty."[33]

Finally, Roberts and Robinson pointed out, the South seemed to be moving into his camp. This would be an historic event, a turning away from the one-party Democratic rule that had existed there since the 1870s. Democrátic loyalties in other parts of the country also remained unclear. Such conditions, they felt, required a strategy of involving others in courting a reluctant candidate. Meanwhile, Eisenhower's legislative aide, Wilton Persons, took the position that, while Army Regulations prevented the general from being a candidate while on active duty, "if somebody else wanted to enter the general's name without the general's permission," there was nothing in the regulations that "would oblige the general to demand that his name be withdrawn."[34]

Eisenhower had much to accomplish and, if everything occurred as anticipated, a strict timetable. Still, much remained to be done at SHAPE, as Eisenhower explained in January 4 letter to George Sloan. He and his staff had been working "at top speed . . . to produce concrete steps in the development of a European army and of some form of continental European political union. Without the latter," he said, "I do not believe there is any permanent and assured peace of the western world as long as the communist menace exists in its present form and with its present intentions." Eisenhower said he disagreed with a friend who believed him "privileged to consider myself a private citizen and to act accordingly." An individual with his responsibilities, he said, "can leave an important duty only when called to a higher one—he can scarcely, in advance, merely 'resign.'"[35]

He now sent Truman a progress report and also a request for action. The European countries lacked resources, he said, so he was attending to three areas where "significant accomplishment was possible without great expenditure of money." Two of them—the Schuman Plan and the European Defense Community (EDC)—"partake of the political and economic more than the military," and when completed would have a direct influence on the achievement of the third—a political and economic union of Western continental Europe. The Schuman Plan, he said, already was moving toward implementation of a European Coal and Steel Community. A six-nation agreement on a "broad plan for rapid development of a European Defense Force" also was in process. EDC posed a special problem because a division of opinion had developed. France, Germany, and Italy, Eisenhower reported, advocated a common budget; "arrangements to avoid discrimination against any member, including Germany; and partial surrender of sovereignty to responsible central executives." But Belgium and Holland disagreed, looking to Great Britain as their traditional protector and political mentor. Eisenhower suggested that Truman talk with Prime Minister Churchill, then on a visit to Washington to address a joint session of Congress. If the president could get the prime minister to make a "ringing statement" endorsing "early establishment of an effective European army (if for no other reason than as a long step toward political union)," Eisenhower said, it "could not fail to have a profound effect in Europe."[36]

Lodge's press conference in New Hampshire, meanwhile, was scheduled for January 6. The Luce publications set the stage. *Time* carried reprinted speeches in which Eisenhower had opposed New Deal social programs. *Life* appeared on the New England newsstands with an article entitled "The Case for Ike." The general, it said, "understood war without being a militarist; had enormous administrative experience; opposed 'unbridled' government; and would 'boost' national morale." *Fortune* soon thereafter celebrated Eisenhower's "matured grasp of the fundamentals of world power and politics."[37]

It was in this atmosphere that Lodge called a press conference and read the letter he had sent to Governor Adams, affirming that Eisenhower was a Republican. When reporters sought verification of the statement, Lodge referred them to SHAPE. In Paris, unexpectedly besieged by reporters asking if he was a Republican, Eisenhower responded that Lodge and his associates had a "right to place before me next July a duty that would transcend my present responsibility."[38]

With that statement, Eisenhower crossed into the realm of partisan politics. It was not a graceful crossing. He complained to Clay that he had agreed only to make "some personal comment on the matter . . . to clinch the sincerity of the statements." Even this, he said, was not enjoyable to him." As it turned out, he was caught in "a bit of a trap."[39] In fact he was not, as was confirmed in a letter from General Snyder to Robinson. Generals like to have contingency plans, and in this case

Eisenhower's staff had helped to draft a statement to the press. Snyder said he hoped Roberts and other friends "were not disappointed" by the general's announcement. "It removes the large measure of insecurity which had developed in the NATO organization with reference to the [Eisenhower's] term in office by a direct statement of intentions. It also places before the American people and the friends of the general in the political party machinery a decision which enables them to act positively in his connection if they are intent upon doing so."[40]

The effect of Eisenhower's statement, as Lodge had hoped (probably expected), was dramatic. It may have damaged the candidate's image of being the pursued, but only slightly, and it did no damage at all to either NATO or his standing at home. If anything, it enhanced them.

Robinson called the general's announcement "a classic of its kind."[41] Burnham wrote Eisenhower the next day that nothing pleased him more. He characterized the statement as saying, "All right, boys, if you want me for President, draft me. It removed you from the cat and dog fights of primaries and pre-convention maneuvering, and puts it squarely to your political backers in the United States to get to work and to organize," something that "to date, has been lacking." Burnham told of a friend who, on the evening of the announcement, had found himself in a Waldorf-Astoria elevator with General MacArthur. The general had turned to him—a stranger—and said, "Well, General Eisenhower dropped a bomb today, didn't he?"[42]

In other quarters, the Chicago radio commentator Paul Harvey referred favorably to Eisenhower, saying that the nation needed "a statesman, not a politician as a candidate in '52."[43] George Sloan wrote that "the Eisenhower declaration has had a most clarifying effect upon people who have been perplexed largely by the propaganda from the other side."[44] Bullis congratulated the general on his "decision to be a Republican candidate for President! Your historic statement has given hope and encouragement to the majority of our people, who have shown a hunger for your leadership."[45] The "announcement bought to me one of the deepest senses of satisfaction I have enjoyed for a very long time," said George Whitney. "I truly thank God for all it implies."[46] Ed Clark characterized the remarks as "a great historical document and the natural result of which will be your selection as the Republican candidate at the convention in Chicago in July."[47] The Wiesenberger Investment Report for January 11, 1951, predicted that an Eisenhower election might send the Dow Jones industrial average over the 500 mark.[48]

Throughout these weeks, Mamie Eisenhower had sensed something of the machinations that were leading toward yet another duty assignment. Certainly she suspected something was afoot when her Christmas holiday party at Villa-St. Pierre for their wartime friends, James "Jimmy" Gault and his wife, Peggy, expanded to include Robinson and Roberts. She and Ike, she later recalled, received an avalanche of some two thousand Christmas cards. If this was not suspicious enough, Robinson and Roberts arrived at Christmas dinner with "I Like Ike" ties and "I Like Ike" caps and buttons. She recalled that Ike blushed, "but we had to laugh when we saw them because they looked so silly. . . . Poor Ike, they really put it on him," she wrote in a letter to her mother. "He doesn't know which way to turn."[49]

According to Roberts, Mamie disliked the prospect of a political candidacy. "When this Presidential business began to build up to more and more important terms, why Mamie made no secret of the fact that she was definitely opposed to it." She had a good sense of what their responsibilities would be as president and first lady, and "that wasn't her idea of a proper future for Ike and herself. She wanted to live a quiet, happy, enjoyable life as soon as NATO was over."[50]

The extent to which Eisenhower consulted with his wife is not clear. Two strong-willed and very different individuals, they nevertheless loved each other and, as much as possible, shared decisions. Early in their career, however, Mamie had determined that the best way to ensure harmony was to help her husband discover what he wanted to do and then to support him in it. Unlike during World War II, this time she was at his side as he struggled with the conflicting issues of duty, self-image, ambition, and personal comfort. No record exists of their conversations, but it seems logical that, in the words of her granddaughter, Mamie adhered to her "characteristic unwillingness to intervene in his decision-making process."[51] "When it comes to making business decisions, and under business I included politics," Mamie told Cliff Roberts, "I never interfere. . . . He makes the decision alone. And I abide by it."[52]

It was on the evening of December 31, 1951, that Eisenhower's aide, Bob Schulz, sensed that another, larger duty was approaching. At a New Year's Eve party that the Eisenhowers held for the SHAPE staff, the five-star general confided to Schulz that he might be returning permanently to the United States in the near future, and if he did, he wanted Schulz to go too.[53]

☆ 13 ☆

DECIDING
STRATEGY

THE PRESSURES of December and January had passed, but Eisenhower had gained another master: the expectations of Republican professionals and volunteers across the country. Knowing he was vulnerable to charges of conflict of interest, he realized by mid-February that he had to either drop out or announce his intention to run. Considering how far he had come since October, the first option was no longer easily available. Only with considerable awkwardness, and with good reason, could he now withdraw.

Despite his efforts to downplay it, the meaning of his declaration of party affiliation was clear. Eisenhower was a candidate for the presidency. Contradicting what he had claimed in his letters to Clay and Lodge about being embarrassed by press questions, he told Luce on January 8 that the editorial entitled "The Case for Ike" in the latest issue of *Life*, about his "personal potential for public service and responsibility," was "one of the factors that helped influence me to break my policy of complete silence." He revealed the difficulty of his job by referring to the fact that the French government had just fallen. "The longer I live, the more I thank the good Lord that he allowed me to be born an American," he wrote.[1] In the days that followed he arranged for Luce to come to Paris.[2]

Events were moving Eisenhower inexorably toward active involvement. He simply could not get out of his mind the possibility that history would repeat itself, taking the United States and the world into yet another period of great danger and sacrifice. He recorded in his diary his views at the time—a means by which he had become accustomed to changing and justifying them to himself. The federal government, in his view needed to balance mobilization for defense with a careful monitoring of its effects on the nation's economy. Responding to a report that President Truman had submitted a budget for 1953 of more than $85 billion, with a deficit of $14 billion and $65 billion for military preparedness, the supreme commander saw a failure to adjust to the changed nature of international relations. The "only justification for an expenditure program that foresees a minimum $14 billion deficit," he wrote in his diary, "is an immediate prospect of war." There is, he said, "no greater probability of war today than there was two years ago. . . . We can only say that properly balanced strength will promote the probability of avoiding war. Since the purpose of America is to defend a way of life . . . everything done to develop a defense against external threat, except under conditions readily recognizable as emergency, must be weighed and gauged in the light of probable long-term, internal, effect." The two extremes, he said, were, first, lack of preparedness similar to what had led to "neglect of the armed forces to the extent of folly" before World War II; and, second "excessive expenditures for non-productive items" that could lead to "national bankruptcy" resulting in "government control and confiscation of property." This was the great equation. He reviewed his unsuccessful efforts before retirement in 1948 as army chief of staff to obtain a $15 billion defense appropriation. The problem then was insufficient spending. By the time he left the Pentagon he was trying to "bring certain of my convictions to the attention of the public."

National strength, he said, referring to the situation in 1952, must be balanced between moral, economic, and "purely military power." The United States should keep sufficient appropriations to support the Republic of Korea, a nation whose independence was essential to access to the raw materials in East Asia. But the federal government, he argued, still could cut spending across the board from 10 to 20 percent. One of the purposes of his book *Crusade in Europe*, he said, was to "warn of the dangers of deficiency in military strength" without reciting "the many instances in which his recommendations and those of his associates had been disregarded." Now, he said, the war in Korea had placed the nation on "the other horn of the dilemma—the danger of internal deterioration through the annual expenditure of unconscionable sums on a program of indefinite duration." This "has great political significance at home and I have already publicly stated that, if the Republicans decide to place a political mandate upon me, I would not attempt to evade it."[3]

In the weeks that followed his declaration of party affiliation (and his private leanings toward candidacy), he continued to explore the ingredients of national strength. He compared "governmental participation in the industrial, financial, and other affairs of the people to the taking of drugs—each dose increases the need for the next one." "Doctors," he said, "use opiates to alleviate suffering; but only in emergency, and then with the greatest caution and care."[4] Unless each member of the society "has a real incentive to produce, the result will finally be a society that has nothing with which to reward."[5]

The interesting thing in all this contemplation—and perhaps one of the reasons for the delay by historians in coming to an understanding of it—is that Eisenhower still considered himself to be a noncandidate, able to step aside if he decided to do so. He told Cliff Roberts of his unhappiness at being trapped by reporters at the time of the New Hampshire statement by Lodge. "If any attempt is made to push me beyond the limits set by my own ideas of my duty there will be an explosion," he said. He said he had already "gone much further in making myself available than I ever thought I would."[6] To his son he wrote that he had heard "It is impossible to nominate anyone in [a] modern day convention unless he himself works for the nomination. If this is true, then I am automatically excluded because I shall do nothing in that line."[7] But even John was now advocating a larger duty for his famous father. It was his feeling, he said, that the country "is absolutely desperate for leadership." He said the American people, rather than having to choose between Truman and Taft in November, "deserve a better break." He suggested that his father "unbend a little and give

Lodge & Co. a little more help than you are doing. I think you can make your stand on what issues they wish known and get yourself squared away with the public without stooping to real campaigning, attacking opponents, etc. . . . Your word for this probably is 'conniving.' Maybe so. But it is a worthy cause."[8]

Perhaps it is only human to think one thing while doing another. In Eisenhower's case it was, as Herbert Brownell remarked, "politically astute . . . and strategic."[9] The pull between the demands of conscience and inclination, of duty versus yearning, stemmed from the distaste of a small-town Kansan and career army officer for the greed, selfishness, and compromise of politics. Ambivalence, it is also possible to argue, was part of leadership. Eisenhower needed the nomination on terms he found acceptable, and he knew that a nomination would depend upon the inspiration and activity of his followers. He had to convey that even a war hero could not do it alone. They, however, needed assurances from him that their work was essential, even to his decision to run. His public announcement of his candidacy had thus to be timed to produce the appearance of a response to adequate justification and a real groundswell of popular support.

The day-to-day problems of SACEUR, as he had hinted to Luce, were daunting. The fall of the French government put his efforts in what he called a "temporary state of suspended animation."[10] He was worried as well about the weakness of the French economy.[11] On January 28 he wrote disgustedly to Bedell Smith, now director of Central Intelligence, that France, to establish that it recognized the Saar district (along its northeast border in long-disputed Alsace-Lorraine) as an independent country, had sent an ambassador there. The German chancellor, in retaliation, had said he could not "possibly bring Germany into a European coalition to maintain security against Russia." In the United States, meanwhile, both former President Hoover and Senator Taft were asserting that the United States should retreat to its oceanic boundaries and leave the nation's defense to the navy and the air force. "Just how we are going to maintain this navy and air force after there has been established in Africa, Malay, and India the kind of governments that adhere to Moscow," Eisenhower said, "is not explained."[12] Smith replied sympathetically and pointed to the new French premier's proposal to reduce drastically his country's contribution to Western rearmament. The situation in French Tunisia (where an anti-colonial revolt was in progress), he said, was "more acute than people realize," and he pointed out too that the Viet Minh were making progress in Indochina—the Communist insurrection against French colonial rule led by Ho Chi Minh. At home, he said, General Bradley was frustrated by the slowness of decisions from the joint chiefs.[13]

Eisenhower was now uncertain about the success of his mission. He worried about the possibility that the French Assembly would reject the European Defense Community. In this event, he told Smith, "the bright promise of German help will have temporarily disappeared, and morale will suffer markedly. Moreover, America will undoubtedly and justifiably begin to despair of ever obtaining real cooperation."[14] The general explained the difficulties on February 9 in letters to Hoffman and President Truman. He told Hoffman that "the central fact in all our difficulties is the threatening economic situation, particularly in France" because of the "Indochina drain." Rising prices, he said, had brought "greater costs for planned military formations than they can afford," and at the same time America had found it impossible to deliver items "at the rate originally promised."[15] He told Truman that the French, because of their historical experience, had a greater fear of the Germans than of the "aggressive and implacable, great Communist dictatorship." His main hope was that the Lisbon meeting of the NATO ministers would bring some "real accomplishments," for there was "no acceptable alternative to success."[16]

It is interesting to note that at this time of discouragement, the idea of universal military training again surfaced. Smith referred to it, this time as a means to generate a trained and respectable but relatively inexpensive national power. It seemed, he told Eisenhower, "that some individuals retained a forlorn hope" [for it], but most advocates had given up. This included Marshall, who had resigned as secretary of defense the previous September. Now, Smith said, the general was "ready to abandon the sinking ship."[17] In a futile attempt to keep hope from dying, Eisenhower dictated a letter to Congressman James W. Wadsworth of New York, a longtime proponent of UMT and chairman of the National Security Training Commission. He was, he said, "intensely interested" in the congressman's work and wished him good luck and warm personal regards."[18]

Appeals to Eisenhower's "transcendent duty" were thus becoming greater, but the advice about what to do next was often confusing to him. "Having a candidate who is out of the country," said Burnham, "is something new for the politicians. . . . It is the novel which always worries the pros." "The job is up to Duff, Lodge, Dewey, etc," with the first two having to "buckle down to the serious work of getting candidates."[19] Eisenhower's brother Edgar continued to oppose a candidacy because of the effect it would have on Ike's health and because, he said, "no man can live up to the hopes the American people have placed on him."[20] But Philip Reed—chairman of General Electric, member of the Council on Foreign Relations study group on aid to Europe, trustee of the CED, and president of the International Chamber of Commerce—made the case for a campaign. Taft he said, would be unable to win if nominated; a Democratic victory would result in 25 percent inflation and perhaps socialism; Eisenhower would be elected if nominated, but unless he returned to campaign, he had only "a little better than even" chance of being nominated; NATO, while important, "is less so than the Presidency." He urged Eisenhower to convey, if possible by making a trip home, "his current views on three or four major points."[21] Arthur Sulzberger, publisher of the *New York Times*, recommended finding "some terminal point to your services in Europe after the NATO conference in Lisbon." This should occur, he advised, much earlier than June 1952.[22] Sulzberger wrote that people he trusted doubted that Eisenhower could secure the nomination "unless you are here to stimulate the campaign prior to convention time." The crisis, he said, "is now, not June."[23] Bedell Smith agreed, writing with some urgency on February 1 that "the pot is beginning to boil in earnest here. As of today, the Eisenhower-Taft situation is just about a 50-50 bet. If Eisenhower were campaigning, there would be no question about the outcome—nor would there be if the decision [about whom to nominate] rested on the expression of popular will." Unfortunately, he said, it would be made largely by professional politicians.[24]

Clay, Cliff Roberts, Burnham, and Hoffman, meanwhile, kept their candidate briefed. To Eisenhower's expression of unhappiness with the New Hampshire press conference, Clay reported that he had warned Lodge and Duff never again to put the general in such a corner. Friction apparently had recurred between Dewey and Duff, and both Clay and Robinson agreed that Lodge tended not to listen and "is easily rattled." Fortunately, Roberts told Eisenhower, despite the general's apparent dismay with what had transpired at the news conferences in New Hampshire and at SHAPE, the public thought everything went according to plan. Reaction was excellent. Considering the "material available," he said, Lodge was probably the best choice as chairman.

Roberts reported that "top leaders now realize that people like Clark and Burnham were a disturbing influence and caused confusion so, I am told, they no longer pay any attention to them. They now talk business with L.D.C. [Lucius D. Clay]. Clark has graciously retired—partly I suspect because Brownlee and Clark may have realized it was best for him to do so." Robinson, though, was doing good work and "was constantly in touch with the 'pros.'"[25] Arthur Vandenberg, Jr., Clay reported, had agreed to become both chief of staff to Lodge and head of the various citizens' movements for Eisenhower. Stassen appeared to be running behind Taft in both Wisconsin and Minnesota. In Pennsylvania, they said, the campaign needed to court someone other than Duff, who now lacked sufficient support to carry the state.[26]

Hoffman joined the chorus. Lodge, he said, had done a good job at the San Francisco meeting, and Vandenberg was "off to a good start" in organizing the National Committee for Eisenhower. Hoffman said he would establish a Sponsors' [fund-raising] Committee of nationally known people who were "all for Ike." So far, these individuals included John D. Rockefeller III, Clare Boothe Luce, Reed, Tom Mc-

Cabe, Clinton Golden, Fred Gurley, Leonard Firestone, Bill Levis, and John Collyer. Many labor leaders, he reported, also were falling in line behind Eisenhower.[27] Roberts, meanwhile, had urged Clay to tell the organization people "there is no chance of your coming back here before the convention."[28]

Still, Robinson sensed more difficulty. Following discussions with Lodge, Vandenberg, Sigurd Larmon—head of one of the nation's leading advertising agencies, Young and Rubicam—Brownell, and others on January 28, he wrote a memorandum on strategy. "Two-thirds of the professional politicians who will control delegates," he noted, "not only want Taft but are becoming a little more convinced every day that he cannot only become nominated but elected." The argument that the rank and file of the party "want Eisenhower as the nominee will begin to fade . . . unless an organization of the personnel, implements, and strategy of the public side of the organization is developed at once." He recommended a task force under Arthur Vandenberg to work with the Eisenhower clubs, to provide a constant flow of propaganda to them, and that "an over-all promotion organization be set up under Sigurd Larmon comprised of expert newsmen, feature writers, radio, TV, direct mail and movie experts." Unlike 1944 and 1948 when "Taft and the other candidates were fighting it out for the favor of the professional politicians," in 1952, Robinson said, only two candidates were in the race, with Taft favored by the professionals—an advantage he would probably keep until the convention. The memorandum concluded with an exhortation and an admonition. "The only possibility for the nomination of General Eisenhower is an organized public opinion that can be dramatized and make itself felt on the politicians so that they will not dare repudiate the will of the rank and file of the party. There is no similar pattern in recent political history."[29]

Clay ventured another proposal. Eisenhower, he said, should consider going to Abilene in the spring for the ceremony laying the cornerstone of the Eisenhower Memorial Foundation (the first of a series of events that would result in the Eisenhower Museum and ultimately a presidential library). It would be an opportunity to outline broad principles in a "non-political address." In any event, Clay said he planned to come to Paris in February.[30]

Eisenhower now decided to soften his resistance. The campaign organization was receiving continuous advice from Dewey, who met regularly with Lodge and who in fact had supplied material for the Lodge's San Francisco speech.[31] By early February 1952 Clay had reported excellent grassroots organizing work by Senator Darby in Oklahoma, which had caused half its GOP convention delegation to switch from Taft. Eisenhower now told Clay that he wanted to let the "professionals" know that, unlike Willkie, he would never ignore the rank and file of the established Republicans or any other organization. He asked what his co-conspirator thought of the idea of friendly notes from him [Eisenhower] directly to Lodge, Duff, Carlson, Roberts, and Darby, thanking them for their actions in his behalf. With regard to the Abilene idea, Eisenhower said, "until I can come for an indefinite stay, I dread the thought of a so-called 'quick' visit. However, I agree with your observation that circumstances change, a fact that of course compels changes in plans and ideas."[32]

These first weeks of February, it turned out, were the beginning of the process by which Eisenhower moved inexorably to a public announcement. Two thought-provoking letters arrived at Rocquencourt. The first, from Arthur Sulzberger, contained excepts from a newspaper column by Arthur Krock. "From the moment Ike decided to announce publicly that he belongs to the opposition to the party in power," said Krock, "and would accept its nomination under proper circumstances . . . his qualifications for his military post underwent a fundamental and diminished change." The general, Krock wrote, was now "associated with an inevitable attack on the President's record." He should therefore "remove this major obstacle to what he so deeply believes in by turning over his post to a military man totally unconnected with politics. That should be done quickly." Eisenhower, perhaps anticipating that such an attack was bound to occur, scribbled, "How about this one?" in the left-hand corner of the letter, and passed it to General Persons.[33]

The second letter, interestingly, was from Truman. The president had written to reassure his supreme commander. The "news hounds are trying to drive a wedge between us," he said on January 14. "As far as I am concerned, that will never happen."[34] On January 31 he wrote again. Eisenhower, he said, could "rest assured that no matter what the professional liars and the pathological columnists may have to say, you and I understand each other. . . . We are approaching a condition in world affairs where we can become powerful enough to ward off a third world war, if we continue the foreign policy which we have been pursuing. I think you understand it as thoroughly and completely as I do."[35]

On February 11 another acquaintance of Eisenhower, the famous aviatrix Jacqueline Cochran, made a dramatic appearance at Villa-St. Pierre. She had flown to Paris by commercial airliner, bringing with her a two-hour film of an Eisenhower-for-President rally held the previous evening in Madison Square Garden. It was, she had been told, "the greatest spontaneous ovation that has ever been received in the history of our country by a potential for the presidential candidacy." The sight of 33,000 people jammed into the Manhattan sports arena, cheering for him and singing a song entitled "I Like Ike" (adapted from an Irving Berlin song for the Broadway musical *Call Me Madam*), had the intended effect. Watching it, Eisenhower and Mamie both were moved. The general wrote Hazlett the next day that the film "brought home to me for the first time something of the depth of longing in America today for change. . . . I can't tell you what an emotional upset it is for one to realize suddenly that he, himself, may become the symbol of that longing and hope."[36]

As it happened, Henry Luce was visiting the Eisenhowers when Cochran arrived. Upon his return to the United States the magazine publisher said he enjoyed "the sound of the man's voice" and "the twinkle in his brightest blue eyes." He had been "under the agreeable spell of a great personality and with a sense of confidence that the Republican party had a winner."[37]

The conventional wisdom, meanwhile, was a continuing source of concern. The *Kiplinger Washington Newsletter*, for example, reported that the Eisenhower movement lacked momentum. The campaign, it said, seemed poorly organized, with many professionals beginning to ask when Eisenhower would return home. The Taft machine, of course, was well oiled and seemed to know where it was heading. And MacArthur would have a sizable number of convention delegates.[38]

Eisenhower contacted Clay. Cochran, he said, had asked him for words "of hope," to provide confidence and inspiration. He had put her off, saying he needed to consult his political friends to see if such a statement would be appropriate and useful, but he had told her she should call Clay, who might come to Paris soon. He asked Clay if he concurred "that this question of time is really important and think you should come over here quickly?" If he did, said the supreme commander, Clay should call Cochran's husband, the financier Floyd Odlum, for suggestions for a statement that would meet her requirements. He also asked that Clay discuss the matter secretly with the "Board of Directors" (the Dewey and Duff group). He explained—with some foreboding, now that events had begun to accelerate—that he was leaving soon for the king's funeral (King George VI of England had died) and could see Clay in London if he believed there was "any great rush about this business."[39] Clay needed no prompting.

A letter the next day from Roberts reviewed developments. He had obtained $15,000 from Pete Jones to pay Defiance College so that its president, Kevin McCann, could rejoin Ike's personal staff to help with political affairs. For his part, Cliff had urged Clay to "get on over to see you." He also had convened "the gang" (Eisenhower's personal friends) for a second meeting to be held at Pete's New York apartment on March 12, the night after the New Hampshire primaries. Roberts said he would like to spend a week in Paris beginning March 2 or 3.[40]

Clay's biographer, Jean Smith, has written that Eisenhower made his "irrevocable decision" to run for the nomination during a conversation with Clay at the residence of Eisenhower's former British aide, General James Gault, on the day of King George's funeral, February 16, 1952. According to this account, Clay told Eisenhower that the race for the nomination was so close that "unless he was willing to declare . . . we were all working in an effort that would not mean anything." Clay then had to press Eisenhower "for a definite answer and the general still didn't want to give one." As probably no one else could have done, Clay then gave Eisenhower an ultimatum. This was, he said, "the final moment of decision."[41]

This dramatic account fails to encompass the many influences at work. Clay, a willing persuader, was, it is now clear, recommending activities being orchestrated by the man he served. But as yet everything remained theoretical, contingent on the results of the first state primaries. As the Eisenhower biographer Stephen Ambrose has pointed out, the general had determined that he probably would need to become an official and active participant in the campaign. He also did not wish to return to the United States until June. It would be that long, he felt, before the NATO meeting in Lisbon was over, his report written, his mission accomplished.[42] So on February 16 he was deciding not whether to run—he was already running; he was deciding the timing, location, and nature (the content) of the next phase of his campaign—the announcement. This, he told Clay, would occur sometime after June 1 in Abilene, Kansas. This timetable assumed that the results of the New Hampshire and Minnesota primaries were favorable. Clay understood this. After a conversation with Clay on February 17, Don Cook, the *New York Herald Tribune*'s Paris correspondent, wrote that Eisenhower was coming to the conclusion that "he should make some direct effort to get the nomination at some time—meaning in June." He should not become involved in campaigning before then because he and Taft have split 900 convention delegates, with the other 300 uncommitted. In June, "when the heat is on for the latter, Eisenhower will be a fresh figure . . . and a certain Republican winner."[43]

☆ 14 ☆

ENTERING
THE FRAY

FAR FROM INTERFERING with his NATO assignment or his reputation, Eisenhower's public announcement of candidacy, like his earlier declaration of party affiliation, brought widespread approval. A decade later, during his retirement, he recalled that the New Hampshire primary "plus the enormous write-in vote in Minnesota" were "almost the conclusive factors in my final decision to stand for the Presidency."[1] His political assistant and speech writer, Kevin McCann, agreed. "The Minneapolis–St. Paul crowd did a tremendous promotion job there [in Minnesota]. . . . That's when he [the general] began to realize, really realize, that he had to fight this thing out."[2] But it now seems clear that by "final decision to stand," Eisenhower meant that considering the circumstances at home, with Taft's strong position, and since the New Hampshire primary had gone the way his advisers had said it would, he had no choice but to resign from his duties at SHAPE and personally enter the preconvention campaign. He had already accepted what he called a "transcendent duty." His showing in New Hampshire, followed in quick succession by Minnesota, persuaded him that he had the support not just of the promoters but of the public. He did not know whether he could overcome Taft's hold on the convention delegates, but his showing in New Hampshire and Minnesota convinced him that he had an obligation to try and that this required personal intervention.

The stream of letters encouraging him to run that began in January turned into a cascade in the weeks that followed. Phil Reed wrote that if Eisenhower could "somehow be seen and heard (in person or on radio and TV) by millions of Americans expressing your views on peace, the economics of a free and prosperous people, and the return to high standards of decency, honesty, and the observance of promises . . . it would encourage and give meaning to so much that is being done here by others."[3] Nineteen Republican congressmen, including Hugh Scott of Pennsylvania, Norris Cotton of New Hampshire, Christian Herter of Massachusetts, and Gerald Ford of Michigan, relaying the sentiments of their constituents, urged him to come home to inspire them with the "dynamic honesty and the forthrightness of your statesmanship."[4]

Eisenhower, now mainly for show (one last remnant of his strategic dilemma), continued to resist. The overtures, he told Milton, "come down to this: 'You can be nominated only by fighting for it. Unless you are nominated, the country is down the drain, either overtaken by socialism and worse on one side, or its foreign affairs so bungled as to lead to an eventual destruction or loss of liberty.' They say that Taft is in at a walk or, failing this, that MacArthur will certainly be the compromise candidate. All these letters ignore the fact that the second I should make a move in this direction, I would no longer be regarded as honest or wanting nothing. I would be just another political seeker."[5] Still, his commitment to the activity was now clear. He "thought out loud," not just in his diary but in letters to friends. He sent George Sloan a copy of a column by David Lawrence in the *New York Herald Tribune*. Eisenhower, it said, "has integrity, good judgment, is fairminded, can work with other people, is opposed to socialism, believes in free enterprise, supports international cooperation and will protect American interests."[6] He was working on a plan, he told Sloan, to get his views more clearly stated and widely disseminated, and "recoiled from anything that would appear artificial and deliberately manufactured." Timing was important. "A premature consumption of all ammunition in a battle," he said, "is certain to bring defeat—everything must be so calculated that the effort constantly increases in its intensity toward its ultimate maximum, which is the moment of victory."[7]

A student of history, Eisenhower drew upon the Progressive tradition of American politics—to the turn of the century and his childhood fascination with Theodore Roosevelt, whose concept for a stronger America was the cooperative commonwealth. "The principal causative factor" in America's currently serious problems, Eisenhower wrote to Sloan, was "the trend toward disunity." Political freedom for the individual was "the greatest single characteristic of western civilization" and depended on the "existence of certain economic rights," including the "right to work at the place and occupation of one's choice, to save the fruits of one's labor, and to obtain some return on investment of the capital thus saved." The "great chasms separating economic groupings" reflected the "fatuous but vicious doctrine of class warfare and obviously ignore our common American destiny." A hundred and fifty million fully united Americans were capable of "accomplishing anything within the realm of human potentiality" but divisiveness, economic in origin, "prevents effect cooperation" and "adversely affects everything we try to do, domestic and foreign." Wealth, said Eisenhower, "is measured by production," and maximum production was possible only when "management, labor, and capital work in harmony." No prosperity for one economic group is "permanently possible except as all groups prosper." An efficient economy, he said (echoing Lincoln's statement about a nation half slave and half free), could not be half governmental and half private, because having one supported by taxation dominating the other would destroy the conditions necessary for individual freedom. Government should be "the most disinterested and impartial authority available for the development and enforcement of needed regulations" to keep those who control the capital of production from having "unwarranted or dictatorial influence over the opportunities and livelihood of the great masses."[8] Such were the general's considerations, political indeed, in the weeks preceding the New Hampshire primary.

Stassen, meanwhile, told Lodge that he would enter the New Hampshire primary because it was "his understanding that Eisenhower did not intend to engage in a pre-convention campaign." He believed that if he [Stassen] stayed out of the race, Senator Taft would win the nomination "as a result of solidifying Wisconsin, Illinois, Ohio, and many other states." He considered the Wisconsin primary to be "a crucial contest," but to avoid the charge of being merely a stalking horse, he would enter the New Hampshire primary as well as all the Midwest primaries.[9]

Cliff Roberts arrived in Paris on March 3 with misgivings about the general's unwillingness to engage in "pre-convention activities." Ike's personal adviser replied that he was prepared to support this position and "let the chips fall where they may." He admitted, however, that a groundswell in Ike's favor did not yet exist, and a draft was far from certain. The politicos, he said, despite the appearance of working smoothly together, had been "unable to organize properly or to function effectively." Lodge was not "confidence-inspiring and shrewd"; many of the others were "not organization people"; the most capable pros—Dewey, Brownell, and Sprague—were trying to stay in the background; and Clay was "trying to stay under cover." The list went on. Not one of the nine leaders, he said, had ever agreed with the statement that he Eisenhower should remain at NATO and take no part in the effort to obtain the nomination. They lacked confidence and except in New York had raised little money. More delegates, Roberts said, "are solid to Taft than they claim for you, in part a result of the lack of opposition." MacArthur, who has a "surprising number of followers in New Hampshire," had advised them to vote for Taft. They supported Eisenhower by a 5 to 4 margin in the popular preference poll, but since Taft was an effective campaigner, the odds might actually be fifty-fifty or worse (paralleling what the national polls were saying). "The Eisenhower movement," Roberts declared, "will begin losing ground with anything short of a surprising victory in New Hampshire—meaning around 7 to 5 popular choice" and "practically all the delegates." Even then, Eisenhower would need to act. Roberts suggested at least one "non-political speech in Kansas on peace and another at the American Assembly on the evils of inflation"—these in addition to returning on June 1. Most ominously, Eisenhower's friend speculated that a failure to carry the convention in Chicago would weaken Eisenhower's influence in Europe and his "ability to influence Congressional support for European appropriations."[10] The "gang," he said, in summary, was "hopeful but not confident." They agreed that he at least must return for a speech and then come home for good on June 1, "if you are to win."

Roberts laid out three scenarios. In the first, Eisenhower would not return before the convention. This, he said, would mean defeat. The second was to take the recommendations of the gang, which he knew was distasteful. A third possibility was that Eisenhower could "go whole hog by resigning from the Army and Columbia." This would free him, finally, to "speak plainly and campaign vigorously" in behalf of a change in Washington and a sound American economy; generate a large response in the press; demonstrate sincerity; electrify the organization; cause Truman to act more promptly than otherwise; and draw attention both to the magnitude of Eisenhower's accomplishments and the strength of his position. He could explain to Truman—and to anyone who asked the reason for such a departure from his stated intent—that his mission in Europe was largely achieved and that a large number of callers and an "avalanche of mail" were beginning to detract from that military effort.[11]

Robinson was similarly discouraged. He and Hoffman had traveled by train together for a speech in Philadelphia, and Robinson had conveyed Eisenhower's wishes that Hoffman join the campaign on a "full-time basis." The current operation, said Robinson on March 6, was "disorganized and leaderless" and to blame for adverse comment in the press. The problem, he reported to Eisenhower, was lack of "decisiveness and aggressive action" by Lodge and animosity between Duff and Dewey. Hoffman was prepared to become executive director of the campaign.[12]

A letter from Hoffman (written two days earlier) also arrived at SHAPE. Its content was only slightly less bleak. The New Hampshire campaign, he said, was being handled by Governor Adams, with help from Lodge, Duff, and himself. He enclosed a copy of the talk he had been giving in New Hampshire. Thoughtful people, said Hoffman, were convinced "you're the one man who can pull the world out of the mess it's in." "Even the Taft people," he added, "admit that if you do come home, you're a certain winner." Failure to campaign (making at least a limited number of appearances), however, would put the nomination in jeopardy.[13]

Winter and early spring usually brought arctic weather to northern New England, and 1952 was no exception. Adams used snowshoes to get to his office; Robinson recalled that his car had to be pulled out of the snow twice by wreckers.[14] Although it was not visible in the results, the New Hampshire primary—as Wellington said of the battle of Waterloo—was a closely run thing. Indeed, if one excludes the Stassen vote, too closely. Thanks to last-minute efforts by key individuals, including Jackie Cochran, who raised $25,000 in the week before the election, a total of $49,000 reached the Eisenhower forces in New Hampshire.[15] "Later, as we became better organized," Robinson recalled, "we always had enough money."[16] What he may have been referring to was the fact that Pete Jones arranged with him to provide money for Eisenhower's presidential campaign "whenever you can use money legitimately." How much of this reached New Hampshire is uncertain.[17]

On the day of the primary, March 11, Eisenhower was tending to NATO business, with Roberts by his side, on a quick inspection trip to Germany. In the plane on their way back they received word of the victory in New Hampshire. The turnout had been 92,225. Of this, Eisenhower received 46,497 to Taft's 35,820, Stassen's 6,549, Schneider's 216, and MacArthur's write-in of 2,974. Ike had won all fourteen of the state's convention delegates.[18] Upon landing in Paris, his plane was surrounded by newsmen. The general-turned-politician descended the stairs and told the reporters coyly that he "didn't know what had happened in New Hampshire, that they would have to tell him." It caused a great outpouring of shouting and congratulations and questions about how he felt about his new victory. "It did make him feel good," he told Roberts, "when that many people who don't know you at all would express that kind of confidence."[19] Roberts could only smile.

The individuals most responsible for the victory were Adams and his supporters—younger voters and state Republican leaders, including, early on, Leonard Finder, and later Burroughs.[20] Also helpful was unrelenting favorable coverage by newspapers such as the *New York Herald Tribune*, the *New York Times*, and the Luce magazines. Article after article in *Time* had urged Eisenhower to come home and of course trumpeted the activities of Hoffman's Citizens for Eisenhower committee.[21]

Harry Bullis, finance chairman of the Minnesota Eisenhower committee, was joyous. "We are all jubilant over that result." Hoffman, he said, was a "master sales executive."[22] Eisenhower replied that he had had nothing to do with setting up the organization but that he understood "there is a general reinforcement going on of the whole organization."[23] He then dictated letters conveying his humility, telling members "how deeply complimented" he was by the "personal convictions that have led you to devote so much effort to the business of placing before me a highly political duty."[24] He credited Clay, telling Lodge that "When he [Clay] gives me advice he takes off his gloves and pounds pretty hard, but my friendship for him is so deep that I still enjoy it."[25] Lodge assured him that "no man ever had a more loyal, tireless and effective friend" than Eisenhower had in General Clay.[26] Robinson, now upbeat, wrote that it was "heartening, amusing, and amazing," he said, "to see the complete turnabout of all the 'expert' prophets of doom." Reed, Slater, and he felt that "with proper organization from here on, there would be at least an even chance for your nomination," even without returning before the convention. But he forwarded Pete Jones's belief that the "nomination seems impossible unless you have on your own terms completed your task in Europe, to return here early in May."[27]

Here at last was the evidence Eisenhower had sought that the GOP nomination was more than just a possibility. Roberts recalled that after the New Hampshire primary "everybody and his brother from all over the country was demanding that the general go ahead and announce his candidacy." It was only a matter of Eisenhower "deciding whether it would be fitting for him to retire from the army and ask to be relieved of his duties at NATO and make himself available . . . or whether he would continue to sit on his perch and say, 'Well, all right. If you want me to run, go ahead and nominate me, and when you can come to me and hand me the nomination, then I'll take it and be your candidate.' "[28] The New Hampshire primaries "decided that he was going to have a go at being a politician and the American people really made up his mind for him, and he became convinced that he had a duty to run for President." "If he hadn't come out as a candidate and worked hard," said Roberts later, "he never would have been nominated. . . . I would say that the Nevada gamblers never would have given him one chance in four of being the nominee of the party, even after the New Hampshire primary."[29] Eisenhower confirmed this in his 1967 memoirs: "I was sure that the Taft forces within the Republican party were strong enough to deny anyone else the nomination. In this belief I was steadfast until the New Hampshire primary."[30]

And the write-in vote for Eisenhower in the Minnesota primary, the week following New Hampshire's, was in some ways more impressive. The Minnesota delegation—by 129,000 votes—went to Stassen. But while Eisenhower was not on the ballot, he received an amazing 108,692 write-ins.[31] Roy Roberts wrote Eisenhower from Kansas City that this was "one of the biggest things that ever happened in an American political campaign." It demonstrated that "down-at-the-people-level there was a strong, overwhelming sentiment for you." Dewey, he said, handled himself well, and the campaign would benefit because his people, Brownell and Sprague, "are starting to move over the country." The Taft forces were failing because they had deviated from their plan to concentrate only in places like Wisconsin and Illinois where they were strong. Believing the Eisenhower organization was about to fall apart, they went instead for a knockout blow by entering the primaries in New Hampshire and New Jersey, where Eisenhower also won. But the Eisenhower vote in Minnesota, Roberts said, did not mean that the senator from Ohio was "licked," and he asserted that it was now politically possible for Eisenhower to come home where there was a "higher call."[32]

Bullis again was jubilant. Hoffman and Walter Williams, he said, were "the two best men in the United States." He credited Abbott Washburn—former assistant to Stassen and to Clay's Crusade for Freedom—and Bradshaw Mintener for organizing the write-in in Minnesota. They would now begin to "get some real money from Minnesota for your campaign."[33]

For Eisenhower the New Hampshire primary was thus the point of no return, and he now swung into action. At the recommendation of his friend, Clarence Francis, he invited Howard Chase, one of the leading Republican strategists, to Paris. Chase arrived on Friday, March 14, and remained over the weekend. (Before going to SHAPE, he conferred with Time Inc. president Roy Larsen and Eric Gibbs, head of the Paris bureau of Time-Life.) Ike told Chase that foreign policy, the first order of concern in an "inter-dependent and inter-related world," should be tied to a "widely shared confidence" among the public "that there is a future" and to "economic soundness." "If the fundamental soundness at home is jeopardized now, as I believe it is, then the job of the Presidency [if one had to choose between that and the job of SACEUR] is certainly the most important." Chase asked him whether he could take the abuse of a campaign. It was not a major concern, Eisenhower replied, but he worried about its effect on Mamie. He mentioned the rumored relationship during the war between him and his driver and correspondence secretary Kay Summersby. "While he would refuse to discuss it publicly," he assured Chase privately that "he never saw Kay except while she was driving or in groups and that was that." (Nor, for that matter, he went on, "Was there truth in other rumors about a girl with whom he dined and danced occasionally in social gatherings with friends in the Philippines in the 1930s.) He did not like the fact that Mamie, who had been unhappy about the allegations of wartime infidelity, would have to stand up against such questions, "but," he said—apparently convinced that political enemies would have little to chew on in this area—"if that's what he had to take, he was prepared to face it." Chase explained that the victory in New Hampshire had brought a "new stage," that it was now necessary to decide on a plan. Eisenhower agreed.

To Chase the general expressed his dissatisfaction with the Truman administration. The president, he said, had "rare courage and charm when necessary," but lacked philosophy and convictions. He had disliked the influence of Truman's crony and aide, General Harry Vaughn, in Pentagon appointments after Eisenhower's departure as chief of staff, and the president's tendency to turn the "sublime into the ridiculous." "One of the silliest damn things," he said, referring to Truman's conferences on atomic energy, was "the strain of pretending to defend Europe without ever mentioning the atomic bomb."[34]

The last day of Chase's visit, March 17, included a day-long conference with Hoffman and Walter Williams, who had just arrived from the United States. (The two men had agreed to be co-chairmen of the Independent Citizens Committee for Eisenhower.) With the three men present, Eisenhower turned first to policy in Europe. "Germany," he said, "is the prize for which the international game is being played." A reconstructed Germany tied to Russia would change the balance of world power; tied to the West, though, it would mark "one more step in the downfall of communism."[35] General Biddle, Eisenhower's intelligence chief, advised that Russia "will use all means short of war between now and the middle of summer to achieve disunity, confusion, and unrest in the NATO countries." His staff had identified twenty-five Russian divisions in "total war strength actually on the frontier" (which NATO was prepared to contain). In the event of an attack, said the SACEUR, a rain of weapons "of all kinds" would fall behind Russian lines "from bases ranging from northern Norway to Turkey." In Eisenhower's opinion, "logic" would prevent an attack, "but the men in the Kremlin are not informed and do not believe what they are told about the strength that even now can be brought to bear against them."[36]

The general told those gathered in his office that he would submit his resignation, effective June 1, to Secretary of Defense Robert Lovett on April 5—"three days after the release of the Annual Report of SHAPE." Hoffman and Chase then recommended that Eisenhower leave Paris on May 16; fly directly from Paris to Abilene to dedicate the Eisenhower Memorial with a speech on world peace; go from Abilene to Washington, D.C., until May 31; to New York City until June 15; and then to the Brown Palace Hotel in Denver. During these travels, they said, he should give two or more speeches—on integrity and on the American dream. The mission would be to "introduce in person to General Eisenhower, every Republican convention delegate."[37]

Hoffman saw that it was time for an expanded and tightened budgeting, financing, public relations, and publicity program for the Citizens-for-Eisenhower committee. Mary Lord became co-chairman; Sigurd Larmon, vice chairman; and Chase, acting general consultant. Hoffman accepted chairmanship of the advisory committee with Mildred McAfee Horton, former commander of the Women's Naval Forces, as co-chairman.[38] He was enthusiastic about publicity. "Never has there been manifested for a candidate," Hoffman told Eisenhower, "as much good will as there is for you in the whole communications field." This included the publishers of "all the great weeklies, the radio and television people, and almost without exception, the motion picture moguls will break their neck for you." Hoffman also wanted to find a way to use Dewey, Brownell, and Talbott "without creating the impression that Dewey had taken over." He suggested doing this by putting the "spot light" on Cabot Lodge.[39] Hoffman began raising funds, writing individuals such as Alfred P. Sloan and reminding them that they could increase their contribution $20,000 beyond their $5,000 to the National Committee for Eisenhower by contributing to state and county Eisenhower committees.[40]

Meanwhile, Eisenhower's NATO mission—what he had been able to accomplish in a year—was winding down. On March 4, Harriman in a speech at the *Philadelphia Bulletin* forum, reported the results of the just-concluded meeting of the NAC. "Long strides," he said, had been taken there "towards the security of the free world." France and Germany had voted to accept the principle of merging their military forces. The member nations had worked out procedures for analyzing their "several capabilities and deciding among themselves a combined plan of action for common defense." This was the first time in history that "free nations in peacetime had joined together in submitting all the necessary information to analyze what the military program of each country was, whether it was effective, and whether each was doing its fair share." A draft treaty of a European Defense Community (EDC) of six nations—France, Germany, Italy, Belgium, Luxembourg, and the Netherlands—"with supranational authority," was "virtually completed." It would include an assembly made up from representatives of the various national assemblies, a council of ministers, a defense commission, and a court to adjudicate differences and interpret agreements. It would be associated with the "larger, less tightly knit" NATO and would thus be part of the alliance's total force—"the Eisenhower army, as they call it in Europe."[41]

The United States could not arm itself without raw materials from the rest of the world, or "maintain our present preponderance of industrial capacity" if the resources and skills of western Europe were "added to those already controlled by the Kremlin," Harriman continued—repeating Eisenhower's geopolitical argument. Thus the American investment of $8 billion to strengthen "our friends and allies abroad is the best and least costly way to add to our own security." Member nations had agreed to provide approximately fifty divisions, half combat-ready and half "capable of rapid mobilization"; four thousand operational aircraft in Western Europe, and "strong naval forces." The American contribution included expanded military forces and a Mutual Security Program (by then 12 percent of the defense budget) which replaced with military assistance the postwar reconstruction aid of the European Recovery Program.[42]

Eisenhower was pleased with Harriman's remarks but privately had misgivings about how things were unfolding. The fall of the French government, he said, was "bad, indeed." "The more bitter the fight, the more confusing the situation becomes." The "political partisans" of both France and Germany, he said, had "seized upon the effort [to create an EDC] as one in which to make a bid for power. . . . What will come of all these things, I cannot tell, but I must say that if we here at SHAPE were easily discouraged, we would certainly have a few spiritual sand traps to dig our way out of this minute."[43]

Much remained to be done. On March 20, Eisenhower dictated

another long letter (this one ten single-spaced pages) to George Sloan with copies to Clarence Francis and the organizers of the campaign for his nomination, including Lodge, General Persons, and Chase; and to staff members McCann and Gruenther.[44] At once a summary, rationale, dire warning, hopeful scenario, and treatise on the national interest, it was a statement—as direct as one can find—of what would become American national strategy in the 1950s. Eisenhower warned that a "ruthless, implacable, Communist dictatorship" was attempting to "extend the limits of its power over all the earth." It was doing this not by military aggression in most instances but rather by military intimidation, propaganda, bribery, subversion, and corruption. Its strength lay not in its overall productive capacity or in the spontaneity of its people, but rather in the fact that a centralized dictatorial system was free to channel resources to military uses at the expense of the civilian economy, and, in the world, to choose the "areas selected for concentrated attack." More important, its strength derived also from a lack of resolve and disunity in the free world—a failure, as had occurred in Czechoslovakia in 1948 and before the Korean aggression, to devise collective arrangements and allocate sufficient resources for preparedness. Soviet strength also was a consequence of the possibility that free world economies would allow poverty, privation, and suffering that inhibited the ability to create effective armies and sound fiscal policies. "Solvency and security are," Eisenhower said, "mutually interdependent." National power is the mathematical product of spiritual, economic, and military strength. "If any one of these falls to zero, then the product of the equation—the influence of the nation in the international field—likewise falls to zero." Returning to an earlier theme—now echoed by Harriman—he warned of the urgent threat that Soviet communism would exploit Western weakness, thereby denying it access to raw materials including manganese, tin, tungsten, uranium, cobalt, platinum, many drugs, copper, lead, zinc, and oil. Maintaining access to and trade with "all areas of the world from which we draw vital supplies," Eisenhower said, required an ability both to deter aggression and to prevent the "collapse of orderly and free government in any area in which the Soviets are interested."

The biggest such prizes were western Europe and Japan, both of which were important to the "great production advantage in favor of the non-Soviet world." If the Soviet Union gained control of western Europe it also would have the Middle East (and its oil); the technical skills of the German, Dutch, and Italian scientists; and the products of the industrial heart of Europe, the Ruhr and the Saar, with "equally grave consequences" for both the United States and "all the other areas of the world."

The general nevertheless foresaw an excellent result from proper and timely action. It would "confront the Soviet Communists with the certainty that they cannot hope successfully to attack the free world." From a position of strength, he said, "we can begin to negotiate on a practical basis for the development of a plan of co-existence in this world," along with a program of gradual disarmament. "More than this we possibly cannot hope for until the Soviet dictatorship will begin to deteriorate, as all others have in the past, because of the essentially evil, selfish purposes of those controlling it." After the free world achieved the material forces "that will provide military equilibrium, we have faith that, thereafter, the virtues and appeal of our own system will in the long run, triumph over the desperate doctrines of communism."

Eisenhower refused to specify the costs of this effort. His duty, he said, was to advise the United States "what military strength could be produced in this area if the necessary munitions were available." The "real answer," he said, was "a political and economic federation among West Germany, France, Italy, Holland, and Benelux at least." He recommended that the United States provide initial supplies of armaments with the understanding that the European countries would establish "at least one source of production" for each item of equipment in Europe. An overriding need was to "inspire European nations to maximum effort in our common security program."[45]

That same day, March 20, Harriman wrote an encouraging letter to the SACEUR. Eisenhower's identity as a presidential candidate, said the president's assistant, was helping, not hurting, his mission at NATO. He commiserated with Eisenhower about the situation in

France, blaming the country's fundamental instability on its system of proportional representation; but he gave France credit for having originated the concept of the EDC and the Schuman Plan, and he agreed with Eisenhower that "we are at a crossroads. Europe could either move forward in integration and defensive strength or backwards, with not only Schumaker in West Germany and De Gaulle in France, but Bevan in England and a communist stooge in Italy." "What happens in Congress," Harriman said, "is perhaps decisive," but, he hastened to add, "we're on the road and the job can be done."[46] Interestingly, considering Harriman's credentials as a lifelong Democrat, he now thanked Eisenhower for the efforts of his preconvention campaign organizers. In the battle for mutual security under way on Capitol Hill, he said, he had testified five times, and while there he had detected "more optimism among our friends on getting the program through, of no small importance [because of] the fact that a fellow by the name of Eisenhower seems to be getting a lot of support in the primaries. It is making Congress stop and wonder whether the people of the country aren't ahead of Congress on international matters."[47]

In retrospect, one can see that Eisenhower's decision to enter the political arena sprang from his belief that only he had the necessary vision and experience to lead in a time of peril. After the outbreak of war in Korea, the Truman administration had been unable to agree on either the nature of the Communist threat or what to do about it. Paul Nitze and the policy planning staff of the State Department thought the United States needed to gain a position of superiority before the Soviet regime achieved nuclear parity in 1954. If the United States failed to do so, the Soviets would become intractable and, from their position of strength, willing to take risks.

Soviet experts George Kennan and Charles Bohlen, on the other hand, asserted that the occupants of the Kremlin were chiefly interested in remaining in power. The Communist party of the Soviet Union had experienced war and knew its horrors. More important than a huge American and allied military buildup was the overall allied capacity to "confront the Soviet Union with the prospect that an attack by it would bring serious threat to its regime." In Bohlen's view there was no year of "maximum danger" as NSC-68 had asserted (1954) but rather a danger of "Soviet cumulative piecemeal expansion by subversion, political and economic warfare, or possibly local aggression in unstable, peripheral areas."[48] Attempts at rollback, said Bohlen, would be needlessly provocative, for eastern Europe was both a vital security interest of the Soviet Union and firmly under its control.[49]

While the Truman administration deliberated, after the Lisbon meeting in February 1952 the Europeans began retreating from the force goals they had adopted. The French, because of the drain on their resources of their war in Indochina, asked for increased American assistance. In London, Prime Minister Churchill was determined to reduce defense spending to ease the strain on the British economy. France soon refused to ratify the EDC treaty, and both French opponents and the German Social Democratic party stalled plans for rearming Germany.[50] Simultaneously U.S. assistance lagged, with shipments of only $3.2 billion of the allocated $11.2 billion in aid reaching Europe by January 1953.[51]

In these circumstances Eisenhower espied the end of his tour. On March 18, after his lengthy and revealing talk with Chase, he invited Herbert Brownell to Paris. Without question the party's most able and influential campaign manager, Brownell had organized Dewey's presidential campaigns in 1944 and 1948 and had served as Republican national chairman. His political wisdom was legendary, his knowledge of convention delegates and state Republican politics unsurpassed. He had first met Eisenhower in 1948 at the Century Club. Two years later, around Christmas of 1950, before the general's departure for Paris, he had accompanied Dewey, Clay, and Sprague to a party for Eisenhower at the Columbia University faculty club. It was the occasion on which Dewey had announced his decision not to run for the presidency in 1952 and had touted Eisenhower as his replacement.[52] By December 1951, Brownell was aware that the main group working for Eisenhower's nomination included Lodge and was meeting regularly at the Commodore Hotel. He also knew that another group—including, in addition to Cliff Roberts and Bill Robinson, Ellis Slater, Bob Woodruff, president of Coca-Cola; Sid Richardson, a Texas oilman;

Pete Jones; and George Allen, a Democrat and friend of Harry Truman— ostensibly nonpolitical personal advisers to the candidate, were
acting toward the same goal. This group of "personal advisers" had invited Brownell to a Christmas party in 1951 at the Jones residence.
There Robinson told Brownell that "the group would undertake to
raise the funds necessary for the preconvention campaign, along with
the existing fund-raising efforts of Harold E. Talbot."[53]

Brownell, of course, accepted Eisenhower's invitation. He liked
the general's appeal to independents and Democrats and his position
on foreign policy. More than Dewey, Eisenhower listened patiently to
all shades of opinion and to people he didn't like personally.[54]
Brownell was impressed as well by the absence of any conflict between
Eisenhower's thinking as a military man and as a national politician.
The general, he recalled, had "the skill and expertise to seal once and
for all the Republican party's commitment to internationalism."[55] His
experiences in the war, where he was closely associated with
Churchill and Roosevelt, had taught him to "meld the use of military
force with diplomatic negotiations" and made him more knowledge-
able than any man in the country about American policies in both Europe and China, something the American people sensed.[56] Brownell's
job, he later wrote, was to "take a full-time active role in the campaign
to garner delegates for Ike." With instructions from Clay to travel
under an assumed name (since he was widely recognized by journalists as a GOP strategist), Brownell arrived in Paris on March 24 and the
next day spent ten uninterrupted hours with the candidate.

Brownell later would recall the day as "the experience of a lifetime." A "legendary world figure," he said, the general was "plainspo-
ken, and warm . . . ready to approach the nation's problems and apply
his considerable experience to solving them."[57] Eisenhower had
"known about and expressed appreciation to various friends and volunteer groups advocating his nomination and done nothing to stop
them," being "strategic in his political moves." The general nevertheless had been "surprised" when Brownell told him it was "unrealistic
to expect a draft" and that he "would have to fight for the nomination."
This was probably either an error of memory or a misperception on

Brownell's part. It was often Eisenhower's practice to ask plenty of questions when he wanted to find something out, and it is likely that he probed Brownell, the skilled and seasoned politico. Face to face, Brownell now confirmed what he had been saying to the Dewey team in New York—that to obtain the nomination Eisenhower would need to return to the United States "at least a month before the convention, declare himself a candidate, speak in various parts of the country on the issues, and above all, meet personally with as many delegates as possible before and at the convention."[58] Brownell later wrote that after that day Eisenhower remained "genuinely undecided about waging what was sure to be an acrimonious intraparty fight against Senator Taft."[59] But this contradicts an earlier, more likely oral history statement by Brownell that when he left Paris, he was convinced that the general would "follow the program as to dates and everything else that I had outlined for him."[60] Indeed, two days later Eisenhower wrote to Edward Mead Earle, who—unaware of how far things had progressed—had suggested that the supreme commander's remaining at SHAPE appeared to be the "shrewdest politics" considering his victory in New Hampshire and "the spectacular outcome in Minnesota."[61] Eisenhower thanked the professor for "an astute bit of reasoning" because "it conforms completely with my instincts." He then noted, probably alluding to his meetings with Chase, Hoffman, and now with Brownell, that a scheme was developing that would have him "seeking relief from here to be dated somewhere between May 1st and June 1st."[62]

Eisenhower now wrote to Clay. He wanted Lodge and John Foster Dulles, Republican senator from New York and the party's expert on foreign affairs, to come to Paris the first week in April. Despite a SHAPE command-post exercise scheduled for that time, Eisenhower's office had an April 2 deadline for completion of his annual report. Then, in what must have sent chills down Clay's spine, the SACEUR spoke of a larger duty. He revealed that he had agreed to write letters "to set in motion the chain of events that you people believe to be necessary or at least highly desirable. I trust you can see why my life seems to be a bit crowded."[63]

To soothe him in "these strenuous days," Harry Bullis sent a prayer to Ike. "Oh, God, give me sympathy and sense and keep my courage high, God give me calmness and confidence, and please a twinkle in my eye."[64] Eisenhower needed the boost. It was, he said, "a devil of a chore to smile over the whole business."[65] In the crush to get everything done, he strained his eyes and came down with such a severe case of conjunctivitis that Dr. Snyder had to administer a salve. Eisenhower wrote to Robinson that despite his efforts to keep political and military affairs separate and "to make certain that the military, neither through individual nor group action, could seek to dominate the civil power," and to "remain aloof from political turmoil"—he [Eisenhower] seemed "to have miscalculated a bit somewhere along the line." The New Hampshire and Minnesota primaries, he said, "were really only incidental to this development. . . . Last December, you, Cliff and I all decided that one mere statement would probably get everything on the rails. I assure you we were wrong."[66]

He related to Clay an incident from his boyhood in Abilene. He had enjoyed standing at the corral as the men tried to get a loop over the neck of a horse that he wanted to ride. The general recalled that he always "pulled for the horse" as it "ducked and dodged and snorted and stomped. Little did I think, then, that I would ever be in a position of the horse!" He said he was now arranging farewell visits to European capitals and major troop headquarters in Germany and "desperately trying . . . to secure an early signing of the treaty for the European Defense Force." He was uncertain how long this would take. At the same time he was urging the European governments to consider a "convention to begin planning of economic union in Western Europe. To allow it to be announced that I shall be . . . coming home, before this treaty is signed," he said, "strikes me as being little short of imbecilic. But time rushes and I seem to be trapped."[67] His co-conspirator and friend responded sympathetically. "I feel terribly guilty and contrite," confessed Clay, "for being a party to what is happening to you. All I can ever say is that our country needs you so badly, I could not do otherwise. There is no one else."[68]

Truman, suspecting what was happening, held a press conference

on March 20 and sent Eisenhower a transcript. It revealed a far different president than the one who had fired MacArthur or, for that matter, had distrusted Eisenhower's disavowals in 1948. "My duty," the
president had told the reporters, "is to see that we attain our objective
in Europe. General Eisenhower is the key man in attaining that objective and he understands the situation, I think, very much better than
Walter Lippmann or anybody else." In response to questions about
Eisenhower's actions having political implications, Truman said he
"was not interested in his [Eisenhower's] political career. He has a per-
fect right to do whatever he pleases in that line, and I told him that
personally. . . . I have told him that he can use his own judgment with
regard to his return. Whenever he feels that it is proper and safe for
him to return, he is at liberty to do so."[69] Before putting the transcript
in the "outgoing" box to Eisenhower, the president scribbled a note to
the general at the bottom. This transcript, it said, is "factual and
correct and speaks for itself."[70] Nine days later, on March 29, Truman
announced publicly his intention not to run for reelection.[71]

Eisenhower sent the letter asking Truman to relieve him from military duties on April 2, three days earlier than he had promised
Howard Chase. (By separate letter he requested the secretary of defense to "initiate action to bring about my relief from my current
post . . . on or about June 1".) While the long-term mission of SHAPE
had just begun, he reported to the president in generally accurate but
carefully worded fashion, those phases of the work that he had agreed
to perform in their conversations in October and December 1950 were
essentially complete. The nations of NATO were ready, in his words,
"to cooperate effectively" and had "achieved, thus far, a marked degree of success in the task of building a viable defense structure in this
critical region."

As for himself, he said partisan activities had forced his hand. "The
situation has changed from one of exploration and initial negotiation
to one of confident planning and development." He requested that, in
order to complete certain tasks, public announcement of his resignation be delayed until April 11. "Having maintained for years the position that I did not aspire to political office," he wrote, "I clearly

miscalculated last January in assuming that by publicly reasserting that attitude, I could avoid the impingements upon my time and attention of political movements then in progress. This view is no longer tenable, and I deem it necessary to seek early termination of my military assignment so that any political activity centering about me cannot possibly affect the military service." This, he said, "contemplates transfer to inactive status," and "in the event that I should be nominated for high political office, my resignation as an officer of the army will be instantly submitted to you for approval." He thanked the president for his "staunch support and encouragement to all there at SHAPE."[72] In retrospect it is clear that Eisenhower had determined that completion of his NATO mission—a unified and stable Europe with West German participation and the reduced possibility of war—required that he become a candidate for the presidency.

☆ 15 ☆

THE NOMINATION

EVENTS IN THE YEARS since the end of World War II had convinced Eisenhower that both national security and world peace were threatened by a failure of leadership in Washington. The American people and their allies, he believed, had to understand that the United States would be prepared to prevail over the long term, or in his words to "wage peace." In his view this meant a willingness on the part of the American people for the foreseeable future to sacrifice for the larger good—to serve in the military, to pay taxes to help countries overseas in their efforts to resist aggression, and by their presence at military bases around the globe, to be a mediator of age-old animosities among new allies: for example, between Germany and France in Europe, and in the Far East between Japan on the one hand and South Korea, the Philippines, and Taiwan on the other. This willingness was the price of peace. But just as important as overcoming the isolationist impulse was, in Eisenhower's view, resisting the opposite impulse—of attempting to overcome the threat by unnecessary spending on arms and armies, of seeking security in hardware and a continuously mobilized populace, a "garrison state." Such a society would simultaneously threaten opponents and risk both the nation's economic vitality and its individual liberties. Eisenhower had become persuaded that of all the potential candidates for president, he was best suited by background, stature, and understanding to provide the needed leadership. He was also convinced that he had a good chance to win. After the treaty creating the European Defense Community was signed by the European foreign ministers on May 27, Eisenhower returned to the United States and announced his candidacy.

After requesting relief from active duty, one of the first acts was to thank Paul Hoffman. Eisenhower told his friend that he had "accomplished the first step of the program that I intimated to you I would undertake." In words that revealed the conflicts that yet existed in his mind about the propriety of what he was doing, he said he did not want to be "overly influenced by political thinking," but he was not going to pretend that "the political pressures have no influence on my thinking." He was basing his request "primarily upon the situation of NATO and not exclusively upon the political situation in the U.S."[1]

Hoffman reported progress in the campaign. In the New Jersey primary, Taft's forces had used trickery but without success. Taft had withdrawn from the campaign while leaving his name on the ballot. His man, Carrol Reese, then had returned to the state and sent out paid workers to generate support. The Eisenhower organization there was short of money, so Hoffman raised it and reached people via radio and television. The Eisenhower forces had hoped for 55 percent of the vote if the weather was good. Despite a downpour, Eisenhower received 60 percent.

Hoffman credited Williams, Lord, Larmon, Chase, and Washburn for the forward momentum. He said Lodge had had a "magnificent response at the meetings and rallies," and that Brownell was "making excellent progress in softening up and lining up delegates." Philadelphia bank president and former undersecretary of the army Howard Petersen had taken over as finance chairman because of Talbott's and Whitney's close ties with Dewey and a desire to avoid association with the twice-defeated candidate.[2]

Harmony in the organization was now, more than ever before, essential. Clay again had expressed concern about Duff. Eisenhower responded, giving Clay some (but hardly all) of the background. He liked Duff despite his "rough edges," because "probably no other individual was as influential in getting me to keep my mouth shut about the developing political situation." Duff, he said, along with Dewey, Hoffman, Lodge, and "numbers of others, persuaded me to avoid open repudiation." If the campaign was to be successful, it must "keep all of them harnessed so as to pull generally in the same direction." Lodge must "be boss in fact as well as in name." Moving to the matters at hand, he asked for a "logical plan of what I am expected to do after I come home . . . [and the] size and location of the organization and where he should go, to the East or to the middle of the United States."[3]

Eisenhower announced his resignation, as scheduled, on April 11. Letters from Stassen and Bermingham brought reassurance. Stassen said he would continue with activities aimed at preventing Taft from "buttoning up sufficient strength for a nomination," which he believed he had already done in New Hampshire and New Jersey, and planned to do in Pennsylvania and Ohio.[4] Bermingham said the campaign was making "astounding inroads" in the Rocky Mountain states, where Lodge had been speaking. Lodge, he reported, "is a far different person" from what he had been before his Paris visit, "due solely to the lift you gave him." Hugh Scott was "happy again, all is on the beam, and we are really rolling."[5]

Hoffman again went on the hustings. On May 6, at Romanoff's restaurant in Hollywood, California, he addressed a dinner for Eisenhower supporters hosted by Samuel Goldwyn, the Warner brothers, and Darryl Zanuck, raising $31,000. He met with "young, dynamic, and enthusiastic" volunteers in northern California and expected to raise another $25,000 at a luncheon in San Francisco. He even breached Taft's hometown of Cincinnati. Attending as the Eisenhower delegate on a panel at the national convention there of the League of Women Voters, Hoffman soon discovered that the invitation had been a mistake. The panelists were supposed to be individuals representing candidates *other than* the leading contenders, Eisenhower and Taft. Hoffman refused to leave and, over objections by Taft's supporters, answered questions about his man by drawing upon material from Eisenhower's speeches and letters. The program reached a television audience of ten million, and Eisenhower's name drew more applause than "all the other candidates put together."[6]

It is difficult to exaggerate the importance of television, which was making its political debut. Although eighteen million Americans now owned television sets, Clay underestimated the power of the new medium and Eisenhower's advantages because of it. Television, Clay thought, would be less important than "an enthusiastic response from a live audience." He failed to consider Ike's following among the network reporters and owners. David Schoenbrun, Paris correspondent of CBS, for example, wrote Eisenhower on May 16 to tell him that he had been a soldier under Eisenhower's command "from London to Algiers, Italy and across into Germany." These years had been "some of the most inspirational years of my life." Then, as chairman of the SHAPE correspondents association for radio and television, Schoenbrun had reported Eisenhower's "successes and great public service." Now he noted that Eisenhower's old friends at CBS—Bill Paley, Ed Murrow, and the new president of CBS radio, Adrian Murphy, "who worked for you in SHAEF, have asked me to bring back their best regards" and "to make available network facilities in both media [radio and television] to provide the most complete and swift public coverage of your views and activities," including "full national broadcasting of your Abilene address."[7] Larmon, who was one of the nation's leading experts on public relations, sensed that television had changed electoral politics as much as radio had twenty years earlier. He purchased air time to push the themes "Eisenhower Can Win" and "You Can't Defeat Corruption with Corruption."[8]

Eisenhower's NATO tasks, meanwhile, now merged with the politics of foreign policy. In mid-April he met with John Foster Dulles. Eisenhower had received two papers that Dulles had written on nuclear strategy, advocating "massive retaliation" in the event of a Soviet invasion of Europe. The supreme commander liked Dulles's proposal because it focused on the key American security priorities: western Europe and deterrence. He was as "deeply impressed as ever with the directness and simplicity of your approach to such complex problems," he told the senator. His only misgiving was Dulles's exclusive emphasis on strategic nuclear capacity. The theory of "massive retaliation" fell down, he told Dulles, if the aggression was political, as in the instance of Czechoslovakia in February 1948, where the Soviet Union took a country into its sphere through subversion and murder rather than direct military force. The purpose of NATO, he said, was in the current circumstance political—the ability to resist attack as a means of creating "confidence to exposed populations . . . that will make them sturdier in their opposition to Communistic inroads," an "atmosphere in which *internal* aggression can be defeated."[9] Dulles quickly admitted that the general had "put his finger on a weak point in my presentation," which he would "try to cover in a revision that he would bring to Paris the first week in May."[10] On May 27 the foreign ministers of France, West Germany, Italy, and the Benelux countries, by signing a treaty creating the European Defense Community, put a "punctuation point" to Eisenhower's work.[11]

Ike and Mamie had feelings of nostalgia and regret about leaving Europe, and—considering the reason for their departure—certain qualms, too. Could he live up to the expectations of supporters? Mamie had enjoyed France; their residence at Marne la Coquette and the beautiful *petite chateau*, Villa Saint-Pierre; their visits to London, Istanbul, Athens, and Naples. Now, having recently finished renovations to their residence, she once more had to pack. The farewell ceremony this time was at Les Invalides, Napoleon's tomb. Eisenhower, in full dress uniform, received France's highest military honor, the Medaille Militaire, from Premier Antoine Pinay. (Later he also received the Grand Cross of the Order of Malta.) Mamie received the Cross of Merit "for unselfish service to mankind."[12]

Eisenhower now turned full attention to Taft and the Republican Old Guard. By late spring 1952, the stalemate in Korea and right-wing Republican accusations of disloyalty in the State Department combined with scandals in his administration to cause the president's public opinion ratings to plummet. Truman, accordingly, announced his decision not to seek reelection. Having done everything in its power to publicize the president's problems, the Old Guard now saw a chance to redeem the party's earlier failures with middle-of-the-road, internationalist candidates—Willkie in 1940 and Dewey in 1944 and 1948. Their candidate—the Senate minority leader, son of a former president (William Howard Taft), and a demonstrated vote-getter—had been campaigning since October. GOP bosses expected to use their control of the party apparatus, especially in states such as Texas, Georgia, and Louisiana, to ensure that Taft received the nomination. When they arrived at the national convention in Chicago, the Taft forces already had 500 of the 604 delegates needed for the nomination.[13]

Eisenhower strategists, who had some 450 delegates, knew that except in a few locations—such as New York, New Hampshire, and New Jersey—the GOP machine was their enemy. Lodge counseled Eisenhower not to appease the conservatives because, in his view, the nation had no intention of "taking a turn to the right."[14] Crucial areas of contention were the states that either had favorite-son candidates, such as Maryland (McKeldin), California (Warren), and Minnesota (Stassen), or in which delegations were split, such as Pennsylvania and Michigan. Personal visits or the momentum of the convention might persuade additional delegates. In places such as Texas and Georgia they were of doubtful value.[15] Eisenhower lieutenants would have to court delegates, bringing them to meet "Ike" or taking him to meet them. They also had to counter the protests of those who felt Eisenhower was a neophyte, insufficiently concerned with Communists in government, or those who charged that as Roosevelt's former European supreme commander, Eisenhower was guilty of appeasing the Soviet Union. (They might, for example, televise the newsreel film of him standing with Stalin on Lenin's tomb reviewing the sports parade of August 1945.)[16]

The soldier from Abilene entered a new and largely unfamiliar realm as he arrived in Washington, D.C., on June 1. His mentor, Brigadier General Fox Conner, in the 1920s had admonished him to "take his job seriously, never himself," but this was not an easy thing to do when the current issue of *Life* magazine had his photograph on the cover, with a story entitled "What Is Ike Like?"[17] Ike and Mamie discovered also—as Ike had anticipated in his conversation with Howard Chase—that they had become fair game. News stories appeared in print that Mamie had a drinking problem. (This was nonsense. She suffered from a chronic inner ear ailment that often affected her sense of balance.) And, as they had suspected, wartime gossip about a love affair between the general and his pretty Irish driver, Kay Summersby, resurfaced in the press. Fortunately the homecoming had its happy moments as well—his invitation to the White House, where, in a five-minute ceremony, President Truman pinned a fourth oak-leaf cluster on his Distinguished Service Medal. The president declared that the first SACEUR had "inspired the confidence and united the efforts of the several member nations of the North Atlantic Treaty Organization." He called it "a monumental achievement without historical peacetime precedent."[18]

The first national televised political event of its kind, Eisenhower's announcement of his candidacy on June 4 in Abilene, did not go well. The location was the stadium in the town's rodeo, softball, and picnic area, recently renamed Eisenhower Park. In later years it also would feature a World-War-II-vintage medium tank, stripped of its armaments and engine and thus available as a climbing apparatus for children. The day was blustery, with white cumulus clouds lined with blue-grey scudding across the sky. The candidate's prepared text took the "middle road." It reassured Republicans that he opposed inflation, excessive government, high taxes, dishonesty, and corruption. He opposed the secrecy within which, he said, Roosevelt at the Yalta Conference had acceded to Stalin's postwar control of eastern Europe in 1945 and the so-called loss of China to the Communists. Unfortunately for the dramatic effect, soon after the candidate began to speak a sudden cloudburst drove half the crowd from the unsheltered stadium. The general, covered by a raincoat, his sparse strands of hair blowing in the wind, continued to read. The sparse audience that remained was drenched and inattentive.

Eisenhower retrieved the situation with a televised press conference the next day. The event this time was indoors—in Abilene's sole movie theater, the Plaza. After a brief extemporaneous statement, Ike took questions. In the relaxed style he had mastered as supreme commander briefing correspondents on the progress of the war in Europe, he captivated the political reporters with his earnest and confident air. Going over the main points of his remarks the previous day, he admitted that he had no formula for ending the Korean War but promised to seek a decent armistice. He favored civil rights but opposed a federal

Fair Employment Practices Commission. Racial justice, he said, reassuring his supporters south of the Mason-Dixon line, was the responsibility of the states. He opposed socialized medicine but favored "the right of every American to decent medical care." He refused to speak against the red-baiting Senator Joseph R. McCarthy of Wisconsin and proposed that subversive influences be "uprooted from responsible places in our government."[19]

In the weeks that followed, Eisenhower met delegates. He met them in Abilene, at Morningside Heights in New York City, on a picnic at his farm in Gettysburg, Pennsylvania. After taking a train to Denver—and stopping en route in Detroit to speak to forty thousand people—he invited delegates from the Midwest and West to his suite in the Brown Palace Hotel. In contrast to the views of Taft and MacArthur, he cautioned that any invasion of the Chinese mainland or all-out air offensive against the People's Republic of China risked general war. Rather than protecting South Korea, Japan, and Formosa, such action would place them in jeopardy.[20] His would be a "firm and reasonably practical approach to a difficult Eastern problem."[21] After being introduced to the delegates, he and Mamie checked out of the Brown Palace and went eastward across the plains, campaigning for the nomination.

Before the mid-1970s and the advent of carefully staged and orchestrated public relations spectaculars, national political conventions were spontaneous, sweaty, often unruly affairs, most often controlled by the party's dominant faction. Party officials and delegates first decided upon procedures. Then, through a combination of behind-the-scenes maneuvering, deal-making, and pageantry, they chose their candidates and presented them to the public. The purpose was to inspire the faithful.

The Republican party in 1952 was split just as it had been in 1912. That year Theodore Roosevelt and the "Bull Moose" Progressives tried to take the nomination away from the conservative Republican president, Robert A. Taft's father, William Howard Taft. But delegates from the conservative Midwest and South aligned themselves against those from the liberal West and Northeast. The Bull Moosers, led by the nation's popular and dynamic former president, failed chiefly because the conservatives controlled the rules and procedures of the convention. Eisenhower's manager, Brownell, knew this history and recognized that the Eisenhower forces had somehow to loosen the grasp of the Republican National Committee on the convention.

Brownell, having mastered the ethos and folkways of modern Republican conventions, now drew upon his contacts and friendships in key states, his mastery of past Republican nominating conventions, and his skill in writing legal briefs to act as impresario. (This was all the more remarkable because he had to work quietly and away from the glare of the media because of his association with Dewey.) Having noticed the parallels with 1912, Brownell, remarkably, had gone to the New York Public Library where, holed up for a week, he read the minutes of the 1912 convention and of later ones as well. The focus of the effort in 1952, he then determined, had to be the opening day, when delegates voted on whether to accept or amend the rules of the previous convention. In normal circumstances, no amendments were proposed. If this occurred in 1952, Brownell quickly saw, all the delegates, including those from disputed Texas, Georgia, and Louisiana—a total of sixty-eight—would be able to vote on who was to receive permanent seating, to the detriment of the Eisenhower forces. In 1912 the victorious Taft machine had prevailed by presenting their arguments against changing the rules in a clear, concise manner. Brownell, accordingly, worked with a Boston lawyer, Ralph Boyd, to draft an amendment, to change the rules so that only the delegates from states without disputed representation could vote to decide which delegations would receive permanent seats.[22]

Brownell then called upon a friend, the pro-Eisenhower Republican chairman in Texas, to allow preconvention events and an accompanying newspaper and television campaign in that state. At the May 3 precinct conventions, large numbers turned out to vote for Eisenhower delegates. Old Guard Texas national committeeman Henry Zweifel was not happy with this exercise in grassroots democracy. His machine control depended upon voter apathy. He thereupon initiated a smear campaign, and when pro-Eisenhower delegates appeared at the state convention at Mineral Wells on May 27, he refused them admission. In accordance with his wishes, the state convention then selected a slate of national convention delegates committed to Taft. Anticipating such high-handedness, Brownell pounded the pro-Taft machine in the press, charging in tones of moral outrage that their actions were dishonest and corrupt. The Eisenhower forces, with Brownell's assistance, then held their own convention and elected a majority of Eisenhower delegates.

Ten days before the convention opened, Lodge and James Hagerty, Dewey's former press secretary, arrived in Chicago and began churning out press releases, two a day, for the morning and afternoon papers, television, and radio shows.[23] Brownell, with Aldrich's help, also went to Pennsylvania to talk with the moderates and to Detroit where he conferred with Republican national committeeman Arthur Summerfield. Neither of these trips produced sure results.[24]

In Chicago the Eisenhower campaign reserved a ballroom at the Stevens Hotel, and on the floor of the International Amphitheater, the site of the convention, arranged for a specially built air-conditioned room equipped with telephones, typewriters, and mimeograph machines.[25] When the Eisenhower delegates began to arrive at the convention, Brownell's people greeted them with instructions. They quickly picked up the drumbeat, staging a demonstration for the benefit of the television cameras with placards reading "Fair Play" and "Rob with Bob" in front of the closed doors of the meeting room where the credentials committee, as expected, gave temporary convention seats to the disputed delegations. The public, the demonstrators insisted, had a right to know what was happening in the "smoke-filled" room.[26]

The strategy was shrewd and involved considerable spadework. The month before, in Washington, Lodge had turned his attention to the California delegation. Governor Earl Warren controlled it, so Lodge told his Senate colleague, California's junior senator Richard M. Nixon, that Eisenhower was considering him for the vice presidential slot. Dewey confirmed this on May 8 when Nixon spoke in New York City. Needing no further persuasion, by the time he arrived in

Chicago Nixon was in the Eisenhower camp. He now charged that the Texas machine was corrupt. Talking with California delegates individually and then in caucus, he persuaded them to vote in favor of a "fair play" resolution designed to prevent delegates with disputed credentials (like those from Texas) from voting on whether they would receive permanent credentials.[27] Then, on July 1, Dewey, along with Dan Thornton of Colorado, John Davis Lodge of Connecticut, and New Hampshire governor Sherman Adams, persuaded all twenty-three governors in attendance at the GOP governors' conference in Houston to sign a telegram to Republican national chairman Guy Gabrielson urging him to support an amendment to the convention rules that "no contested delegate may vote to determine the outcome of any contest."[28] By this time the Taft forces sensed trouble. They tried to patch together a compromise, but Lodge, having counted his delegates, refused.

Now events began to go Eisenhower's way. General MacArthur, rather than "fading away" as he had suggested he would in his now-famous farewell speech to Congress a year earlier, had remained an imposing figure and, from his suite at New York's posh Waldorf-Astoria, hopeful. When he realized he could not be the nominee in 1952, he had accepted the advice of Robert E. Wood and former president Herbert Hoover (also a resident of the Waldorf-Astoria) to take the vice presidential slot on a Taft ticket and give the keynote address at the convention. Both these decisions, it turned out, were mistakes. (Later, when it became clear to Hoover that Taft could not win, he attempted to get the senator to stand aside and move his delegates to MacArthur. Taft refused.)

Instead of sparking enthusiasm in the delegates, MacArthur's keynote address was partisan and dull, reflecting, if anything, the old soldier's fading interest.[29] Thereafter the convention went progressively better for Eisenhower. Senator Joe McCarthy, the next speaker, stridently denounced Communists in the federal government. Senator Everett Dirksen of Illinois bitterly derided Dewey for taking the party to defeat in two previous elections. A misguided attempt by Taft forces to offer a weak proposal to exclude seven of the Louisiana delegates went nowhere, and the convention adopted the "fair play" amendment 607 to 531.

For all intents and purposes, Eisenhower now had the nomination. The balloting soon revealed that Dewey controlled New York; Stassen could deliver Minnesota; Governor Fine held Pennsylvania; Arthur Summerfield retained control in Michigan; and Nixon held California. When Texans-for-Eisenhower, Georgians-for-Eisenhower, and Louisianans-for-Eisenhower took their seats, only formalities remained. The first ballot brought 595 delegates for Eisenhower (still nine votes short), 500 for Taft, 81 for Warren, 20 for Stassen, and 10 for MacArthur. Stassen then asked to be recognized, and as leader of the Minnesota delegation—true to his word—he gave his votes to Eisenhower. The remaining delegations followed, and with 841 votes the general had won.

Having watched the count on television with friends and family members in his suite at the Blackstone Hotel, Eisenhower went to tell Mamie, who had not been feeling well and had gone to lie down. Milton recalled that his brother, now the Republican candidate for President of the United States, was gone for some time. When Milton heard a commotion on the street, he peered out the window and saw Ike pushing through a crowd of reporters and cameramen toward Senator Taft. He watched as his brother, surrounded by news photographers and reporters, graciously extended his hand to the Senate Republican leader, now the defeated candidate for the nomination.[30]

When the cheering stopped, Cliff Roberts wrote to his friend, the nominee. In one instance at the convention, he said, Eisenhower floor leaders had forced a Virginia delegate back in line by arranging a deluge of three thousand telegrams from constituents after he and two fellow delegates had defected to Taft. The "fair play" strategy, said Roberts, had been "masterful." He credited Brownell and praised Clay, who had been active on the convention floor.

Eisenhower's friend, stockbroker, and political adviser then turned to issues of presidential image. The campaign to follow, Roberts said, needed more money not from a few people, most of them from New York, but from small contributors. And Eisenhower should consider joining a church in order to make himself appealing to the evangelical Protestants in the South. He should not participate in big golf gambling pools; and, perhaps most important, he should send a personal note thanking Pete Jones, a good friend and major donor.[31] (Roberts would later reveal that at various times beginning in 1952, Pete Jones gave him a total of $250,000 in cash to use in Eisenhower's campaigns.)[32]

The turn of events even caused General Marshall to break his silence. Eisenhower's wartime boss sent congratulations on the "fine victory." The former secretary of state and defense said he had remained "incommunicado because he feared that the attacks on him [Marshall] by various Republicans might cause any communication with you to be detrimental to your cause."[33] Eisenhower replied immediately, expressing his "deep appreciation" for the general's "fine note." If he had suggested in the spring of 1942 that this would happen, he said, he "ventured a guess that you would have had me locked up as a dangerous character." He was "buoyed up," he said, "by the belief that I am performing a real service and I am doing my duty." Eisenhower said he intended to fight as hard as he could to end the domination of government by one party, especially one with which he disagreed "on so many points of policy."[34]

The road from the first hints of presidential possibilities in 1943 to the nomination nine years later had been long and difficult for Eisenhower, but also fascinating and exhilarating. After the convention, Dewey stopped by Lodge's hotel room one more time to say goodbye. Lodge was out and Dewey missed him. When Lodge returned, he dictated a letter to the man behind the scenes. Dewey, he said, had been "not only a tower of strength but an indispensable one. Your one thought was always, 'what can I do to help the cause?'. . . It must be a deep satisfaction to you, as it is to me, to feel that we have really wrought a fundamental reform in the Republican Party and that we have nominated such a great man for President. For me, there is the added satisfaction of having worked with you, of having really come to know you well and of appreciation of your own great qualities. Faithfully yours."[35] MacArthur might have taken satisfaction in the accomplishments of the officer who had served him and the nation so well. Instead he took the outcome as another personal rebuke. The disagreements, and now the perceived wounds, were too great. "Eisenhower," the disconsolate former Far East commander muttered to friends, "was a lightweight."[36]

The urgency of the times and the sacrifices that Ike and Mamie faced as they moved directly into the political spotlight bore down on them the day after the nomination in a personal way. They had to escort their son, John, an infantry captain, from the Blackstone Hotel to the airport for his departure for combat duty in Korea. "All the three of us could do was stand and stare until it was time to kiss Johnnie," Mamie recalled. "As Ike and I choked back our feelings while waiting for the take-off . . . flashbulbs went off. I don't blame the photographers and reporters, they had their jobs to do; it was just that we would have liked to keep our private grief to ourselves."[37]

An important ingredient of this success was probably Eisenhower's ability to make it appear that the office came to him. Sherman Adams later reflected that for Eisenhower, as for "any American, to become President was the ultimate achievement. I have no doubt that back of all the persiflage Eisenhower really felt during this time that if it could become apparent he could marshal substantial delegate support, he would go for it."[38] But the reticence—what Adams called "persiflage"—came naturally. It stemmed, after all, from a humility instilled into a child by hardworking parents, by the playing fields of Abilene, by West Point, and in the Panama Canal Zone in the early 1920s by General Fox Conner. This ethic, had been reinforced by Eisenhower's encounters with MacArthur's vanity and had been tempered by supreme command in war. If he was ambitious for the presidency, Eisenhower handled himself in such a way that it was not evident.

What came forward instead was an earnest warmth, quiet confidence, and desire to do what was best for his nation. Norris Cotton, congressman and delegate from New Hampshire, was an early convert to Eisenhower. Just before the GOP convention, Senator Homer Capehart, a Taft supporter and delegate from Indiana, pleaded with Cotton not to support Ike. The general, Capehart said, had "approved the policy of appeasing the Russians in Europe and was chief of staff when Marshall and Acheson abandoned Chiang Kai-shek to the communists in Asia. . . . Unless we nominate Taft, the New Deal will take over the Republican party." Unmoved, the New Hampshire congressman politely thanked the senator and filed the letter.[39] Cotton later recalled his conversion to Eisenhower. He had visited SHAPE for five days in June 1951 as a member of a subcommittee of the Congressional Appropriations Committee. Not once had he or any of the delegates talked with the supreme commander about his political plans. Nevertheless, by the time he came away, Cotton, like so many others, believed he had a good sense "of Ike's way of thinking. . . . I admit that I fell under the spell of General Eisenhower's personality and came away his ardent admirer." Ike, he said, could have had the presidency "on a platter" if he had been willing to declare himself a Democrat. He was a "genius as an administrator," and as a candidate "he can break into the South, win the border states, and make the Republican party a national party once more."

Lodge later elaborated this theme—and the usefulness of the appearance of a presidential draft. He recalled in a letter to the president in June 1954 (by that time Lodge was ambassador to the United Nations) that as campaign manager he had been able to tell potential contributors that their giving involved no specific obligation on Eisenhower's part. "I always made it clear that you did not want the job. If ever there was a 'draft' in American history, your nomination was it."[40] Such was the approach—by Lodge, Hoffman, and Petersen—that brought in $788,000 in contributions by mid-May. More money had arrived by the time of the convention.[41]

The media, of course, found Eisenhower irresistible. Everything he said or did was newsworthy, and especially his insistence—which made him even more appealing to them—that he was not a candidate. The mystery surrounding his decision to run was a foolproof angle for selling newspapers and magazines. Of course, this was especially useful to those media moguls who were on a crusade of their own to obtain Ike's election. William Robinson, after all, was acting both as a citizen and in behalf of the *New York Herald Tribune*, as was Leonard

Finder of the *Manchester Union Leader*. Robinson credited Henry Luce and Roy Larsen as the individuals who more than anyone else created the atmosphere that brought about the general's candidacy. Looking back on the events, Robinson told Larsen in July 1952 that he "always knew, despite the sneering and scoffing of the professional politicians, that the people would have to nominate Eisenhower by bringing pressure on the delegates. That is exactly what happened in Chicago, and I don't know any single instrument of public opinion that wielded a stronger force in that direction than your organization. I happen to believe personally that you represented entirely the margin for victory."[42]

One question worth asking is whether Eisenhower would have entered the race if he had believed NATO would be secure without his leadership as president. What if someone other than Taft or MacArthur had been the Republican nominee—someone, say, with Dewey's beliefs but with sufficient public following to win in both July and November (Hoffman comes to mind)? The evidence suggests that Eisenhower would not have run.

☆ **16** ☆

A QUESTION
OF DUTY

DWIGHT DAVID EISENHOWER was one of the most popular and
trusted individuals of his time. In the years after World War II, as questions arose about the size and role of the federal government and how
the nation ought to respond to Communist expansion, his fellow
countrymen increasingly turned to him, the general who had led the
victorious crusade against Italy and Germany in World War II. No
sooner had the war ended than pundits, and even President Truman,
began to discuss the possibility that he would be a presidential candidate. By 1947, with the outbreak of cold war, and, in the spring of 1948,
the Soviet blockade of land routes to Berlin, the possibility that Eisenhower—having left his position as army chief of staff to become president of Columbia University—would enter national politics was
increasingly appealing. Before the national conventions of 1948, both
parties courted him. When the GOP lost its fourth consecutive presidential election that year, Republicans especially urged him to become their candidate.

Eisenhower, though he refused to enter partisan politics, found
the idea intriguing. He had been frustrated by Truman's inability to
persuade Congress to pass the appropriations that he considered a necessary minimum for national defense. The United States had adopted
a policy of containing Soviet expansion—the so-called Truman Doctrine—and had implemented it by passing the European Recovery

Program, the Marshall Plan. After the Berlin crisis it became a sponsor of the North Atlantic Treaty Organization. Following these events, Eisenhower accepted the president's request that he return to Washington in early 1949 as acting chairman of the Joint Chiefs of Staff in order to mediate disputes within the armed services and develop a strategic concept upon which to base budget requests. But the exhortations that he enter partisan politics became more frequent as world affairs seemed to spiral downward. The Soviet Union tested an atomic bomb, and the Chinese Communist Peoples' Liberation Army overran the mainland, forcing the Nationalist government to the island of Formosa. Then, in June 1950, war broke out in Korea after the Soviet-backed army of Kim II Sung's Communist regime in the North invaded the South. Eisenhower returned to active military duty—this time as NATO supreme commander—that winter; but by this time, unbeknownst to the president (or very many others, for that matter), he was cooperating with Republican groups who were studying the feasibility of an Eisenhower presidential candidacy in 1952. After he became convinced in early 1951 that the most likely GOP nominee, Senator Robert A. Taft, opposed American policies aimed at ensuring European security, Eisenhower secretly—and in violation of Army Regulations—authorized and cooperated with efforts to forward his own nomination instead.

Skeptics might ask whether Eisenhower's motivation was any different from that of another general, Douglas MacArthur, who had sought the nomination in 1948 and 1952: vanity and egotism, and an accompanying insistence that his view of American strategy was correct. Both individuals, it seems, were politically ambitious. Eisenhower, like MacArthur (only a few years earlier), had moved upward through army ranks and had no doubt about his political potential. Mention of his name in connection with presidential politics had begun as early as 1943 with the liberation of North Africa by an Allied force under his command. One could argue that he saw an opportunity in 1952—with the advent of such technology of warfare as long-range bombers and bombs of heretofore unimaginable destructiveness, along with Communist hostility—to exploit the national anxiety. This interpretation raises interesting questions. Did Eisenhower, for example, manipulate and perhaps exaggerate the nature of the Communist threat for his own purposes? (Was the Red Army, given Stalin's intentions, really a threat to western Europe?) Critics of cold war policies, including the expensive and dangerous nuclear arms race that began in the 1950s, would point to this political general from Abilene as the president who institutionalized an American strategy that led to what Eisenhower himself, in his farewell address, called the military-industrial complex.

According to this view, Eisenhower was not drafted but wanted the presidency. He acted in such a way, ingeniously, as to produce the appearance of a draft—a fiction that was essential to remove any suspicion about what he really had in mind. Meanwhile he quietly courted the politicos, having them hold out to the Eisenhower-for-President groups the possibility that, if they worked hard enough and established sufficient following, he would accede to their wishes and become a candidate. The appearance of a draft, according to this scenario, once again demonstrated his remarkable skills as a strategist—this time in the partisan political arena, this time for his personal purposes.

In truth, Eisenhower's decision to become a candidate was less complicated, not to mention less devious, and more honorable. Certainly in later years, as revealed in his memoirs, he liked to think of himself as having succumbed to a draft. Before publicly announcing his candidacy, he received continual and mounting pressure to run for office from public opinion polls, journalists, opinion leaders, and politicians. But if being drafted meant that he did nothing to forward his candidacy until he was nominated by the party convention (something that he often mentioned as desirable), then he was not. Did he thus prove the skeptics correct? The answer is, no. Unlike MacArthur, his chief satisfaction came from serving. While ambitious, he scorned preoccupation with himself. His favorite slogan, from his mentor, General Fox Conner, was "take your job seriously, never yourself." He had become famous but had no time for those who traded on their fame, especially the kind that came through sacrifice in war. Although willing to seek high office, he worried about the possible effects on the army should he be perceived as politically ambitious. Nor would he have remained in contention had he not believed that as president his policy goals would have their best chance of being realized. He feared, after much soul-searching, that if he did not run for president, his NATO mission would fail and the world would slip into turmoil.

It is now clear that Eisenhower's perceptions were accurate. While Stalin, from the evidence now available in Moscow, was not planning an invasion of western Europe, he was willing to use any method that did not endanger his regime to expand his influence. His miscalculation of U.S. interest and ability to respond, for example, persuaded him to promise Soviet support to the North Korean invasion of South Korea. Soviet interests also required a weak and disunited western Europe. Eisenhower decided he had a duty—which he called "transcendent"—to make the United States a stabilizing force in the postwar world. It was this sense of overweaning responsibility—his West Point code of "duty, honor, country" and his satisfaction at leading an enterprise in which he believed—that sustained him and brought him, finally, to enter the race.

Eisenhower's motives for this decision derived first from the knowledge he had gained at the highest levels of military and national security policy and his study of the history of American foreign relations. They reflected his belief by 1946 that the United States, in demobilizing its armed forces, had followed the same path it had taken after World War I—rendering itself, despite sole possession of the atomic bomb, considerably less influential in international relations. In an era of transoceanic bombers, the United States was vulnerable as never before to a surprise aerial attack, a fact that gave the nation an unprecedented interest in maintaining the postwar balance of power. He advocated unifying the armed services under a secretary of defense and a presidential military adviser, the chairman of the Joint Chiefs of Staff; retaining possession of the atomic bomb; and establishing a system of universal military training similar to that of Switzerland. These elements, together with support for recovery and reconstruction in war-torn western Europe and Japan, he felt, would go far to remedy the nation's weakness.

But as late as mid-1947 Congress had passed none of these measures. The United States had a loosely organized national military establishment but not a true department of defense; it possessed the atomic bomb but had only a few of them and no feasible plan or doctrine for their use in war. Congress, while cutting the defense budget to less than $12 billion, had refused to pass universal military training. The Soviet Union, meanwhile, had retained an army of 175 divisions; become intransigent over policy in occupied Germany and Poland; and begun to solidify its hold over eastern Europe. Western Europe—having lost many, though not yet all, of its colonial possessions and accompanying natural resources in Africa, the Middle East, and Southeast Asia—lacked the economic and political stability and confidence necessary to resist intimidation. The United States, despite its lack of respectable strength, had nonetheless proclaimed in the Truman Doctrine that the world was divided into two camps, slave and free, and that it would support free peoples anywhere who were resisting outside aggression or internal subversion. Not until the autumn of 1949, with the advent of the Soviet Union atomic bomb and the Communist takeover of mainland China, did Truman even order large-scale production and stockpiling of atomic bombs and the development of a hydrogen bomb. All these events brought Eisenhower deep concern.

With the outbreak of war in Korea and then Red Chinese intervention, he decided that the nation's security was in jeopardy. The United States needed to identify its vital interests, regain the capacity to uphold them, and, to prevent miscalculations, let potential enemies, including the Soviet Union and the People's Republic of China (both of which were involved in the Korean conflict), know what they were. His goals now included, in approximately the following order: an armed and unified western Europe within the NATO alliance; a reinforced American army through selective service; a strategic and tactical nuclear bombing capability to either deter or, if necessary, retard a Soviet attack; a revitalized and democratic Japan under American protection as the keystone of Far Eastern defense; and a favorable negotiated end to the military stalemate in Korea.

Eisenhower also knew that none of these objectives was possible without the support of the American people and their representatives in Congress. In the spring of 1951, because of setbacks in Korea and the strategic controversy that surrounded Truman's sacking of General MacArthur as his Far East commander, the president's public opinion rating had sunk so low that he could not win reelection. The most likely Republican nominee and possible winner in 1952 would be Taft, a senator who had voted against rearming NATO and who had refused both publicly and in private conversations with Eisenhower to support the concept of collective security. Indeed, the senator had determined, after listening to MacArthur, that the United States should allocate more strategic resources not to western Europe but to the Far East. Eisenhower's decision to run in 1952 flowed from these events and his abiding sense of responsibility.

NOTES

Preface

1. David Fromkin, *In the Time of the Americans: FDR, Truman, Eisenhower, Marshall, MacArthur—The Generation that Changed America's Role in the World* (New York: Alfred A. Knopf, 1995), p. 520.

2. Herbert A. Brownell, Eisenhower Library Symposium, "The Great Crusade: The Road to the White House, 1952" (videotape, Nov. 6, 1992).

3. Dwight D. Eisenhower, *Mandate for Change: The White House Years, 1953–56* (New York: Signet, 1963), p. 48.

4. Stephen E. Ambrose *Eisenhower*, Vol. I: *Soldier, General of the Army, President-elect, 1890–1952* (New York: Simon and Schuster, 1983), pp. 489–490.

5. Peter Lyon, *Eisenhower: Portrait of the Hero* (Boston: Little, Brown, 1974), p. 426.

6. Blanche Wiesen Cook, *The Declassified Eisenhower: A Divided Legacy of Peace and Political Warfare* (New York: Penguin Books, 1984), pp. 68–75, 85.

7. Milton Eisenhower, Oral History [OH], Sept. 6, 1967, Eisenhower Library; Jean Edward Smith, *Lucius D. Clay: An American Life* (New York: Henry Holt, 1990), pp. 591–592.

8. Underlying the dramatic tension between the two generals and the president was the fact that the generals had known each other from years of close association before World War II (indeed, Eisenhower, as aide to MacArthur when the latter was army chief of staff in the early 1930s, had drafted reports for his signature) and that the cold war required a renewal of the competition for American resources and strategic priorities that they had experienced as European and Asian theater commanders, respectively, in that war. Unfortunately, just as in the earlier conflict, American cold war strategy relegated the senior officer to the theater of secondary importance. It would have been a difficult arrangement for anyone, but for an individual of MacArthur's temperament, knowing he was reaching the end of his career, it was no doubt troublesome indeed.

9. The individuals whose efforts he cultivated and who both encouraged him and helped him win the nomination were enormously skillful, in most instances selfless and well connected, but invariably dedicated and loyal. While not exhaustive, the

list—mentioned below—included family members and friends, political professionals, and the Citizens for Eisenhower movement.

The first group included, of course, his wife Mamie, who supported and encouraged him in whatever he desired to do; his son, John S. D. Eisenhower, who was at
times a "sounding board" for his father; his childhood friend Everett "Swede" Hazlett,
who encouraged him to enter politics; and William E. Robinson, executive vice president of the *New York Herald Tribune*, who saw to it that Eisenhower published his
memoirs and helped to organize Citizens for Eisenhower. Leonard Finder, publisher
of the Manchester, New Hampshire, *Union Leader*, worked in Eisenhower's behalf
from the moment the general removed himself from the presidential race in 1948;
Brigadier General Edwin Norman Clark began exploratory activities for Eisenhower
in the autumn of 1947 and later served as secret emissary to Republican politicos in
New York; Milton Eisenhower served as information gatherer and confidential sounding board for most decisions; Edgar Eisenhower was always a voice for skepticism and
prudence; General Lucius Clay husbanded Ike's reputation, raised money, and, after
Eisenhower became NATO supreme commander, was liaison with the professionals.
General Walter Bedell Smith, his wartime chief of staff, gave encouragement and ap-
praisals of his political standings, and, as U.S. ambassador to Moscow and later director of Central Intelligence, kept him abreast of relations between the United States
and the Soviet Union. Clifford Roberts, New York investment banker and president of
the Augusta National Golf Club, was Eisenhower's personal financial adviser and
"chairman" of his informal circle of close friends. General Howard Snyder, his personal physician, concealed from public view his physical ailments.

Other important friends were Winthrop W. Aldrich, chairman of the Chase National Bank; John Hay "Jock" Whitney, New York financier and venture capitalist;
George Sloan, former president of the Cotton Textile Institute, director and member
of the finance committee of United States Steel Corporation, and chairman of the
Metropolitan Opera Association; George Whitney, chairman of J. P. Morgan and
Company; Joseph E. Davies, Washington attorney, philanthropist, and former U.S.
ambassador to the Soviet Union; Alton "Pete" Jones, president of Cities Service Corporation; Henry R. Luce, publisher of *Time, Life,* and *Fortune* magazines; Russell
Davenport, editor of *Fortune* and political strategist; Philip Young, dean of the Columbia University School of Business; Philip Reed, chairman of General Electric; Douglas Southall Freeman, author and historian; Edward Mead Earle, fellow at the
Institute for Advanced Study in Princeton; Averell Harriman, former U.S. ambassador
to the Soviet Union and White House national security adviser and liaison with
NATO; and Harry Bullis, chairman of General Mills.

The most important of the professional politicians were Senator James Duff of
Pennsylvania, who cooperated with the earliest efforts to get Eisenhower the nomination; Governor Thomas E. Dewey, former two-time GOP presidential candidate, who,
working behind the scenes, provided expert guidance; Senator Henry Cabot Lodge,
Jr., of Massachusetts, who agreed in late October 1951 to become campaign manager;
Herbert Brownell, former GOP national chairman, Dewey's campaign manager, and
mastermind of the 1946 GOP congressional victory, who was in charge of the campaign; and Harold Stassen, former governor of Minnesota and president of the University of Pennsylvania, who was a stalking horse for Eisenhower in the presidential
primaries of 1952 and swung his delegates to Eisenhower at the end of the first ballot at
the GOP convention.

The third group included, among others, two individuals who also were close friends of the general: William Burnham, a Wall Street investment banker who also was president of the 1948 Citizens for Eisenhower organization and Eisenhower's part-time political assistant at NATO; Paul G. Hoffman, former president of the Studebaker Corporation, administrator of the Marshall Plan, chairman of the Committee for Economic Development, member of the Committee on the Present Danger, and president of the Ford Foundation; Howard C. Petersen, New York attorney, head of the international studies division of the Committee for Economic Development, and later finance chairman of Eisenhower's campaign; and Edward Bermingham, a trustee of Columbia University and GOP national committeeman from Chicago.

The important point here is that while various groups whose purpose was to draft or support Eisenhower for president came into existence at various locations and at various times, each of these individuals in one way or another remained in contact with Eisenhower, received encouragement from him, and in turn helped move him toward the 1952 GOP presidential nomination. Clifford Roberts to DDE, June 5, 1961, Eisenhower Post-Presidential Papers, box 15, Roberts, Cliff (3); W. Howard Chase, Memorandum of Visit with General Eisenhower, July 20, 1961, Clarence Francis Papers, Eisenhower Library, box 10, DDE, 1961.

Chapter 1. War Hero

1. John S. D. Eisenhower, *Allies: Pearl Harbor to D-Day* (Garden City, N.Y.: Doubleday, 1982), p. 288.

2. George Van Horn Moseley to DDE, Sept. 29, 1943, Dwight D. Eisenhower Pre-Presidential Papers, 1916–1952 series, Dwight D. Eisenhower Library, Abilene, Kansas, [hereafter: DDEPP], box 84, file: Moseley.

3. Daniel D. Holt and James W. Leyerzapf, eds., *Eisenhower: The Pre-war Diaries and Selected Papers, 1905–1941* (Baltimore: Johns Hopkins University Press, 1998), p. 230.

4. Geoffrey Perret, *Old Soldiers Never Die: The Life of Douglas MacArthur* (New York: Random House, 1996), p. 213.

5. Holt and Leyerzapf, p. 363.

6. Ibid., pp. 424, 430.

7. Ibid., pp. 440, 453.

8. DDE to Moseley, Oct. 7, 1943, DDEPP, box 84, Moseley.

9. Henry Cabot Lodge to DDE, Jan. 7, 1943, DDEPP, box 72, Lodge.

10. DDE personnel records, DDEPP, box 4, awards, Aug.–Dec. 1943.

11. Edgar Eisenhower to DDE, Aug. 21, 1944, DDEPP, box 172, Edgar (3).

12. Averell Harriman to DDE, June 24, 1944, DDEPP, box 55, Harriman (6).

13. DDE to Harriman, July 7, 1944, DDEPP, ibid.

14. Harriman to DDE, Aug. 28, 1945, DDEPP, box 110, Stalin.

15. David McCullough, *Truman* (New York: Simon and Schuster, 1992), p. 398; *New York World-Telegram*, June 19, 1945, clipping in vertical file, United States Military Academy Archives, West Point, Eisenhower, file 5.

16. McCullough, pp. 429–430.

17. Besides Roosevelt, he later told an admirer, Benjamin Franklin, George Washington, Abraham Lincoln, and Robert E. Lee were the historical figures who influ-

enced him most. DDE to Schreyer, Nov. 30, 1963, Eisenhower Post-Presidential Convenience Series, Eisenhower Library, Abilene, Kansas [hereafter: DDEPPCS], box 1, "DDE personals"; Clarence Frances papers, Eisenhower Library [hereafter: CFP], box 10, file: DDE, 1961.

18. Lucius D. Clay, Oral History, Eisenhower Library, February 5, 1971, p. 533.

19. DDE to Walter Winchell, Dec. 18, 1946, DDEPP, box 25, Winchell (6).

20. IBM Corporation, "General of the Army Dwight D. Eisenhower," 1945, DDEPP, box 122, Watson (5).

21. Swede Hazlett to DDE, Feb. 17, 1946, DDEPP, box 56, Hazlett (4).

22. Douglas Southall Freeman to DDE, Nov. 5, 1943, DDEPP, box 43, Freeman, D.S.

23. DDE to Freeman, Nov. 13, 1943, ibid.

24. DDE, OH, July 20, 1967, p. 50.

Chapter 2. Lessons in Politics

1. Richard H. Kohn, ed., *The United States Military Under the Constitution of the United States, 1789–1989* (New York: New York University Press, 1991), p. 1.

2. DDE to John S. D. Eisenhower [hereafter: JSDE], Dec. 20, 1942, DDEPP, box 173, JSDE (1).

3. DDE to Swede Hazlett [hereafter: Swede], Apr. 7, 1943, DDEPP, box 56, Hazlett (5).

4. DDE to JSDE, June 19, 1943, DDEPP, box 173, JSDE (1).

5. DDE to JSDE, Sept. 20, 1943, ibid.

6. DDE to JSDE, Oct. 13, 1942, ibid.

7. DDE to Edgar N. Eisenhower [hereafter: Edgar], Sept. 27, 1943, DDEPP, box 172, Edgar (3).

8. DDE to Edgar, Sept. 26, 1944, ibid.

9. Edgar to DDE, Mar. 1, 1944, ibid.

10. Milton S. Eisenhower to DDE, Mar. 10, 1944, DDEPP, box 174, Milton (2).

11. DDE to Edgar, Apr. 10, 1944, DDEPP, box 172, Edgar (3).

12. DDE to Milton, May 2, 1944, DDEPP, box 174, Milton (2).

13. Eisenhower annotated in his own handwriting the margins of Kenneth C. Davis's book, *Eisenhower: Soldier of Democracy* (Garden City, N.Y.: Doubleday, 1945). Kenneth C. Davis manuscript, Eisenhower Library, p. 401.

14. Ibid.

15. DDE to Jacob L. Devers, July 16, 1945, DDEPP, box 174, Milton (movie file).

16. The scriptwriter may have failed to give sufficient credit to the British. And of course Eisenhower desired to avoid the perception that he or his family would profit from it. DDE to Milton, July 11, 1944, ibid.

17. Franklin D. Roosevelt message to DDE, Nov. 9, 1943, DDEPP, box 100, Roosevelt (1).

18. McCullough, pp. 349–350.

19. DDE memo to Joint Chiefs of Staff, Jan. 16, 1946, in Alfred D. Chandler, Jr., and Louis Galambos, eds., *The Papers of Dwight D. Eisenhower* [hereafter DEP] (Baltimore: Johns Hopkins University Press, 1970–), Vol. VII: *The Chief of Staff*, pp. 760–761.

20. Ambrose, p. 415; Memorandum of DDE's meeting with Harry S. Truman, July 25, 1946, DDEPP, box 116, Truman (4). Instead of moving toward UMT, something that would provide the security he was seeking at a reasonable price, he thus had to spend time wrestling with the issue of the control of nuclear weapons. He believed they must remain under civilian authority but also, for security reasons, under military custody. In an unprecedented and tricky proposition that ultimately reflected the high degree of confidence the United States armed forces had earned for themselves, he recommended that the military branches, acting as agents of the Atomic Energy Commission, store, maintain, and guard these weapons that were so uniquely powerful they could be authorized for use only at the direction of the president. DDE memo to General Norstad, Sept. 20, 1947, DDEPP, box 127, atomic weapons and energy (1).

21. DDE's Speech to Members of Congress, Jan. 5, 1946, President's Secretary's File, Harry S. Truman Library [hereafter: PPSF], box 118, Eisenhower, D.D.

22. Clay, OH, Feb. 11, 1971, p. 98.

23. DDE to Baruch, Oct. 7, 1945, DDEPP, box 10, Baruch (4).

24. DDE to Swede, Mar. 13, 1946, DDEPP, box 56, Hazlett (4).

25. Part of the reason for the tension between the two officers was the awareness of both individuals that the junior lacked combat experience. As one MacArthur biographer put it, unlike MacArthur, "Ike did not wear a single decoration for gallantry." MacArthur would even remark unfairly, considering Ike's huge accomplishments as supreme commander, that the latter "never fought in Europe" but rather "let his generals in the field fight the war for him. . . . Lucky he had Patton." Eisenhower, for his part, while critical of MacArthur's pomposity, vanity, and overt partisan activities, admired his former boss's exploits in the South Pacific. He told one colleague that MacArthur's campaigns in New Guinea and the Philippines "have no equal in history." Perret, pp. 501–502.

26. Joseph E. Davies diary entry of Dec. 7, 1946, Davies Papers, Library of Congress [hereafter: DPLC], box 24, Davies diary. Not long after taking office as army chief of staff, Eisenhower found himself besieged by individuals who wanted to exploit his fame. Authors and Hollywood producers asked him to participate in book and movie contracts about his life and career. One offered 10 percent of gross receipts and an advance of $300,000—quite a sum for a career army officer. James Stack memorandum about Milton Hill, May 29, 1946, DDEPP, box 57, Milton Hill; Hill to DDE, June 2, 1946, ibid.; Truman to the Secretary of War, July 30, 1946, DDEPP, box 116, Truman (4).

27. Perret, p. 501.

28. Forrest C. Pogue, "George C. Marshall on Civil-Military Relationships," in Kohn, p. 194.

29. DDE to Douglas MacArthur, Jan. 28, 1946, DDEPP, box 74, MacArthur (1).

30. Ambrose, p. 442.

31. Ambrose, p. 443.

32. DDE to George C. Marshall, May 28, 1946, DDEPP, box 80, Marshall (5).

33. Tom Clark, Oral History, Truman Library, pp. 166–167; Cabell Phillips, *The Truman Presidency: The History of a Triumphant Succession* (New York: Macmillan, 1966), pp. 196–97; Sam Rosenman, Oral History, Truman Library, p. 81.

34. DDE to MacArthur, Jan. 28, 1946.

Chapter 3. Cold War

1. W. Averell Harriman and Elie Abel, *Special Envoy to Churchill and Stalin, 1941–1946* (New York: Random House, 1975), pp. 501–502; Harriman memoirs, Dec. 8, 1954, Harry S Truman, Post-Presidential Memoirs, Truman Library [hereafter: HSTPPM], box 1, Memoirs, Harriman.

2. DDE to Marshal Georgi K. Zhukov, Mar. 13, 1946, DDEPP, box 126, Zhukov; DDE to Zhukov, Mar. 4, 1946, ibid.

3. Clay, OH, Jan. 19, 1971, p. 634.

4. Eduard Mark, "The War Scare of 1946 and Its Consequences," *Diplomatic History*, 21 (Summer 1997), 387–388.

5. Phillip A. Karber and Jerald A. Combs, "The United States, NATO, and the Soviet Threat to Western Europe," *Diplomatic History*, 22, (Summer 1998), 403.

6. Mark, p. 392.

7. Harriman memoirs; Forrest C. Pogue, *George C. Marshall: Statesman, 1945–1959* (New York: Viking, 1987), pp. 190, 196.

8. DDE to JSDE, Mar. 3, 1946, DDEPP, box 173, JSDE (2).

9. DDE to Milton, Mar. 15, 1946, DDEPP, box 174, Milton, 1946–47 (3).

10. DDE to the Secretary of Defense, Nov. 3, 1947, DDEPP, box 42, Forrestal (5); Zimmerman quote in William B. Pickett, *Dwight David Eisenhower and American Power* (Wheeling, Ill.: Harlan Davidson, 1995), p. 55.

11. DDE to JSDE, May 8, 1944, DDEPP, box 173, JSDE (1).

12. DDE to Hazlett, Nov. 27, 1945, DDEPP, box 56, Hazlett (4).

13. If it were true that administering the "combined armed forces are beyond the capacity of any one man, then it would follow, he said, that 'no man has the capacity to assume the Presidency of the United States.'" Townsend Hoopes and Douglas Brinkley, *Driven Patriot: The Life and Times of James Forrestal* (New York: Alfred A. Knopf, 1992), p. 324.

14. DDE to Gee [General Gerow], February 24, 1943, DDEPP, box 46, Gerow (2).

15. George C. Marshall to DDE, Sept. 20, 1945, DDEPP, box 80, Marshall (5); DDE Memo to Joint Chiefs of Staff, Jan. 9, 1946, DEP, VII, 743; DDE to Baruch, Jan. 5, 1946, DDEPP, box 10, Baruch (4).

16. DDE Memo to JCS, Jan. 9, 1946.

17. Michael J. Hogan, *A Cross of Iron: Harry S. Truman and the Origins of the National Security State, 1945–1954* (Cambridge, U.K.: Cambridge University Press, 1998), pp. 141–156.

18. James Hershberg, *James B. Conant: Harvard to Hiroshima and the Making of the Nuclear Age* (New York: Alfred A. Knopf, 1993), p. 147.

19. DDE to JCS, Jan. 13, 1947, DEP, VIII, 1441.

20. DDE to Lauris Norstad, Feb. 5, 1947, ibid., pp. 1483–1485.

21. DDE to Edward Mead Earle, Feb. 12, 1947, DDEPP, box 37, Earle, E. M.

22. DDE to Walter Bedell Smith, Mar. 18, 1947, ibid., pp. 1609–1610.

23. DDE to JCS, May 10, 1947, ibid., pp. 1700–1701.

24. DDE to James B. Conant, Oct. 20, 1947, DDEPP, box 27, Conant (2); Conant, "The Atomic Age: A Preview 1974 Edition," DDEPP, box 27, Conant (2).

25. DDE to the Secretary of War and the Secretary of Navy, Mar. 3, 1947, DEP, VIII, 1592–1597.

26. DDE to Walter Bedell Smith, Mar. 18, 1947, ibid., p. 1609.

27. Robert H. Ferrell, ed., *The Eisenhower Diaries* (New York: W. W. Norton, 1981), p. 142.

28. DDE to Milton, May 29, 1947, DDEPP, box 174, Milton, 1946–47 (2).

29. DDE to Smith, July 3, 1947, DDEPP, box 109, Smith (1).

30. DDE to Hap [General Arnold], July 1, 1947, DDEPP, box 5, Arnold (2).

31. DDE to Thomas J. Watson, June 14, 1947, DDEPP, box 122, Watson (5); Schulz to Glidden, Aug. 29, 1961, Eisenhower Post-Presidential files [hereafter: DDEPST], box 1, DDE personals.

32. Copies of DDE Speeches and articles in DDEPP, box 21.

33. DDE to Milton, Aug. 2, 1945, DDEPP, box 174, Milton, 1944–45 (movie file).

34. William E. Robinson, notes on origin of *Crusade in Europe* (no date), William E. Robinson Personal Papers, Eisenhower Library [hereafter: WERPP], box 9, Robinson notes for book (DDE), pp. 5–6; DDE to Joseph E. Davies, Dec. 31, 1947, DDEPP, box 33, Davies J. (1).

35. Ambrose, I, 474.

36. Susan Eisenhower, *Mrs. Ike: Memories and Reflections on the Life of Mamie Eisenhower* (New York: Farrar, Straus and Giroux, 1996), pp. 248–249.

37. Cliff Roberts, Bill Robinson, George Allen, Jerry D. Brandon, and Ellis Slater; DEP, XI, 898; Susan Eisenhower, p. 250.

38. Pickett, p. 67.

39. Susan Eisenhower, p. 251.

40. List of Donors, Concert for the Benefit of the Manhattanville Neighborhood Center, Inc., Oct. 16, 1948, Mamie Doud Eisenhower Papers, Eisenhower Library, box 1, Manhattanville.

41. The members of the committee for the function to which Eisenhower was invited included Thomas J. Watson, John D. Rockefeller, Jr., and George Whitney, chairman of J. P. Morgan and Company. Winthrop Aldrich to Robert L. Shultz, Oct. 18, 1948, DDEPP, box 3, Aldrich, W.; Aldrich to DDE, July 9, 1948, ibid. Arthur M. Johnson, *Winthop W. Aldrich: Lawyer, Banker, Diplomat* (Cambridge, Mass.: Graduate School of Business Administration, Harvard University, 1968), p. 40.

42. Johnson, p. 105.

43. DEP, X, 216; Johnson, pp. 283, 313, 333, 336, 340.

44. Purposes of the Bohemian Club, DDEPP, box 181, Clubs and Associations (Bohemian Club).

   45. Julius Ochs Adler to Edwin N. Clark, Aug. 7, 1950, Edwin Clark Papers, Eisenhower Library [hereinafter: CP], box 1, American Military Institute (5); Garfield D. Merner to Clark, Aug. 12, 1950, ibid.

46. DDE to L. F. McCollum, Sept. 12, 1950, DDEPP, box 4, American Assembly (2).

47. Ibid.: DDE to Harriman, June 26, 1950, DDEPP, box 55, Harriman (5); DDE to Harry Bullis, July 10, 1950, Bullis Papers, Eisenhower Library, box 1, Album 75 (1950–52).

48. Walter H. Mallory to DDE, May 10, 1950, DDEPP, box 28, Council on Foreign Relations (3); George F. Kennan to DDE, Mar. 30, 1950, DDEPP, box 64, Kenna-Kenner Misc.; staff members included Philip Bell, Percy Bidwell, McGeorge Bundy, and William S. Dieboldt, Jr.

49. DDE to Dean G. Acheson, Dec. 2, 1948, DEP, X, 338; John Foster Dulles to DDE, Mar. 31, 1950, DDEPP, box 36, Dulles, J. F.; DDE to Smith, Dec. 22, 1949, DDEPP, box 109, Smith W. B. (1).

50. Howard S. Ellis, *Economics of Freedom: The Progress and Future of Aid to Europe* (New York: Council on Foreign Relations, 1950), pp. 481–483. In the days before Eisenhower's departure to take command of NATO forces in December 1950, at his request the group drafted a memorandum of advice and support. Richard Bissell, Oral History, Eisenhower Library, June 5, 1967, p. 4.

51. Pickett, pp. 69–70.

52. For Davenport see DEP, XI, 1191–1192; Robert E. Herzstein, *Henry R. Luce: A Political Portrait of the Man who Created the American Century* (New York: Scribner, 1994). John K. Jessup, introduction to article entitled "Luce in His Own Words," Clare Booth Luce Papers, Library of Congress, box 21, file: 10, pp. 21–23. DEP, VIII, 1835; for C. D. Jackson, see DEP, VIII, 1842, and XII, 230. DDE had lunch with Luce and Clark at 60 Morningside Drive on Oct. 6, 1950, and with media executives A. H. Sulzberger, R. E. McConnell, D. M. Black, William S. Paley, and Helen R. Reid, and Luce on Dec. 12, 1950. DEP, XI, 1646, 1655.

53. DEP, VIII, 1835.

54. R. A. Winnaker to Edwin N. Clark, Dec. 27, 1949, ECPP, box 1, American Military Institute (8).

55. Clark to Henry R. Luce, Apr. 11, 1950, ibid.

56. Luce to Clark, May 19, 1950, ECPP, box 1, American Military Institute (6); Clark to Luce, May 23, 1950, ibid.; Clark to Luce, Aug. 15, 1950, box 1, American Military Institute (5); Luce to Clark, Aug. 9, 1950, ibid.

57. It would study military history; analyze economic and political factors and their relation to American military policies; investigate current U.S. military policies; and be a repository of manuscripts and publications of former military leaders. William T. R. Fox to Clark, Jan. 9, 1952, w/ enclosure, ECPP, box 1, American Military Institute (3).

58. Ibid.; Grayson Kirk to Ralph G. Boyd, Nov. 23, 1951, ECPP, box 1, American Military Institute (4).

59. Karber and Combs, p. 408.

60. Ibid., pp. 409, 411.

61. DDE memo for Secretary James Forrestal, Jan. 31, 1948, DDEPP, box 42, Forrestal (5).

62. Robert H. Ferrell, *Harry S. Truman: A Life* (Columbia: University of Missouri Press, 1994), p. 257.

63. DDE to Forrestal, Sept. 27, 1948, DDEPP, box 42, Forrestal (4).

64. DDE to Forrestal, Nov. 4, 1948, ibid., Forrestal (3).

Chapter 4. The Finder Letter

1. Pickett, pp. 1–21.

2. Martin J. Medhurst, *Dwight D. Eisenhower: Strategic Communicator* (Westport, Conn.: Greenwood Press, 1993), p. 14.

3. James Stack Memorandum for DDE, Dec. 31, 1946, DDEPP, box 155, Presidency, 1948.

4. Medhurst, 23.

5. J. H. Michaelis to James Alan Coogan, Sept. 6, 1947, DDEPP, box 155, Presidency, 1948.

6. DDE to Smith, Sept. 18, 1947, DDEPP, box 109, Smith, W. B. (2); DDE to Milton, Oct. 16, 1947.

7. Ambrose, I, 421.

8. Medhurst, pp. 14–15.

9. Medhurst, p. 12.

10. Ferrell, pp. 142–143.

11. Smith to DDE, Sept. 3, 1947, DDEPP, box 109, Smith, W. B. (2).

12. Robinson, Stray Notes on Pre-nomination, 1952–1952, pp. 1–2, WERPP, box 9, Robinson notes for book (DDE).

13. Robinson notes on visit with DDE, Oct. 17, 1947, WERPP, box 1, Eisen, (Personal), 1944–1947.

14. Robinson, Stray Notes, pp. 1–2; ibid.

15. Robinson, notes on the origin, pp. 3, 4, 7.

16. Hazlett to DDE, Oct. 25, 1947, DDEPP, box 56, Hazlett (4).

17. DDE to Hazlett, Oct. 29, 1947, ibid.

18. Perret, p. 529.

19. DDE to Hazlett, Oct. 29, 1947; Perret, p. 529.

20. Joseph Grew to Leonard V. Finder, Feb. 15, 1948, Finder Papers, Eisenhower Library [hereafter: FP], Box 2, file: Manchester Comm. Forum, 1947–48.

21. DDE to Finder, Oct. 6, 1947, FP, box 1, Finder–DDE corresp. 1947–51; DDE to Finder, Oct. 21, 1947, ibid.

22. Finder to DDE, Jan. 12, 1948, ibid.

23. Kevin McCann, Oral History, Eisenhower Library, Dec. 21, 1966 [hereafter: McCann OH], pp. 4, 113.

24. DDE to Finder, Jan. 22, 1948, DDEPP, box 41, Finder (5).

25. Burnham to DDE, Jan. 23, 1948, DDEPP, box 15, Burnham (6).

26. Finder to DDE, Jan. 26, 1948, DDEPP, box 41, Finder (5); DDE to Finder, Jan. 27, 1948, ibid.

27. Thomas D. Campbell to Milton Eisenhower, Jan. 24, 1948, DDEPP, box 174, Milton 1946–47 (3).

28. DDE to Smith, Jan. 28, 1948, DDEPP, box 109, Smith, W. B. (2).

29. Smith to DDE, Feb. 10, 1948, ibid.

30. Thomas W. Mattingly and Olive F. G. Marsh, "A Compilation of the General Health Status of Dwight D. Eisenhower," Mattingly Papers, Eisenhower Library [hereafter: TMPP], pp. 68, 78–79, box 1, Gen. Health (1).

31. Robert J. Sherwood to John Hoagland, Mar. 25, 1948, DDEPP, box 25, Winchell, Walter.

32. Ibid.; Memorandum of Black visit w/ DDE, Mar. 29, 1948, WERPP, box 1, Eisen. (Pers) 1948. Robinson to Eisenhower, Mar. 31, 1948, ibid.

33. Robinson to DDE, Mar. 31, 1948.

34. Ibid.; Robinson to Helen Reid, Mar. 24, 1948, ibid.

35. Robinson to DDE, Mar. 31, 1948.

Chapter 5. Behind the Scenes

1. William E. Leuchtenburg, *In the Shadow of FDR: Harry Truman to Ronald Reagan* (Ithaca, N.Y.: Cornell University Press, 1985), pp. 25–29.

2. DDE to Finder, Jan. 22, 1948, DDEPP, box 41, Finder (5).

3. Michael Schaller, *Douglas MacArthur: The Far Eastern General* (New York: Oxford University Press, 1989), pp. 147, 152; Harold Ickes diary, Michigan State University, Jan. 25, 1948; Harry Vaughn, Oral History, Truman Library, pp. 119–120.

4. "Republicans Back to Normal," *Time*, Feb. 2, 1948.

5. Schaller, pp. 147, 152; Perret, p. 530.

6. James Forrestal to Harry S. Truman [hereafter: HST], Jan. 22, 1948, Papers of Harry S. Truman, President's Secretary's files [HSTPS], box 118, Gen. File, Eisenhower, DD.

7. Roy Roberts, "A Patriot's Act," *Kansas City Star*, Jan. 27, 1948, in Roberts to DDE, Jan. 27, 1948, DDEPP, box 99, Roberts, Roy A.; Ray Sherer, videotape of a symposium, "The Great Crusade: The Road to the White House, 1952," Eisenhower Library, Abilene, Kans., Nov. 6, 1992.

8. DDE to Ernest Lindley, June 19, 1948, DEP Vo. X, pp. 119–120.

9. Robinson, Stray incidents; Robinson to Leo Perper, June 12, 1948, Robinson Papers, Eisenhower Library [hereafter: RP], box 1, Eisen (Gen.), Jan.–June 1948.

10. Forrestal Memorandum, Mar. 26, 1948, Eben Ayers Papers, Truman Library [hereafter: AP], box 6, general file: D. D. Eisenhower.

11. Claude Pepper to Finder, June 26, 1948 , Finder Papers, Eisenhower Library [hereafter: FP], box 1, Corres. Re: DDE, 1947–51.

12. Finder to Pepper, June 29, 1948, ibid.

13. DEP, X, 125, note 2.

14. Ickes diary, July 3, 1948; McCullough, pp. 612, 613; Phillips, pp. 200, 211.

15. DDE for Mr. Harron, July 5, 1948, Whitman DDE diary, Eisenhower Library [hereafter: WHIT], box 45, DDE dictation; Jules Abels, *Out of the Jaws of Victory* (New York: Holt, 1959), p. 75. Privately he was telling those around him that "all his associations were Republican—his upraising, his background" and most of his family. Kevin McCann, Oral History, Eisenhower Library [hereafter: McCann OH], Dec. 21, 1966, p. 8.

16. DDE to James Roosevelt, July 8, 1948, DEP, X, 129; Robert J. Donovan, *Conflict and Crisis: The Presidency of Harry S. Truman, 1945–1948* (New York: W. W. Norton, 1977), p. 404; Truman's memories about DDE's attitude toward his running for office were that the general had said, "No, I don't think any military man should run for President." Truman Personal Papers–Memoirs, Truman Library, box 5, politics, 1948.

17. Joseph E. Davies to DDE, July 9, 1948, DDEPP, box 33, Davies, J. (1).

18. DDE to Davies, July 16, 1948, ibid.

19. Cliff Roberts, Oral History, Columbia University, Sept. 12, 1968, p. 29.

20. Eben Ayers diary, July 6, 1948, AP box 16, diary, 1948.

21. William Benton to DDE, July 2, 1948, DDEPP, box 10, Benton, W. (2).

22. Robert H. Ferrell, *Harry S. Truman: A Life* (Columbia: University of Missouri Press, 1994), p. 269.

23. C. D. Jackson, Jan. 4, 1954, C. D. Jackson Papers, Eisenhower Library, box 41, Time Inc. Eisenhower thru 1956 (2).

24. Herbert Brownell, Oral History, Eisenhower Library, Jan. 25, 1967, pp. 13–15.

25. Finder to DDE, Jan. 30, 1948, DDEPP, box 41, Finder (5).

26. Finder to Mother and Dad, Feb. 5, 1947 [year probably should be 1948], FP, box 1, family correspondence, re: Eisenhower, 1947–51.

27. Finder to Mother and Dad, Jan. 30, 1948, FP, box 1, Finder family correspondence, re: DDE.

28. Finder memorandum of meeting with DDE on Feb. 10, 1948, at Fort Myer, Virginia, Mar. 31 or Apr. 2, 1948, DDEPP, box 41, Finder (5); Finder, "Eisenhower Can Be Drafted," manuscript of article, FP, box 1, Finder on DDE, 1948–1955.

29. Finder memorandum of conversation with Roy Roberts, Feb. 16–17, 1948, FP, box 2, Interview Notes.

30. Finder telegram to DDE, Mar. 29, 1948, FP, box 1, DDE correspondence, 1947–51; Finder to DDE, Apr. 26, 1948, ibid.

31. Finder to DDE, Apr. 5, 1948, FP, ibid.

32. Ambrose, p. 464.

33. DDE to Davies, Feb. 6, 1948, DDEPP, box 33, Davies (2).

34. DDE to William H. Burnham, Jan. 29, 1948, DDEPP, box 15, Burnham (6).

35. Burnham to DDE, July 14, 1948, ibid.

36. DDE to Marquis Childs, July 8, 1948, DEP, X, 128–129.

37. DDE to Harold Stassen, July 12, 1948, DEP, X, 141–142; 143, note 3.

38. Ambrose, p. 464.

39. For a biographical sketch of Edwin N. Clark, see DEP, VII, 1674, and XII, 48–49; see also Clark to Ralph Kent, Mar. 31, 1971, Clark Papers, Eisenhower Library [hereafter: CP], box 4, correspondence, 1933–81 (1); DDE to Russell Davenport June 30, 1950, DEP, XI, 1191–1192.

40. Perhaps the largest obstacle to this was Eisenhower's belief that it would be unseemly for him to benefit personally from a motion picture about his participation in a war. DDE to Clark, Nov. 3, 1948, DEP, X, 279–280.

41. Clark to DDE, July 23, 1947, DDEPP, box 23, Clark, E. N. (2); DDE to Clark, July 24, 1947, ibid.

42. Edwin N. Clark, "Eisenhower for President: Pre-Convention Activities," (draft manuscript, nd, CP, box 4, CV: DDE for Pres. [hereafter: CEFP]), p. 10.; DDEPP, box 127, file: appointment schedule, Mar. 1948–Dec. 1950 (3); DEP, X, 139.

43. CEFP, p. 11.

44. Ibid., p. 10.

45. Ibid., p. 11.

46. Ibid., p. 12.

47. Ferrell, *Truman*, p. 278.

48. Ibid., p. 281.

49. DDE to Thomas E. Dewey, Sept. 10, 1948, DEP, X, 184.

50. Roberts, OH, pp. 38–39.

51. Roberts, OH, pp. 37, 147–148.

52. Richard Norton Smith, *Thomas E. Dewey and His Times* (New York: Simon and Schuster, 1982), pp. 505–506.

53. Elmer Davis to Joseph E. Davies, Nov. 27, 1948, in Davies to DDE, Dec. 3, 1948, DDEPP, box 33, Davies (1); Dwight D. Eisenhower, *Crusade in Europe* (New York: Avon Books, 1948), p. 471.

54. Edward Mead Earle, "The Man Who Might Have Been President: Dwight D. Eisenhower," *Atlantic Monthly* (December 1948), DDEPP, box 123, Wedemeyer (1).

55. DDE to Clark, Nov. 3, 1948, DEP, X, 279–280, notes 1 and 2.

56. DDE to Douglas MacArthur, Dec. 7, 1948, DDEPP, box 74, MacArthur, D. (1).

Chapter 6. The Communist Menace

1. Roberts, OH, p. 451.

2. DDE to H. H. Arnold, Mar. 14, 1949, DDEPP, box 5, Arnold (1).

3. ASB 508, Advanced Study Branch, Plans Group, P&O Division, General Staff, United States Army, "Pattern of War in the Atomic Warfare Age," DDEPP, box 127, Atomic Weapons and Energy (1) [hereafter: Pattern], p. 3.

4. Ibid., pp. 8–9.

5. Ibid., pp. 10, 13.

6. Robert R. Bowie and Richard H. Immerman, *Waging Peace: How Eisenhower Shaped an Enduring Cold War Strategy* (New York: Oxford University Press, 1998), p. 13.

7. Ibid., pp. 14–15.

8. John McCone, Oral History, July 26, 1976, p. 4; Conant to Karl T. Compton, Sept. 18, 1949, DDEPP, box 62, Johnson, L. (2); DDE to Edwin F. Black, Oct. 5, 1949, ibid.

9. DDE to Bernard Baruch, Oct. 10, 1949, DDEPP, box 10, Baruch (2).

10. Churchill elaborated this view. A nuclear threat, he said, was needed to deter a Soviet offensive in Europe. David Holloway, *Stalin and the Bomb: The Soviet Union and Atomic Energy, 1939–1956* (New Haven: Yale University Press, 1994), p. 229.

11. Bowie and Immerman, p. 16.

12. W. Stuart Symington memorandum to Secretary Johnson, Nov. 8, 1949, in Symington to DDE, Nov. 10, 1949, DDEPP, box 113, Symington, W. S. (2). Highlighting the seriousness of the situation was an extract from a report that arrived in Eisenhower's office three months later. It was dated June 1949, and its author was Dr. Walter Dornberger, former commanding officer of the German guided missile development center at Peenemunde. Russia, it said, had obtained from its liberation and occupation of Germany the three industries essential for modern war in which it had been deficient: aeronautical, electrical, and optical. The Soviets thus had the capability to build both a "strong up-to-date air defense, including guided anti-aircraft missiles, and long range guided missiles." Symington to DDE, Feb. 27, 1950, ibid., containing extract from a report prepared for AEDC by Dr. Walter Dornberger, June 1949, and James R. Dempsey memorandum for Thomas G. Lanphier, Jr., Feb. 16, 1950.

13. Bowie and Immerman, p. 14.

14. DDE memorandum for the Secretary of Defense, July 14, 1949, DDEPP, box 62, Johnson (2).

15. Bowie and Immerman, p. 15. For additional background and analysis of this planning activity, see Melvyn P. Leffler, *A Preponderance of Power: National Security, the Truman Administration, and the Cold War* (Stanford, Calif.: Stanford University Press, 1992), p. 276.

16. DDE memorandum for the Secretary of Defense, Feb. 4, 1949, DDEPP, box 42, Forrestal (1); DDE notes used in conversation with President Truman, Feb. 9, 1949, DDEPP, box 116, Truman (2); DDE note to Forrestal, Feb. 25, 1949, DDEPP, box 42, Forrestal (1).

17. Bowie and Immerman, p. 14.

18. Bowie and Immerman, p. 22; Leffler, pp. 264–265.

19. HST to DDE, Aug. 11, 1949, DDEPP, box 116, Truman (2).

20. Bowie and Immerman, p. 17.

21. Ibid., p. 21.

22. Ibid., p. 22.

23. Ibid., p. 19.

24. Hershberg, p. 496.

25. Smith to Charlton Ogburn, May 2, 1949, BSP, box 26, correspondence of military or historical signif. (1).

26. Lucius Clay, Oral History, Mar. 13, 1971, p. 760.

27. John W. O'Daniel to S. LeRoy Irwin, Feb. 1, 1950, DDEPP, box 87, OD-OE.

28. Holloway, p. 247.

29. Ibid., pp. 232, 264, 267, 272.

30. DDE, Oral History, Eisenhower Library [hereafter: DDE, OH], July 13, 1967, p. 10.

31. Holloway, p. 264.

32. Walter Bedell Smith to Kenneth Strong, July 26, 1950, Bedell Smith Papers, Eisenhower Library [hereafter: BSP], box 26, correspondence on military or historical significance (1); for a similar analysis see Symington to DDE, July 17, 1950, enclosure of July 15, 1950.

33. DDE to Symington, July 31, 1950, DDEPP, box 113, Symington, W. S. (1).

34. Ferrell, p. 175; DDE to Strong, June 29, 1950, DDEPP, box 112, Strong, K.

35. DDE to Johnson, July 31, 1950, DDEPP, box 62, Johnson, L. (1).

36. DDE to Harriman, June 16, 1950, DDEPP, box 55, Harriman (5).

37. Strong to DDE, Sept. 29, 1950, DDEPP, box 37, Strong, K.; DDE to Strong, Nov. 6, 1950, DDEPP, box 112, Strong.

38. Holloway, p. 272.

39. DDE to MacArthur, Oct. 28, 1950, DDEPP, box 74, MacArthur (1).

40. MacArthur to DDE, Nov. 4, 1950, ibid.

41. List of participants, College Presidents' Conference, Waldorf Astoria Hotel, Sept. 28, 1950, DDEPP, box 27, Committee for the Present Danger, and box 136, Conference, Roundtable; Conant memorandum for conference of Sept. 28, 1950, in Conant to DDE, Sept. 22, 1950, DDEPP, box 27, Conant (1).

42. Ferrell, *Truman*, p. 260.

43. DDE to Conant, Sept. 16, 1950, DDEPP, box 27, Conant (1).

44. DDE to George C. Marshall, Oct. 18, 1950, DDEPP, box 80, Marshall (4); Marshall to DDE Jan. 23, 1950, ibid.

45. Roy Roberts to DDE, Oct. 4, 1950, DDEPP, box 99, Roberts, Roy.

46. DDE to Roy Roberts, Oct. 9, 1950, ibid.

47. Hershberg, p. 494.

48. Ibid.

49. Ibid., p. 498.

50. Ibid., p. 272.

51. Ibid., p. 496.

52. Ibid., p. 497.

53. "The guest list shown at the College Presidents' Conference held at the Waldorf on September 28, 1950, was the forerunner and 'cover' for the activities of a group known as the Committee for the Present Danger. DDE withdrew from the activities which are described in various parts of the file." Robert L. Schulz memorandum, Nov. 1, 1952, DDEPP, box 27, Committee for the Present Danger.

54. Hershberg, p. 496.

55. Ibid., pp. 498–500, 504; Emergency surgery prevented Conant from attending the Waldorf conference, but he sent Eisenhower his thoughts. The allied purpose, he said—referreing to Czechoslovakia—was to prevent the remainder of Western Europe from "going the way of Czechoslovakia."

Nobody can be sure, he said, that the Russians would not occupy Western Europe without the existence of the U.S. strategic air force and ground defense. With the "uncertain technological [atomic] arms race now in progress," the possibility existed that the Kremlin [leaders] might consider themselves by 1952–1954 to have countered American air power and might decide to start a war to obtain their goal. As a "guide to policy," he said—and this was perhaps the key point—it would be dangerous to proceed on any other basis. He recommended both American assistance in rearming Western Europe and two years of military service in the United States for every American male between the ages of eighteen and twenty. The latter, he said, would allow the United States to keep 3.5 to 5 million men under arms. Conant to DDE, Sept. 22, 1950.

56. Bowie and Immerman, p. 23.

57. Ibid., p. 24.

58. Lawrence S. Kaplan, *The Long Entanglement: NATO's First Fifty Years* (Westport, Conn.: Praeger, 1999), pp. 7–22.

59. Thomas G. Patterson and J. Garry Clifford, *America Ascendant: U.S. Foreign Relations Since 1939* (Lexington, Mass.: D. C. Health, 1995), p. 77.

60. Alfred G. Gruenther to DDE, Sept. 12, 1950, DDEPP, box 48, Gruenther (1).

61. HST to DDE, Oct. 19, 1950, DDEPP, box 116, Truman (1); DDE, OH, July 20, 1967, p. 9.

62. Schulz, OH, July 23, 1972, Eisenhower Library, p. 184.

63. DDE to Hazlett, Nov. 1, 1950, DDEPP, box 56, Hazlett (2).

64. Kaplan, p. 21.

65. Paul T. Carroll to DDE, Nov. 19, 1950, DDEPP, box 21, Carroll, Paul T.; DDE to Gruenther, Nov. 30, 1950, DDEPP, box 48, Gruenther (1); DDE to Winston Churchill, Dec. 6, 1950, DDEPP, box 22, Churchill (2); DDE to Marshall, Dec. 12, 1950, DDEPP, box 80, Marshall (3); Arthur S. Nevins to DDE, Dec. 14, 1950, DDEPP, box 28, Council on Foreign Relations (2).

66. DDE to President Truman, Dec. 16, 1950, DDEPP, box 116, Truman, H. S. (2).

67. DDE to Harriman, Dec. 30, 1950, DDEPP, box 55, Harriman (5); DDE to Ferdinand Eberstadt, DDEPP, box 37, Eberstadt, Ferd. (1).

Chapter 7. The Politics of National Security

1. DDE to Hazlett, Feb. 24, 1950, DDEPP, box 56, Hazlett (2).
2. Dwight D. Eisenhower, *At Ease: Stories I Tell to Friends* (New York: Avon Books, 1967), p. 337.
3. DDE to Johnson, May 25, 1949, DDEPP, box 62, Johnson, L. (3); DDE to Johnson, May 3, 1949, ibid.
4. The discovery of evidence by his cardiologist, Mattingly, and confirmed by historian Robert Ferrell, that it was a life-threatening heart attack and that Snyder was attending to the general's political viability is in keeping with evidence of Eisenhower's partisan interests that began as early as the summer of 1948. Robert H. Ferrell, *Ill Advised: Presidential Health and Public Trust* (Columbia: University of Missouri Press, 1992), pp. 68–71. A more recent study by Clarence G. Lasby entitled *Eisenhower's Heart Attack: How Ike Beat Heart Disease and Held onto the Presidency* (Lawrence: University Press of Kansas, 1997) doubts that Eisenhower suffered a heart attack before 1955. The individual who later was perhaps Eisenhower's closest confidant, Clifford Roberts, believed Eisenhower's ileitis attacks were related to stress and that high blood pressure followed. He saw "a connection between stomach upsets and heart strain, not only with his illness in Denver [1955], but in subsequent heart attacks." Clifford Roberts, *The Story of the Augusta National Golf Club* (Garden City, N.Y.: Doubleday, 1976, pp. 165–166.
5. Robinson, Stray Notes, pp. 3–4.
6. DDE interview by David Lawrence for *U.S. News and World Report*, Jan. 17, 1950, DDEPP, box 70, Lawrence, D.
7. Lawrence to DDE, Mar. 4, 1952, ibid.
8. Robinson to DDE, Mar. 4, 1949, DDEPP, box 99, Robinson (6).
9. Robinson to DDE, May 5, 1949, ibid.
10. William Burnham phone memorandum concerning L. F. McCollum, May 8, 1950, DDEPP, box 75, McCollum L. F. (2).
11. Burnham to DDE, May 15, 1950, DDEPP, box 15, Burnham (5); Eisenhower, elated, asked Burnham to discuss with McCollum and others the proposition that the chief responsibility of "our educational institutions is to establish a sharper understanding of the American system"—the value of opportunity free from government control, "the dignity of work and thrift." Universities, he insisted, must do more than concentrate on the "material betterment of their graduates." DDE to Burnham, ibid.
12. Ferrell, *Eisenhower Diaries*, pp. 161–162.
13. Robert K. Merton memorandum to DDE, et al., concerning "An Inventory of Communications Addressed to General Eisenhower in the Spring of 1948: A Summary and Digest," as per their conversation of July 19, 1949, DDEPP, box 155, Presidency, 1948.
14. Robert K. Merton, "An Inventory of Communications Addressed to General Eisenhower in the Spring of 1948: A Summary and Digest" (Bureau of Applied Social Research, Columbia University, September 1949), p. 14.

15. Ibid., p. 17.

16. Ibid., p. 22.

17. Ibid., pp. 12–13.

18. Leila Sussman to author, Feb. 26, 1997, and Joan D. Goldhamer to author, May 4, 1997.

19. Joan D. Goldhamer, "Eisenhower in Academe: A Clash of Perspectives and a Study Suppressed," *Journal of the History of the Behavioral Sciences,* XXXIII (Summer 1997), 254.

20. Robinson to DDE, Sept. 6, 1949, RP, box 1, Eisen. (pers), 1949.

21. Robinson, "Eisenhower—A Special Note" concerning Truman's offer of the Democratic nomination for United States senator from New York, Aug. 29, 1949, ibid.

22. Clarence Budington Kelland to Robinson (nd) in Robinson to Kelland, Sept. 9, 1949, RP, box 1, Eisen. (Gen.), 1949; Robinson to Ellis D. Slater, Sept. 9, 1949, ibid.

23. Ferrell, *Eisenhower Diaries,* pp. 163–164; DEP 8, p. 757.

24. DDE to Clare Booth Luce, Oct. 1, 1949, DEP, X, 764.

25. Ferrell, *Eisenhower Diaries,* p. 164.

26. Ibid., p. 165.

27. Ibid., p. 166.

28. Ibid., pp. 169–173.

29. DEP, XI, 888.

30. DEP, XI, 1040, note 4.

31. Ibid., pp. 1043, 1046.

32. Ibid., p. 1045.

33. J. Earl Schaefer to DDE, Aug. 26, 1950, DDEPP, box 106, Schaefer (2).

34. He said that as chief of staff he had recommended more and better equipment, more protection for Alaska, and universal military training; and that later, as temporary presiding officer of the joint chiefs, he had sought a $15 billion defense budget, which had then been cut to $13.2 billion. DDE to Schaefer, Aug. 31, 1950, Earl Schaefer Papers, Eisenhower Library, box 1, Eisen/Schaefer personal (1).

35. Kenneth C. Royall to DDE, Aug. 1, 1950, DDEPP, box 100, Royal, K. (2).

36. Freeman to DDE, Sept. 6, 1950, DDEPP, box 43, Freeman, D. S.

37. DDE to Freeman, Sept. 12, 1950, ibid.

38. Ferrell, *Eisenhower Diaries,* pp. 177–78.

39. George Lodge, "The Campaign to Win the Republican Nomination for Dwight D. Eisenhower, November 16, 1951–July 12, 1952," as told to Lodge by his father, Henry Cabot Lodge, Jr. (unpublished manuscript, 39 pp.), Whitman Administrative Series, Eisenhower Library, box 23, Lodge campaign memo. p. 1.

40. Henry Cabot Lodge, Jr. [hereafter: Lodge] memorandum entitled "Estimate of the Situation," June 2, 1950, Confidential Journal, Henry Cabot Lodge, Jr., Papers, Series II, Massachusetts Historical Society, Boston, Mass. [hereafter: LP-II].

41. Eisenhower's speech at American Legion groundbreaking ceremonies, Aug. 19, 1950, Denver, Colorado, RP, box 1, Eisen. (Gen.) 1950.

42. Robinson to Freeman F. Gosden, Sept. 13, 1950, ibid.; DEP, XII, 337.

43. Burnham to DDE, July 31, 1950, DDEPP, box 15, Burnham (4).

44. CEFP, p. 15.

45. Clark to DDE, Jan. 16, 1950, and Feb. 9, 1950, DDEPP, box 23, Clark, E. (1).

46. Brownlee to DDE, Feb. 24, 1950; DDE to Brownlee, Mar. 17, 1950.

47. Alan R. Raucher, *Paul G. Hoffman: Architect of Foreign Aid* (Lexington: University of Kentucky Press, 1985), pp. 17, 24, 37, 58.

48. Ibid., p. 51.

49. Ibid., p. 52.

50. Ibid., pp. 54, 58.

51. Ibid., p. 63.

52. Ibid., p. 60.

53. Ibid., p. 59.

54. Ibid., pp. 60, 62.

55. Ibid., pp. 82, 85–86.

56. Lodge memorandum of conversation with DDE, Nov. 30, 1950, LP. That the situation was perhaps not quite so dire he revealed in a letter to George C. Marshall on December 12. The president, he told his former boss, "clearly indicated that he would not ask me to undertake this task unless the advance political and military arrangements were such as to give justifiable promise of success." DDE to Marshall, Dec. 12, 1950, DDEPP, box 80, Marshall (3); Marshall to DDE, Dec. 21, 1950, ibid.

57. Robinson to Ralph D. Moores, Oct. 27, 1950, RP, box 1, Eisen (Gen), 1950.

58. Robinson to John Orr Young, Nov. 1, 1950, ibid.

59. CEFP, pp. 17–19.

60. Ibid., p. 26.

61. Russell W. Davenport to DDE, Nov. 28, 1950, DDEPP, box 33, Davenport, R. W.; DDE to Davenport, Dec. 5, 1950, ibid.

62. Burnham to DDE, Dec. 27, 1950, DDEPP, box 15, Burnham (3).

63. CEFP, pp. 20–21, 28–29; Burnham to DDE, Dec. 7, 1951, DDEPP, box 15, Burnham (1).

Chapter 8. NATO Command

1. DEP, XII, 7.

2. J. H. Burns memorandum for James S. Lay, Jr., Apr. 5, 1951, Elsey Papers, Truman Library, box 65, Foreign Rel., West Eur. Defense.

3. Susan Eisenhower, p. 256.

4. Transcript of DDE's meeting with HST and the Cabinet, Jan. 31, 1951, Elsey Papers, Truman Library [hereafter EP], box 73, Korea–DDE's report to cabinet, p. 3.

5. Pickett, p. 79.

6. Transcript of DDE's meeting, pp. 2, 10.

7. Ibid., p. 12.

8. Ibid., p. 8.

9. Ibid., p. 13.

10. Ibid., p. 16.

11. DDE's report to Congress, "Unity of Purpose Urged for Security of North Atlantic Area," *Department of State Bulletin*, Feb. 12, 1951, EP, box 65, For. Rel. W. Eur. Defense, pp. 246, 248.

12. Ibid., p. 245.

13. Ibid.

14. Edward J. Bermingham to DDE, Feb. 14, 1951, DDEPP, box 11, Bermingham (4).

15. William B. Pickett, *Homer E. Capehart: A Senator's Life, 1897–1979* (Indianapolis: Indiana Historical Society, 1990), p. 122.

16. James T. Patterson, *Mr. Republican: A Biography of Robert A. Taft* (New York: Houghton-Mifflin, 1972), pp. 456, 469.

17. Ibid., pp. 470–471.

18. Ibid., p. 470.

19. Ferrell, *Truman*, p. 336.

20. Patterson, p. 477.

21. Ibid., pp. 474–475.

22. Ibid., pp. 449, 505.

23. Ibid., p. 473.

24. CEFP, pp. 23–25; Andrew J. Goodpaster to the author, Nov. 17, 1998.

25. DDE, OH, July 20, 1967, p. 13.

26. DDE to Robinson, Feb. 16, 1951, RP, box 1, Jan.–Mar. 1951.

27. Susan Eisenhower, pp. 254–257.

28. Susan Eisenhower, p. 256.

29. Susan Eisenhower, pp. 257–258. It would be a compound with four or five other buildings that housed their personal staffs, including the Snyders, the Drys, the Gruenthers, Colonel Cannon and his family, and Lieutenant Colonel Robert L. Schulz, aide to General Eisenhower, and his wife. Schulz to Clifford Roberts, Mar. 7, 1951, RP, box 1, Eisen (pers), Jan.–Mar. 1951.

30. Eisenhower memorandum on his objective as SACEUR, Kevin McCann Papers, Eisenhower Library [hereafter MP], box 1, Misc. notes.

31. Rear Admiral L. C. Stevens address to the National War College, "A National Strategy for the Soviet Union," Jan. 25, 1951, DDEPP, box 55, Harriman (4), p. 36.

32. Ibid., p. 13.

33. Ibid., pp. 20–21.

34. Ibid., p. 27.

35. Ibid., p. 29.

36. DDE to Stevens, Feb. 22, 1951, DEP, XII, 61. In his diary a few days later, he wrote that "[he had read] a remarkable paper on [the] Soviets, by an Admiral Stevens. I think I'll put it in back of this book because, with minor exceptions, it represents my beliefs exactly. But he states the thing clearly." DEP, XII, 90.

37. Alfred Gruenther, Oral History, Eisenhower Library, Apr. 20, 1967, pp. 29, 31.

38. Tapes of Oval Office conversations preceding DDE's meeting with Senator Alexander Smith, Aug. 12, 1954, Eisenhower Library.

39. Henry M. Wriston, Oral History, Jan. 4, 1968, pp. 12–13.

40. Clay to DDE, Mar. 1, 1951, DDEPP, box 24, Clay (6).

41. DDE to Ed Bermingham, Apr. 20, 1951, DDEPP, box 11, Bermingham, E. J. (4).

42. DDE to Bermingham, Feb. 28, 1951 and Bermingham to Ike Mar. 23, 1951, ibid.

43. List of Contributors, The American Assembly, Nov. 10, 1950, DDEPP, box 4, Am. Assy. (2).

44. L. W. Douglas wire to Paul Douglas [nd, probably 1951], DDEPP, box 126, Young, Phil.

45. Cliff Roberts [hereafter: Cliff] to DDE, Apr. 10, 1951, DDEPP, box 98, Roberts, C. (5); DDE to Cliff, Apr. 16, 1951, ibid.; DDE to Philip D. Reed, May 2, 1951, DDEPP, box 97, Reed, Phil.

46. Bowie and Immerman, p. 24.

47. DDE to HST, Feb. 24, 1951, DDEPP, box 116, Truman (1).

48. Kaplan, p. 137.

49. Kaplan, pp. 61–62.

50. Bowie and Immerman, pp. 25–26.

51. Harriman to DDE, Apr. 9, 1951, DDEPP, box 55, Harriman (4).

52. DDE to Harriman, Apr. 20, 1951, ibid.

53. DDE to Harriman, July 9, 1951, DDEPP, box 55, Harriman (5); Edward Meade Earle to DDE July 10, 1951, DDEPP, box 37, Earle; DDE to Marshall, Aug. 3, 1951, DDEPP, box 80, Marshall (1); DDE to Harriman, Sept. 6, 1951, box 55, Harriman (1); Harriman to DDE, Sept. 19, 1951, ibid.

54. Bowie and Immerman, p. 26.

55. Ibid., p. 27.

56. Tom Deligiannis, "Vanguards of the Tactical Nuclear Revolution: Early Army Thinking About the Tactical Use of Atomic Weapons, 1948–1949" (paper presented at the annual meeting of the Society for Historians of American Foreign Relations, University of Colorado, June 1996), pp. 8–9.

57. Ibid., pp. 5–6, 9–10.

58. Ibid., pp. 13, 22–23.

59. Robert A. Wampler, "Nuclear Learning and Nuclear Teaching: The Eisenhower Administration, Nuclear Weapons and NATO Strategy, 1953–1960" (paper presented at the annual meeting of the Society for Historians of American Foreign Relations, Vassar College, June 1995), pp. 4–5.

60. Ibid., pp. 1, 6–7.

61. Lodge, Memorandum for Confidential Journal, Apr. 10, 1951, LP-II, confidential journal, 1948–1963; Lodge to Wilton B. Persons, July 2, 1951, LP-II; Harriman to DDE, Nov. 17, 1951, DDEPP, box 55, Harriman (1); Harriman to HST, Nov. 21, 1951, HST Library, P.P.F.—1191.

62. Harriman to HST, Nov. 21, 1951; HST to Harriman, Nov. 30, 1951, ibid.; HST to Harriman, Nov. 30, 1951, ibid.; DDE to Bob Lovett, Dec. 19, 1951, DDEPP, box 72, Lovett (1).

Chapter 9. Political Fires

1. Finder to Thomas E. Dewey, Jan. 27, 1951, FP, box 1, corres. re: DDE 1947–51.

2. Dewey to Finder, Jan. 31, 1951, ibid.

3. Finder to DDE, Jan. 28, 1951, FP, box 1, Finder–DDE corres., 1947–51.

4. CEFP, pp. 29–31. Clark's trips to Paris had no other purpose than discussions about a possible Eisenhower candidacy. Burnham, after he arrived in Paris, and Clay, also traveling back and forth, were working clandestinely for the same purpose. The

problem was that people recognized them. Burnham to DDE, Feb. 23, 1951; DDE to
Clay, Aug. 25, 1951.

5. Burnham to DDE, Apr. 4, 1951, DDEPP, box 15, Burnham (2).

6. DDE to Clark, Mar. 10, 1951.

7. McCann, OH, Dec. 21, 1966, p. 96; Clay, OH, Dec. 9, 1970, p. 283.

8. Ibid.

9. Perret, pp. 77, 143.

10. Ibid., p. 57.

11. Bermingham to DDE, Mar. 23, 1951, RP, b.1, Eisen (pers) Jan.–Mar. 1951.

12. Robinson to DDE, Apr. 20, 1951, RP, b.1, Eisen (pers) Apr.–Aug. 1951.

13. Patterson, pp. 477–478.

14. Perret, p. 574.

15. Clay to DDE, Apr. 13, 1951, DDEPP, box 24, Clay (6).

16. DDE to Clay, Apr. 16, 1951, ibid.

17. Cliff to DDE, Apr. 18, 1951, RP, box 1, Eisen (pers) Apr.–Aug. 1951.

18. Finder to DDE, Apr. 14, 1951, FP, box 1, Finder–DDE corres. 1947–51; Finder
to DDE, May 9, 1951, ibid.

19. HST to Harriman, Apr. 24, 1951, DDEPP, box 116, Truman (1).

20. HST to DDE, Apr. 12, 1951, ibid.

21. DDE to Hazlett, June 21, 1951, DDEPP, box 56, Hazlett (2).

22. DDE to MacArthur, May 15, 1951, and MacArthur to DDE, May 18, 1951,
DDEPP, box 74, MacArthur (1).

23. DDE to Henry R. Luce, Apr. 17, 1951, DDEPP, box 72, Luce H.

24. Luce to DDE, Apr. 24, 1951, ibid.

25. DEP, XII, 818.

26. Richard Norton Smith, p. 577; Clay to DDE, May 18, 1951; DDEPP, box 24,
Clay (6).

27. Richard Norton Smith, p. 577.

28. Milton Eisenhower to DDE, May 17, 1951 and DDE to Milton, May 30, 1951,
DDEPP, box 174, Milton, 1951–52 (2); William E. Robinson to DDE, May 19, 1951,
DDEPP, box 99, Robinson (3).

29. DDE to Clay, May 30, 1951, DDEPP, box 24, Clay (6).

30. George Allen to DDE, June 6, 1951, DDEPP, box 4, Allen, George.

31. Clay to DDE, June 12, 1951, DDEPP, box 24, Clay (6).

32. Finder to DDE, Aug. 25, 1951, DDEPP, box 41, Finder (2).

33. Finder to DDE, June 27, 1951.

34. Robinson memo of trip to Paris, June 29–July 8, 1951, Robinson Papers, b.1,
Eisen (pers) Apr.–Aug. 1951. Letters of support came during the summer from George
Whitney and Dewitt Wallace, editor of *Reader's Digest.* Whitney to DDE, June 12,
1951, DDEPP, box 123, G. Whitney; Wallace to DDE, June 26, 1951, DDEPP, box 119,
Wallace, B-S (Misc.). Joseph Davies told him in August that "many believe Truman
will not be a candidate if you were [to be] nominated." Davies to DDE, Aug. 21, 1951.

35. Lodge, "Personal Interview with General Eisenhower," July 16, 1951, LP-II.

36. Ibid.

37. Ibid.

38. Robinson to Cliff Roberts Memorandum of Aug. 8, 1951, RP, box 1, Eisen (pers) Jan.–Mar. 1951; DDE to Robinson, Oct. 1, 1953, RP, box 2, Eisen (personal), 1953.

39. Cliff to Robinson, Aug. 27, 1951, RP, box 1, Eisen (pers) Sept.–Dec. 1951.

40. Robinson to Cliff, Sept. 4, 1951, ibid.

41. Milton to DDE, June 18, 1951, DDEPP, box 174, Milton, 1951–52 (2).

42. Dewey "Memorandum," June 24, 1951, DDEPP, box 24, Clay (6).

43. Ibid.; Bernard Shanley, "The Stassen Story," Shanley Diaries, July, August, and October 1951, pp. 7, 13, 28, 50, Eisenhower Library, box 1, delaying action (1) and (2).

44. Clay message to DDE, Aug. 22, 1951, DDEPP, box 24, Clay (6); Clay to DDE, Aug. 22, 1951, ibid.

45. Edgar Eisenhower to DDE, July 24, 1951, DDEPP, box 172, Eisenhower, Edgar (1).

46. Freeman to DDE, Sept. 13, 1951, DDEPP, box 43, Freeman, D.S.; DDE to Freeman, Sept. 20, 1951, ibid.

47. DDE to Finder, Sept. 3, 1951, DDEPP, box 41, Finder (2).

48. Finder to DDE, Sept. 13, 1951, FP, box 1, Finder–DDE corres., 1947–51.

49. DDE to Finder, Sept. 22, 1951, DDEPP, box 41, Finder (2).

Chapter 10. The Duff Letter

1. Roberts, OH, pp. 145–146.

2. William Bragg Ewald, Jr., *Eisenhower the President: Crucial Days, 1951–1960* (Englewood Cliffs, N.J.: Prentice-Hall, 1981), p. 40, and "Ike's First Move," *New York Times Magazine*, Nov. 14, 1993, pp. 56–57.

3. Roberts, OH, pp. 202–204.

4. Ibid., p. 159.

5. J. H. Michaelis to Finder, Sept. 7, 1951, FP, box 1, Eisenhower staff corres., 1948–51.

6. DDE to Clay, Oct. 3, 1951, DDEPP, box 24, Clay (5).

7. Finder to Schulz, Sept. 11, 1951, FP, box 1, Eisenhower staff corres., 1948–51; Schulz to Finder, Sept. 15, 1951, with enclosed manuscript article by Finder, "The Man Who Would Not Be President," ibid.

8. Finder to Folks, Sept. 24, 1951, FP, box 1, Family Corres. re: Eisenhower, 1947–51.

9. Eben Ayers diary, Truman Library, AP, box 17, file: 1951.

10. Clay to DDE, Sept. 29, 1951, DDEPP, box 24, Clay (5).

11. Unknown to Lodge (concerning General MacArthur's speech to the American Legion), Oct. 19, 1951, LP-II.

12. Tracy S. Voorhees to DDE, Oct. 26, 1951, DDEPP, box 118, Vor-VV (Misc.).

13. Clay to DDE, Sept. 24, 1951, DDEPP, box 24, Clay (5).

14. Clay to DDE, Sept. 29, 1951, ibid.

15. DDE to Clay, Sept. 27, 1951, ibid.
16. DDE to Clay, Oct. 3, 1951, ibid.
17. Robert P. Burroughs to DDE, Oct. 1, 1951, DDEPP, box 16, Burroughs, R.
18. Karl E. Mundt to Bermingham, Oct. 5, 1951, DDEPP, box 11, Bermingham (3).
19. Bermingham to Mundt, Oct. 9, 1951, and Bermingham to DDE, Oct. 9, 1951, ibid.
20. DDE to Burroughs, Oct. 11, 1951, DDEPP, box 16, Burroughs, R.
21. DDE to Bermingham, Oct. 18, 1951, DDEPP, box 11, Bermingham (3).
22. Aksel Nielson to DDE, Oct. 10, 1951, DDEPP, box 87, Nielson (1).
23. DDE to Nielson, Oct. 15, 1951, ibid.
24. CEFP, p. 35.
25. Ibid., p. 36.
26. Ibid., p. 37.
27. Ibid., p. 38.
28. "Progress Report," in James H. Duff to Davenport, Oct. 5, 1951, CP, box 5, file: Davenport, Russell: political matters, p. 4.
29. Ibid., p. 6
30. Ibid., p. 16.
31. Ibid., p. 17.
32. Ibid., pp. 1–20.
33. Ibid., p. 12.
34. Duff to Davenport, Oct. 5, 1951, ibid.
35. JHD [James H. Duff] memorandum of current political situation (nd), CP, box 5, Davenport, Russell: political matters. p. 1.
36. Ibid., p. 4
37. Ibid., pp. 6–7.
38. CEFP, p. 40.
39. Ibid., p. 45.
40. Ibid., p. 47.
41. Ibid., p. 45.

Chapter 11. Organizing the Campaign

1. Patterson, p. 506.
2. Ibid., p. 507.
3. Ibid., pp. 500, 505.
4. Ibid., p. 508.
5. Ibid., p. 514.
6. Ibid., p. 517.
7. Ambrose, p. 524.
8. Patterson, p. 529.
9. Smith, *Lucius D. Clay* [hereafter: JES], pp. 583–584; Clay interview by Ann B. Sloane, Feb. 20, 1974, [#B270], Brownell Papers, Eisenhower Library, pp. 1–3.
10. George Lodge, pp. 1–2; Richard Norton Smith [hereafter: RNS], p. 578.

11. Milton to Robinson, Sept. 20 and 26, 1951, RP, box 6, Eisenhower Nom. Campaign (2).

12. Clay to DDE, Oct. 16, 1951, DDEPP, box 24, Clay (5).

13. Milton to DDE, Oct. 20, 1951, DDEPP, box 174, Milton, 1951–52 (1).

14. DDE to Robinson, Oct. 19, 1951, RP, box 8, Election of 1952 (1951).

15. Robinson to Willma, Oct. 19, 1951, RP, box 1, Eisen (pers.) Sept.–Dec. 1951. Interestingly, the next day a letter went out to one of Eisenhower's friends, Syd Richardson in Fort Worth, Texas. It was from the nation's foremost evangelist, Billy Graham. Only one man on the political horizon, said Graham, had the "courage, honesty, integrity, and spiritual insight, who has captured the imagination of the American people as no man in recent generations—and that man is General Eisenhower. I sincerely believe it is the duty of this great General to offer himself to the American people." Billy Graham to Syd Richardson, Oct. 20, 1951, Jackie Cochran Papers, Eisenhower Library [hereafter: JCP], box 1, Eisen gen file, 1952 (1).

16. William E. Robinson's memorandum on the origins of *Crusade in Europe* (nd), RP, box 9, Robinson, note for book.

17. Robinson editorial, "The Time and the Man," reprinted from *New York Herald Tribune*, Oct. 25, 1951, RP, box 1, Eisen (pers) Sept.–Dec. 1951 and in DDEPP, box 108, Sloan, G.A. (2).

18. Robinson to DDE, Oct. 26, 1951, RP, box 1, Eisen (pers) Sept.–Dec. 1951.

19. Philip Young to DDE, Oct. 30, 1951, DDEPP, box 126, Young (1).

20. DDE to Milton, Oct. 31, 1951, DDEPP, box 174, Milton, 1951–52 (1).

21. DDE to Robinson, Oct. 31, 1951, DDEPP, box 99, Robinson (3).

22. Charles E. Wilson's talk, "The Camel's Nose Is Under the Tent," Dallas Chapter of the Society for the Advancement of Management, Oct. 10, 1951, DDEPP, box 124, Wilson, C. E. (2).

23. DDE to Wilson, Oct. 20, 1951, ibid.

24. Craig Cannon to Clay, Oct. 25, 1951, DDEPP, box 24, Clay (5).

25. "Meeting of the President with General of the Army Dwight D. Eisenhower in the Cabinet Room of the White House," 3:15 p.m., Nov. 5, 1951, PPSF, box 118, Gen. File: Eisenhower, D. D.

26. Ibid., p. 8.

27. Ibid., pp. 12–13.

28. Ibid., p. 16.

29. Ibid., p. 10.

30. Robinson to DDE, Nov. 15, 1951, RP, box 1, Eisen (pers) Sept.–Dec. 1951.

31. DDE to Hazlett, Nov. 14, 1951, DDEPP, box 56, Hazlett (1).

32. DDE to Robinson, Nov. 24, 1951, RP, box 8, Election of 1952 (1951).

33. DDE to Cliff, Nov. 8, 1951, DDEPP, Box 98, Roberts, C. (3).

34. Raucher, pp. 87, 92, 93.

35. JES, pp. 584–585, 586–587; RNS, p. 579; George Lodge, p. 2; CEFP, p. 48; Clay OH, Feb. 20, 1967, p. 14.

36. Cliff to DDE, Nov. 15, 1951, DDEPP, box 98, Roberts, C. (3).

37. DDE to Duff, Nov. 13, 1951, DDEPP, box 36, Duff, James, 1951.

38. Paul Hoffman to DDE, Nov. 15, 1951, DDEPP, box 57, Hoffman, P. (2).

39. Bermingham to DDE, Nov. 15, 1951, DDEPP, box 11, Bermingham (4).

40. John K. Jessup, introduction to article, "Luce in His Own Words," Clare Booth Luce Papers, Library of Congress, box 21, file: 10, pp. 21–32. "Certainly from 1946 on, the question of Eisenhower as a presidential candidate was widely discussed, and it was assumed that he might run as a Democrat. But all of that I had no part in. . . . He plainly could have had the nomination in 1948, on the Democratic ticket, but he turned it down, which was the first sign that he might thereafter run on the Republican ticket in 1952. It was felt then that Truman might be re-elected." Clare Booth Luce, Oral History, Jan. 11, 1968, Eisenhower Library [hereafter: CBL, OH], pp. 4–5. Having failed in his efforts to obtain the White House for Wendell Willkie in 1940 and for Thomas E. Dewey in 1944 and 1948, this time, according to one of his former editors, Luce determined to throw the editorial resources of his magazines behind a winner, Dwight D. Eisenhower. This even involved hiring editors of *Time*, Roy Alexander and Max Ways (national affairs editor), who would carry out his bidding. Thomas Griffith, *Harry and Teddy: The Turbulent Friendship of Press Lord Henry R. Luce and His Favorite Reporter* (New York: Random House, 1995), pp. 186–188, 196–198.

41. DDE to Luce, July 16, 1951 in DEP, XII–XIII, 425–426.

42. Edward K. Thompson, *A Love Affair with Life and the Smithsonian* (Columbia: University of Missouri Press, 1995), chapter 9. Eisenhower later would thank Luce profusely, saying that "C. D. Jackson saved my sanity—such part as is salvageable—and is giving us all a lift." He called Jackson, "a God-send . . . in the turmoil of 'running for office.'" DDE to Luce, Sept. 17, 1952, Henry R. Luce Papers, Library of Congress [hereafter: HRLP] box 2, Eisenhower, Dwight D.

43. DDE to Clark, Nov. 15, 1951, DDEPP, box 23, Clark, Edwin (1).

44. Schulz and Clark, telephone conversation transcript (nd), DDEPP, box 23, Clark, Edwin (1).

45. Clay to DDE, Nov. 15, 1951, DDEPP, box 24, Clay (5).

46. Shanley diary, "The Stassen Story," November 1951, p. 142.

47. Duff, "Memo of Political Situation as of November 19," DDEPP, box 36, Duff, James H., 1951.

48. George Lodge, p. 3.

49. Dewey memo to Lodge Nov. 17, 1951, LP-II; Lodge to Dewey, Nov. 21, 1951, HCL-II.

50. Duff, "Memo."

51. Dewey memo to Lodge, Nov. 23, 1951, LP-II.

52. Duff, "Memo."

53. Lodge to DDE, Dec. 3, 1951, DDEPP, box 72, Lodge.

54. DDE to Cliff, Nov. 24, 1951, DDEPP, box 98, Roberts, C. (3).

55. Winthrop Aldrich to DDE, Nov. 26, 1951, DDEPP, box 3, Aldrich, Winthrop.

56. McCann, OH 159, p. 62.

Chapter 12. Republican Affiliation

1. Hoffman to DDE, Dec. 5, 1951, DDEPP, box 57, Hoffman (2).

2. Burnham, Dec. 4, 1951, DDEPP, box 15, Burnham (1).

3. Roberts, OH, p. 133.

4. DDE to Edgar Eisenhower, Dec. 6, 1951, DDEPP, box 172, Eisenhower, Edgar (1).

5. Clay to DDE, Dec. 7, 1951, DDEPP, box 24, Clay (5).

6. Burnham to DDE, Dec. 7, 1951, DDEPP, box 15, Burnham (1).

7. Burroughs to DDE, Dec. 8, 1951, DDEPP, box 16, Burroughs, R.

8. Cliff to DDE, Dec. 5, 1951, DDEPP, box 98, Roberts, C. (3).

9. DDE to Cliff, Dec. 8, 1951, ibid.

10. DDE to Lodge, Dec. 12, 1951, DDEPP, box 72, Lodge.

11. DDE to Clay, Dec. 12, 1951, DDEPP, box 24, Clay (5).

12. Clay to DDE, Dec. 13, 1951, ibid.

13. Dewey, "Memorandum," transmitted by Clay to DDE, Dec. 13, 1951, ibid.

14. Lodge to DDE, Dec. 13, 1951, DDEPP, box 72, Lodge.

15. Log of telephone conversation between Wilton B. Persons and Lodge, Dec. 20, 1951, DDEPP, box 72, Lodge; Lodge to DDE, Dec. 22, 1951, DDEPP, box 72, Lodge.

16. DDE to Clay, Dec. 19, 1951, DDEPP, box 24, Clay (5).

17. Harold Stassen to DDE (handwritten), Dec. 15, 1951, DDEPP, box 111, Stassen (1).

18. George A. Sloan to DDE, Dec. 21, 1951, DDEPP, box 108, Sloan, G. A. (12).

19. HST to DDE, Dec. 18, 1951, Eisenhower Miscellaneous Diary, Eisenhower Library [hereafter: EMD], box 1/1, Jan. 1, 1950–Feb. 28, 1952.

20. Clay to DDE, Dec. 21, 1951, DDEPP, box 24, Clay (5).

21. DDE to Clay, Dec. 27, 1951.

22. DDE to Lodge, Dec. 29, 1951, DDEPP, box 72, Lodge.

23. Clark to DDE, Dec. 31, 1951, DDEPP, box 23, Clark, E. (1).

24. DDE to ENC, Jan. 9, 1952.

25. Robinson memorandum, Dec. 29, 1951, RP, b.1, Eisen (pers) Sept.–Dec. 1951.

26. Roberts, OH, pp. 182–184.

27. Adams to Lodge, Dec. 17, 1951, RP, box 9, N.H. Primary, 1952.

28. Roberts, OH, pp. 152, 154.

29. Ibid., pp. 155–156.

30. DDE to HST, Jan. 1, 1952, EMD, box 1/1, Jan. 1, 1950–Feb. 28, 1952.

31. DDE draft of letter from Lodge to Adams for Jan. 4, 1951, RP, box 9, N.H. Primary, 1952.

32. Lodge to Adams, Jan. 4, 1952, Herbert Brownell Papers, Eisenhower Library [hereafter: BP], box 127, politics, 1951–1952.

33. Robinson memorandum, Dec. 29, 1951, RP, box 1, Eisen (pers) Sept.–Dec. 1951.

34. Roberts, OH, p. 177.

35. DDE to Sloan, Jan. 3, 1952, DDEPP, box 108, Sloan, G. A. (2).

36. DDE to HST, Jan. 4, 1952, DDEPP, box 116, Truman (1).

37. DDE to Luce, Jan. 8, 1952, DDEPP, box 52, Luce, H.; Griffith, p. 188, "The Ike Boom," *Life* (March 31, 1952); "How Much Difference Would a Republican Make?" *Fortune* (February 1952), p. 200.

38. Ambrose, p. 522.

39. DDE to Clay, Jan. 8, 1952, DDEPP, box 24, Clay (4).

40. Howard McC Snyder to Robinson, Jan. 8, 1952, RP, box 8, Election of 1952 (spring–summer).
41. Robinson to Snyder, Jan. 15, 1951 [actually 1952], RP, box 8, Election of 1952 (spring–summer).
42. Burnham to DDE, Jan. 7, 1952, DDEPP, box 15, Burnham (1).
43. Earl Shaefer to DDE, Jan. 7, 1952, Schaeffer Papers, Eisenhower Library, box 1, Eisen/Schaeffer personal (1).
44. Sloan to DDE, Jan. 8, 1952, DDEPP, box 108, Sloan, G. A. (2).
45. Harry A. Bullis to DDE, Jan. 10, 1952, Bullis Papers, Eisenhower Library, box 1, Album 75, 1950–52.
46. George Whitney to DDE, Jan. 10, 1952, DDEPP, box 123, Whitney, G.
47. Clark to DDE, Jan. 10, 1952, DDEPP, box 23, Clark, E. (1).
48. Wiesenberger Investment Report, Nov. 11, 1952, JCP, box 1, Eisen. gen file, 1952 (1).
49. Susan Eisenhower, p. 263.
50. Roberts, OH, pp. 144–145.
51. Susan Eisenhower, p. 267.
52. Roberts, OH, p. 146.
53. Schulz, OH, p. 198.

Chapter 13. Deciding Strategy

1. DDE to Luce, Jan. 8, 1952, DDEPP, box 72, Luce, H.; Griffith, p. 188.
2. DDE to Luce, Jan. 22, 1952, ibid.
3. Ferrell, *Eisenhower Diaries*, pp. 209–213.
4. DDE to Sloan, Jan. 29, 1952, DDEPP, box 108, Sloan, G. A. (2); see also DDE to G. Whitney, Jan. 29, 1952, DDEPP, box 123, Whitney, G. and DDE to Ed, Jan. 30, 1952, DDEPP, box 172, Eisen. Edgar (1).
5. DDE to Sloan, Jan. 29, 1952.
6. DDE to Cliff, Jan. 11, 1952, DDEPP, box 98, Roberts, C. (2).
7. DDE to JSDE, Jan. 11, 1952, DDEPP, box 173, Eisenhower, John S. D. To Aksel Nielson DDE put a double underline under the word "not" when he wrote that "he meant exactly what I said when I put in my statement that I would not seek a nomination." DDE to Nielson, Jan. 14, 1952, DDEPP, box 87, Nielson (1).
8. Susan Eisenhower, p. 264
9. Herbert Brownell with John P. Burke, *Advising Ike: The Memoirs of Attorney General Herbert Brownell* (Lawrence, Kans.: University Press of Kansas, 1993), p. 97.
10. DDE to Burnham, Jan. 17, 1952, DDEPP, box 15, Burnham (1).
11. DDE to Cliff, Jan. 28, 1952, DDEPP, box 98, Roberts, C. (2).
12. DDE to Smith, Jan. 28, 1952, DDEPP, box 109, Smith, W. B. (1)
13. Smith to DDE, Feb. 1, 1952, DDEPP, box 109, Smith, W. B. (1)
14. DDE to Smith, Feb. 11, 1952, DDEPP, box 108, Smith, W. B. (1).
15. DDE to Hoffman, Feb. 9, 1952, DDEPP, box 59, Hoffman (2).
16. DDE to HST, Feb. 9, 1952, DDEPP, box 116, Truman (1).
17. Smith to DDE, Feb. 1, 1952.

18. DDE to James W. Wadsworth, Feb. 13, 1952, DDEPP, box 119, Wachs-Walco.

19. Burnham to DDE, Jan. 14, 1952, DDEPP, box 15, Burnham (1).

20. Edgar Eisenhower to DDE, Jan. 25, 1952, DDEPP, box 172, Eisenhower, Edgar (1).

21. Phil Reed to DDE, Jan. 22, 1952, DDEPP, box 97, Reed, Phil D.

22. Arthur Hays Sulzberger to DDE, Jan. 23, 1952, DDEPP, box 112, Sulzberger, A. H. (1).

23. Sulzberger to DDE, Jan. 31, 1952, ibid.

24. Smith to DDE, Feb. 1, 1952.

25. Cliff to DDE, Jan. 28, 1952, DDEPP, box 98, Roberts (2).

26. Clay to DDE, Jan. 16, 1962, DDEPP, box 24, Clay (4) with Dewey Memorandum of Jan. 14, 1952; Cliff to DDE, Jan. 18, 1952, DDEPP, box 98, Roberts (2).

27. Hoffman to DDE, Jan. 24, 1952, DDEPP, box 57, Hoffman (1).

28. Clay to DDE, Jan. 16, 1952; Cliff to DDE, Jan. 18, 1952.

29. Robinson "memorandum following discussions with Lodge, Vandenberg, Larmon and Brownell," Jan. 28, 1952, RP, box 2, Eisen (gen) Jan.–Mar. 1952.

30. Clay to DDE, Feb. 1, 1952, DDEPP, box 24, Clay (4).

31. Dewey to Lodge, Dec. 15, 1951, HCL-II.

32. Clay to DDE, Feb. 1, 1952, and DDE to Clay, Feb. 9, 1952, DDEPP, box 24, Clay (4).

33. Sulzberger to DDE, Jan. 28, 1952, DDEPP, box 112, Sulzberger, A. H. (1).

34. HST to DDE, Jan. 14, 1952, HSTPSF, box 7, Eisenhower, D. D.

35. HST to DDE, Jan. 31, 1952, DDEPP, box 116, Truman (1).

36. DDE to Hazlett, Feb. 12, 1952, DDEPP, box 56, Hazlett (1).

37. Robert T. Elson, *The World of Time Inc.: The Intimate History of a Publishing Enterprise* (New York: Atheneum, 1973), p. 307.

38. Kiplinger letter, Feb. 15, 1952, Cochran papers, b.1, Eisenhower, gen. file, 1952 (2).

39. DDE to Clay, Feb. 12, 1952, DDEPP, box 24, Clay (4).

40. Cliff to DDE, Feb. 13, 1952, DDEPP, box 98, Roberts, C. (2).

41. JES, pp. 590–591.

42. Ambrose, p. 524.

43. Dan Cook, "Memorandum of Conversation with Gen. Lucius D. Clay in London, Feb. 17, 1952," RP, box 8, Election of 1952 (spring–summer).

Chapter 14. Entering the Fray

1. DDE to Robinson, March 14, 1968, RP, box 9, N.H. Primary, 1952.

2. Kevin McCann, OH, p. 64

3. Reed to DDE, Feb. 20, 1952, DDEPP, box 97, Reed, Philip D.

4. Members of Congress Letter to DDE, Feb. 22, 1952, DDEPP, box 24, Clay (4).

5. DDE to Milton, Feb. 23, 1952, DDEPP, box 174, Milton, 1951–52 (1).

6. David Lawrence, "Eisenhower Friends Called Unwise in Asking His Return," *New York Herald Tribune*, Feb. 18, 1952.

7. DDE to Sloan, Feb. 21, 1952, DDEPP, box 108, Sloan, G. A. (2).

8. DDE to Sloan, Mar. 1, 1952, ibid. (1).

9. Stassen to Lodge, Feb. 22, 1952, DDEPP, box 111, Stassen (1).

10. Cliff memorandum to DDE, March 3–6, 1952, DDEPP, box 98, Roberts, C. (2), pp. 1–8.

11. Ibid., pp. 9–13.

12. Robinson to DDE, Mar. 6, 1952, RP, box 8, Election of 1952 (spring–summer).

13. Hoffman, Mar. 4, 1952, DDEPP, box 57, Hoffman (1).

14. Robinson to DDE, Mar. 16, 1968, RP, box 9, N.H. Primary, 1952.

15. Petersen to Lodge, Mar. 11, 1952, Howard C. Petersen Papers, Eisenhower Library [hereinafter: HPP], box 1, National Committee, Eisenhower for President (3); Gordon W. Blair to Arthur Hampson, Mar. 3, 1952, HPP, box 3, Eisen. Contrib. to State Comm. (4); Jackie Cochran to Clay, Mar. 4, 1952, Jacqueline Cochran Papers, Eisenhower Library [JCP], box 1, Eisenhower, gen. file, 1952 (4); and Florence Walsh to Clay, Mar. 6, 1952, ibid.

16. Robinson to DDE, Mar. 16, 1968.

17. Roberts, OH, p. 268.

18. Burroughs to DDE, Mar. 12, 1952, DDEPP, box 16, Burroughs, R.; Bullis to DDE, Mar. 12, 1952, BP, box 1, Album 75, 1950–52.

19. Roberts, OH, p. 192.

20. Bullis to DDE, Mar. 12, 1952.

21. *Time* (Jan. 14, 1952), pp. 15–16; W. A. Swanberg, *Luce and His Empire* (New York: Scribner, 1972), pp. 325–326.

22. Bullis to DDE, Mar. 12, 1952.

23. DDE to Bullis, Mar. 19, 1952, Bullis Papers, Eisenhower Library [hereafter: BP], box 1, Album 75, 1950–52.

24. DDE to Duff, Mar. 18, 1952, DDEPP, box 36, Duff, J. H.

25. DDE to Lodge, Mar. 18, 1952, DDEPP, box 72, Lodge.

26. Lodge to DDE, Mar. 24, 1952, ibid.

27. Robinson to DDE, Mar. 14, 1952, RP, box 2, Eisen. (pers) Jan.–Mar. 1952.

28. Roberts, OH, p. 200.

29. Roberts, OH, pp. 201–202.

30. Eisenhower, *At Ease*, p. 359.

31. Ambrose, p. 524.

32. Roberts to DDE, Mar. 22, 1952, DDEPP, box 99, Roberts, Roy.

33. Bullis to DDE, Mar. 22, 1952, BP, box 1, Album 75, 1950–52.

34. W. Howard Chase, Aide-Memoir (nd), CFP, box 10, Eisen. D. D., March 1952, p. 11.

35. Ibid., p. 24.

36. Ibid., p. 25.

37. Ibid., p. 20.

38. Hoffman to DDE, Mar. 29, 1952, DDEPP, box 47, Hoffman (1).

39. Ibid.

40. Hoffman to George Whitney, Apr. 16, 1952, Paul Hoffman Papers, Truman Library [hereafter: HP], box 34, 1952 W.; Hoffman to Alfred P. Sloan, Apr. 16, 1952, ibid.

41. Harriman, "Lisbon and the Security of the Free World," address before the Philadelphia Bulletin forum, Mar. 4, 1952, DDEPP, box 55, Harriman (1), pp. 1–4.

42. Ibid., pp. 6–8.

43. DDE to Harriman, Mar. 11, 1952, DDEPP, box 55, Harriman (1).

44. DDE to Clarence Francis, Mar. 20, 1952, CFP, box 10, DDE, 1952.

45. DDE to Sloan, Mar. 20, 1952, DDEPP, box 108, Sloan, G. A. (1).

46. Harriman to DDE, Mar. 20, 1952, DDEPP, box 55, Harriman (1); Eisenhower gained additional evidence of the urgency of congressional passage a few days later when Gruenther sent him the Defense Department's estimate that the Eastern bloc alone had thirty divisions of troops in their geographical area—twenty-two East German, two Polish, two Austrian, two Hungarian, and two Romanian. Gruenther message to SHAPE, Mar. 24, 1952. DDEPP, box 157, Reports, NATO.

47. Harriman to DDE, Mar. 20, 1952.

48. Bowie and Immerman, p. 31.

49. Ibid., p. 32.

50. Ibid., p. 35.

51. Ibid., p. 40.

52. Brownell, p. 94.

53. Ibid., p. 91.

54. Brownell, OH, Feb. 24, 1977, p. 36.

55. Brownell, pp. 91–92.

56. Brownell, OH #B270, pp. 11–12; Brownell, OH, Jan. 25, 1967, p. 28.

57. Brownell, p. 101.

58. Ibid., p. 100

59. Ibid., p. 101.

60. Brownell OH, Jan. 25, 1967, p. 39.

61. Edward Mead Earle to DDE, Mar. 29, 1952, box 37, Earle.

62. DDE to Earle, Mar. 26, 1952, DDEPP, box 37, Earle.

63. DDE to Clay, Mar. 25, 1952, DDEPP, box 24, Clay (3). Despite the crush of business, he found time to answer a long letter to Anna Rosenberg, wishing her well in what appeared to be an increasingly hopeless effort to get UMT through Congress. Anna Rosenberg to DDE, Mar. 27, 1952, DDEPP, box 100, Rosenberg (1); DDE to Rosenberg, Apr. 2, 1952, ibid.

64. Bullis to DDE, Mar. 28, 1952, BP, box 1, Album 75, 1950–52.

65. DDE to Ann and Arthur Nevins, Mar. 28, 1952, DDEPP, box 86, Nevins (1).

66. DDE to Robinson, Mar. 26, 1952, RP, box 8, Election of 1952 (spring and summer 1952).

67. DDE to Clay, Mar. 28, 1952, DDEPP, box 24, Clay (3).

68. Clay to DDE, Mar. 29, 1952, ibid.

69. HST press conference, Key West, Florida, Mar. 20, 1952, transcript, DDEPP, box 116, Truman (1).

70. Ibid.

71. Ferrell, *Truman*, p. 376.

72. DDE to HST, Apr. 2, 1952, DDEPP, box 116, Truman (1).

Chapter 15. The Nomination

1. DDE to Hoffman, Apr. 3, 1952, DDEPP, box 47, Hoffman (1).

2. Hoffman to DDE, Apr. 18, 1952, ibid.

3. DDE to Clay, Apr. 10, 1952, DDEPP, box 24, Clay (3).

4. Stassen to DDE, Apr. 14, 1952, DDEPP, box 111, Stassen (1).

5. Bermingham to DDE, Apr. 23, 1952, DDEPP, box 11, Bermingham, E. J. (1).

6. Hoffman to DDE, May 6, 1952, DDEPP, box 57, Hoffman (1).

7. Clay to DDE, May 17, 1952, DDEPP, box 24, Clay (1) May 17, 1952; David Schoenbrun to DDE, May 16, 1952, DDEPP, box 24, Clay (1).

8. Gurd S. Larmon to DDE, July 18, 1952, Whitman Name Series, Eisenhower Library [hereafter: WNS], box 20, Larmon, Sig.

9. DDE to John Foster Dulles, Apr. 15, 1952, DDEPP, box 36, Dulles; DDE to Clay, Apr. 10, 1952; DDE to Dulles, Apr. 15, 1952.

10. Dulles to DDE, Apr. 25, 1952, DDEPP, box 36, Dulles.

11. Clay to DDE, May 17, 1952; Ambrose, p. 526.

12. Susan Eisenhower, p. 268.

13. Patterson, p. 549.

14. Lodge to DDE, May 16, 1952, DDEPP, box 72, Lodge.

15. Patterson, pp. 550–551.

16. Lodge to DDE, May 16, 1952.

17. Robert T. Elson, "Question: What Is Ike Like?" *Life* (June 2, 1952).

18. Press release on the awarding of the Distinguished Service Medal (fourth Oak Leaf Cluster) to DDE, PSF, Truman Library, box 118, Gen. file: Eisenhower, D. D.

19. Ambrose, pp. 529–531.

20. Ibid., p. 533.

21. DDE to T. J. Davis, Apr. 17, 1952, DDEPP, box 33, Davis, T. J.

22. Brownell, p. 111.

23. Henry Cabot Lodge, Jr., *The Storm Has Many Eyes: A Personal Narrative* (New York: W. W. Norton, 1973), pp. 106–107.

24. Brownell, p. 109.

25. Brownell, p. 108; Lodge, p. 121.

26. Brownell, p. 115; Ambrose, p. 536.

27. Ambrose, p. 538.

28. Ibid.; Richard Norton Smith, p. 588; Lodge, p. 112.

29. Perret, pp. 575–576.

30. Milton Eisenhower, *The President Is Calling* (Garden City, N.Y.: Doubleday, 1974), p. 248.

31. Roberts to DDE, July 23, 1952, WNS, box 27, Roberts, Cliff (2).

32. Roberts, OH, p. 270.

33. George C. Marshall to DDE, July 12, 1952, WNS, box 21, Marshall, George (2).

34. DDE to Marshall, July 17, 1952, ibid.

35. Lodge to Dewey, July 14, 1952, LP-II. The candidate also wrote to Dewey. He thanked the governor, saying he was "still lost in wonder at your performance" in keeping the New York delegation in place and the many "days and weeks" he had spent counseling others and planning—always entirely in the background—to "bring about the result that was finally attained in Chicago." Richard Norton Smith, p. 597.

36. Perret, p. 577.

37. Susan Eisenhower, p. 271.

38. Sherman Adams, Oral History #162, Eisenhower Library, p. 3.

39. Homer E. Capehart to Norris Cotton, May 28, 1952, Cotton Papers, University of New Hampshire, box 16, political papers, folder 13.

40. Lodge to DDE, Aug. 4, 1955, Whitman Administrative Series, Eisenhower Library, box 27, Lodge, H. C., 1955 (2).

41. Statement of Net Assets, National Committee Eisenhower for President, May 16, 1952, HPP, Eisenhower Library, box 1, Natl. Comm. Eisen. For Pres. (5).

42. Robinson to Roy Larsen, July 15, 1952, RP, box 2, Eisen (Gen) July–Aug. 1952. Clare Booth Luce commented on the work of her husband in the campaign by saying that "largely the concern was to keep this man [Eisenhower] in his public position, where he shone and made his greatest public effect, without putting him in the position of a man who wanted to be a candidate—leave him free to say he was making no movement in his own behalf. . . . Of all the political maneuvers I've ever known in quite a long lifetime of political observation, that up to the time of the convention itself, his appearance as a candidate was as about as close to a draft as you could get. I think that no one who understands politics believes that anyone is ever really drafted without any efforts in his own behalf . . . such as keeping the door open to the right people and giving them the private nod." CBL, OH, pp. 6–7. Henry Luce gave the order for *Time* editors to publish a day early the issue that carried the story of the attempted "steal" of the Texas convention delegates, for timely effect on the convention. CBL, OH, p. 92. Ralph G. Martin, *Henry and Clare: An Intimate Portrait of the Luces* (New York: G. P. Putnam's Sons, 1991), pp. 291–296. Henry Luce contributed $21,000 to the various Republican and Eisenhower presidential campaign committees, national and state. He also contributed $3,000 to the campaign of his wife, who ran unsuccessfully for the U.S. Senate, and another $3,000 to the Republican senatorial campaign committee. HRLP, box 96, Contributions, 1949–1955.

BIBLIOGRAPHY

Archive and Manuscript Collections

EISENHOWER LIBRARY, ABILENE, KANSAS

Herbert Brownell Papers (BP)
Harry Bullis Papers (BP)
Edwin Clark Papers (CP)
Jackie Cochran Papers
Dwight D. Eisenhower, Pre-Presidential Papers (16–52 files—DDEPP)
Dwight D. Eisenhower, Post-Presidential Papers (DDEPST)
Dwight D. Eisenhower, Miscellaneous Diary (EMD)
Mamie Doud Eisenhower Papers
Leonard V. Finder Papers (FP)
Clarence Francis Papers (CFP)
C. D. Jackson Papers
Thomas Mattingly Papers
Kevin McCann Papers (MP)
Oval Office Tapes
Howard C. Petersen Papers (HPP)
William E. Robinson Papers (WERPP or RP)
Earl Schaefer Papers
Bernard Shanley Diaries, 1951
Bedell Smith Papers (BSP)
Ann Whitman Administrative Series (WAS)
Ann Whitman DDE Diary
Ann Whitman Name Series (WNS)

HARRY S. TRUMAN LIBRARY, INDEPENDENCE, MISSOURI

Eben Ayers Papers
George M. Elsey Papers (or EP)
Paul Hoffman Papers
President's Secretary's File (PPSF)
Harry S. Truman, Post-Presidential Memoirs (HSTPPM)

LIBRARY OF CONGRESS

Joseph E. Davies Papers
Clare Booth Luce Papers (CBLP)
Henry R. Luce Papers (HRLP)

OTHER COLLECTIONS

Norris Cotton Papers, University of New Hampshire Archives
Harold Ickes Diary, Michigan State University Archives
Henry Cabot Lodge, Jr., Papers (LP-II), Massachusetts Historical Society
Vertical File, United States Military Academy Archives

Articles, Papers, and Correspondence

ARTICLES AND PAPERS

Christian Cook, "How General Ike Became President Eisenhower: The Non-Politician as Presidential Candidate" (senior thesis, department of politics, Princeton University, 1998).
Tom Deligiannis, "Vanguards of the Tactical Nuclear Revolution: Early Army Thinking About the Tactical Use of Atomic Weapons, 1948–1949" (conference paper, Society for Historians of American Foreign Relations, University of Colorado, June, 1996).
Edward Mead Earle, "The Man Who Might Have Been President: Dwight D. Eisenhower," *Atlantic Monthly*, December 1948.
Dwight D. Eisenhower, "First Annual Report, Supreme Allied Commander Europe." Paris: SHAPE, April 2, 1952 (Robinson papers, box 2, file: Eisenhower, General, April–June 1952, Eisenhower Library).
Eisenhower Library Symposium, "The Great Crusade: The Road to the White House, 1952," November 6, 1992 (videotape).
Robert T. Elson, "Question: What Is Ike Like?" *Life*, June 2, 1952.

William Bragg Ewald, Jr., "Ike's First Move," *New York Times Magazine*, November 14, 1993, pp. 56–57.

Joan D. Goldhamer, "Eisenhower in Academe: A Clash of Perspectives and a Study Suppressed," *Journal of the History of the Behavioral Sciences*, XXXIII (Summer 1997), 241–259.

David Holloway, "The Soviet Union and the Origins of the Arms Race," in Melvyn Leffler and David S. Painter, eds., *Origins of the Cold War: An International History* (London: Routledge, 1994).

"How Much Difference Would a Republican Make?" *Fortune*, February 1952.

"The Ike Boom," *Life*, March 31, 1952.

Robert L. Ivie, "Eisenhower as Cold Warrior," in Martin Medhurst, ed., *Eisenhower's War of Words: Rhetoric and Leadership* (East Lansing: Michigan State University Press, 1994).

Phillip A. Karbert and Jerald A. Combs, "The United States, NATO, and the Soviet Threat to Western Europe," *Diplomatic History*, 22 (Summer 1998), 399–429.

David Lawrence, "Eisenhower Friends Called Unwise in Asking His Return," *New York Herald Tribune*, February 18, 1952.

Melvyn P. Leffler, "National Security and U.S. Foreign Policy," in Melvyn P. Leffler and David S. Painter, eds., *Origins of the Cold War: An International History* (London: Routledge, 1994).

George Lodge, "The Campaign to Win the Republican Nomination for Dwight D. Eisenhower, November 16, 1951–July 12, 1952" (draft manuscript, Whitman Administrative Series, box 23, file: Lodge campaign memorandum, Eisenhower Library).

Eduard Mark, "The War Scare of 1946 and Its Consequences," *Diplomatic History*, 21 (Summer 1997), 387–388.

Thomas W. Mattingly and Olive F. G. Marsh, "A Compilation of the General Health Status of Dwight D. Eisenhower" (Mattingly papers, box 1, general health (1) nd, Eisenhower Library).

Robert K. Merton, "An Inventory of Communications Addressed to General Eisenhower in the Spring of 1948: A Summary and Digest" (Bureau of Applied Social Research, Columbia University, September 1949), p. 14.

Roy Roberts, "A Patriot's Act," *Kansas Star*, January 27, 1948.

Thomas A. Schwartz, "Eisenhower and the Germans," in Gunter Bischof and Stephen E. Ambrose, eds., *Eisenhower: A Centenary Assessment* (Baton Rouge: Louisiana State University Press, 1995).

Thomas M. Sisk, "Forging the Weapon: Eisenhower as NATO's Supreme Allied Commander, Europe, 1950–1952," in Gunter Bischof and Stephen E. Ambrose, eds., *Eisenhower: A Centenary Assessment* (Baton Rouge: Louisiana State University Press, 1995).

Charles W. Toth, "Dwight D. Eisenhower: Presidential Candidate—Mid-Victorian Philosophy Toward Government and Economics," reprinted in *Vital Speeches of the Day*, 18 (April 1, 1952).

Marc Trachtenberg, "American Policy and the Shifting Nuclear Balance," in Melvyn P. Leffler and David S. Painter, eds., *Origins of the Cold War: An International History* (London: Routledge, 1994).

Robert A. Wampler, "Nuclear Learning and Nuclear Teaching: The Eisenhower Administration, Nuclear Weapons, and NATO Strategy, 1953–1960" (conference paper, Society for Historians of American Foreign Relations, Vassar College, June 1995).

Robert A. Wampler, "Eisenhower, NATO, and Nuclear Weapons: The Strategy and Political Economy of Alliance Security," in Gunter Bischof and Stephen E. Ambrose. *Eisenhower: A Centenary Assessment* (Baton Rouge: Louisiana State University Press, 1995).

CORRESPONDENCE

John P. Burke, e-mails to author, August 8 and 10, 1998.
Joan D. Goldhamer, to author, May 4, 1997.
Andrew J. Goodpaster, interview, June 2, 1998.
Andrew J. Goodpaster, to author, November 17, 1998.
Fred J. Greenstein, to author, December 18, 1997.
Wilson Miscamble, e-mail to author, April 15, 1998.
Leila Sussman, to author, February 26, 1997.
Abbott Washburn, interview, June 3, 1998.
Abbott Washburn, to author, June 17, 1998.
John E. Wickman, to author, February 4, 1997.

Oral Histories (OH)

EISENHOWER LIBRARY*

Sherman Adams, #162.
Herbert Brownell, January 25, 1967.
Herbert Brownell, #B270.

Lucius D. Clay, January 19, 1971; February 5, 1971; February 11, 1971; March 9, 13, 1971.
Lucius D. Clay (by Ann Sloane in Brownell papers), February 20, 1974.
Dwight D. Eisenhower, July 12, 20, 1967.
Milton Eisenhower, September 6, 1967.
Alfred Gruenther, April 20, 1967.
Clare Booth Luce, January 11, 1968.
Kevin McCann, December 21, 1966.
John McCone, July 26, 1976.
Howard C. Peterson, April 1, 1968.
Cliff Roberts, September 12, 1968.
Robert Schulz, July 23, 1972.
Thomas E. Stephens, January 12, 1968.
Henry Wriston, January 4, 1968.

*Some of these are copies of interviews at Columbia University.

TRUMAN LIBRARY

Tom Clark (nd)
Sam Rosenman (nd)
Harry Vaughn (nd)

Books

Jules Abels. *Out of the Jaws of Victory.* New York: Henry Holt, 1959.
Stephen E. Ambrose. *Eisenhower,* Vol. I. *Soldier, General of the Army, President-Elect, 1890–1952.* New York: Simon and Schuster, 1983.
Robert R. Bowie and Richard Immerman. *Waging Peace: How Eisenhower Shaped an Enduring Cold War Strategy.* New York: Oxford University Press, 1998.
Herbert Brownell, with John P. Burke. *Advising Ike: The Memoirs of Attorney General Herbert Brownell.* Lawrence: University Press of Kansas, 1993.
Alfred D. Chandler, Jr., and Louis Galambos, eds. *The Papers of Dwight D. Eisenhower.* Vols. VII, VIII, X, XI, XII. Baltimore: Johns Hopkins University Press, 1970.
Blanche Wiesen Cook. *The Declassified Eisenhower: A Divided Legacy of Peace and Political Warfare.* New York: Penguin Books, 1984.
Campbell Craig. *Destroying the Village: Eisenhower and Thermonuclear War.* New York: Columbia University Press, 1998.

Kenneth C. Davis. *Eisenhower: Soldier of Democracy*. Garden City, New York: Doubleday, 1945.

Robert J. Donovan. *Conflict and Crisis: The Presidency of Harry S. Truman, 1945–1948*. New York: W. W. Norton, 1977.

Dwight D. Eisenhower. *Crusade in Europe*. New York: Avon Books, 1948.

Dwight D. Eisenhower. *Mandate for Change: The White House Years, 1953–56*. New York: Signet, 1963.

Dwight D. Eisenhower. *At Ease: Stories I Tell to Friends*. New York: Avon Books, 1967.

John S. D. Eisenhower. *Allies: Pearl Harbor to D-Day*. Garden City, N.Y.: Doubleday, 1982.

Milton Eisenhower. *The President Is Calling*. Garden City, N.Y.: Doubleday, 1974.

Susan Eisenhower. *Mrs. Ike: Memories and Reflections on the Life of Mamie Eisenhower*. New York: Farrar, Straus and Giroux, 1996.

Howard S. Ellis. *Economics of Freedom: The Progress and Future of Aid to Europe*. New York: Council on Foreign Relations, 1950.

Robert T. Elson. *The World of Time Inc: The Intimate History of a Publishing Enterprise*. New York: Atheneum, 1973.

Robert H. Ferrell. *Ill Advised: Presidential Health and Public Trust*. Columbia: University of Missouri Press, 1992.

Robert H. Ferrell, ed. *The Eisenhower Diaries*. New York: W. W. Norton, 1981.

Robert H. Ferrell. *Harry S. Truman: A Life*. Columbia: University of Missouri Press, 1994.

David Fromkin. *In the Time of the Americans: FDR, Truman, Eisenhower, Marshall, MacArthur—The Generation That Changed America's Role in the World*. New York: Alfred A. Knopf, 1995.

Thomas Griffith. *Harry and Teddy: The Turbulent Friendship of Press Lord Henry R. Luce and His Favorite Reporter*. New York: Random House, 1995.

W. Averell Harriman and Elie Abel. *Special Envoy to Churchill and Stalin, 1941–1946*. New York: Random House, 1975.

James Hershberg. *James B. Conant: Harvard to Hiroshima and the Making of the Nuclear Age*. New York: Alfred A. Knopf, 1993.

Robert E. Herzstein. *Henry R. Luce: A Political Portrait of the Man Who Created the American Century*. New York: Scribner, 1994.

Michael J. Hogan. *A Cross of Iron: Harry S. Truman and the Origins of the National Security State, 1945–1954*. Cambridge, U.K.: Cambridge University Press, 1998.

David Holloway. *Stalin and the Bomb: The Soviet Union and Atomic Energy, 1939–1956.* New Haven: Yale University Press, 1994.

Daniel D. Holt and James W. Leyerzapf, eds. *Eisenhower: The Pre-war Diaries and Selected Papers, 1905–1941.* Baltimore: Johns Hopkins University Press, 1998.

Townsend Hoopes and Douglas Brinkley. *Driven Patriot: The Life and Times of James Forrestal.* New York: Alfred A. Knopf, 1992.

Arthur M. Johnson. *Winthrop W. Aldrich: Lawyer, Banker, Diplomat.* Cambridge, Mass.: Graduate School of Business Administration, Harvard University, 1968.

Howard Jones. *Quest for Security: A History of U.S. Foreign Relations,* Vol. II: *Since 1913.* New York: McGraw-Hill, 1996.

Lawrence S. Kaplan. *The Long Entanglement: NATO's First Fifty Years.* Wesport, Conn.: Praeger, 1999.

Richard H. Kohn, ed. *The United States Military Under the Constitution of the United States, 1789–1989.* New York: New York University Press, 1991.

Clarence G. Lasby. *Eisenhower's Heart Attack: How Ike Beat Heart Disease and Held onto the Presidency.* Lawrence: University Press of Kansas, 1997.

Melvyn P. Leffler. *A Preponderance of Power: National Security, the Truman Administration, and the Cold War.* Stanford, Calif.: Stanford University Press, 1992.

Henry Cabot Lodge, Jr. *The Storm Has Many Eyes: A Personal Narrative.* New York: W. W. Norton, 1973.

Peter Lyon. *Eisenhower: Portrait of the Hero.* Boston: Little, Brown, 1974.

Ralph G. Martin. *Henry and Clare: An Intimate Portrait of the Luces.* New York: G. P. Putnam's Sons, 1991.

David McCullough. *Truman.* New York: Simon and Schuster, 1992.

Martin J. Medhurst. *Dwight D. Eisenhower: Strategic Communicator.* Westport, Conn.: Greenwood Press, 1993.

Thomas G. Paterson and J. Gary Clifford. *America Ascendant: U.S. Foreign Relations Since 1939.* Lexington, Mass.: D. C. Heath, 1995.

James T. Patterson. *Mr. Republican: A Biography of Robert A. Taft.* New York: Houghton-Mifflin, 1972.

Geoffrey Perret. *Old Soldiers Never Die: The Life of Douglas MacArthur.* New York: Random House, 1996.

Cabell Phillips. *The Truman Presidency: The History of a Triumphant Succession.* New York: Macmillan, 1966.

William B. Pickett. *Dwight David Eisenhower and American Power.* Wheeling, Ill.: Harlan Davidson, 1995.

William B. Pickett. *Homer E. Capehart: A Senator's Life, 1897–1979*. Indianapolis: Indiana Historical Society, 1990.

Forrest C. Pogue. *George C. Marshall: Statesman, 1945–1959*. New York: Viking, 1987.

Alan R. Raucher. *Paul G. Hoffman: Architect of Foreign Aid*. Lexington: University of Kentucky Press, 1985.

Michael Schaller. *Douglas MacArthur: The Far Eastern General*. New York: Oxford University Press, 1989.

Jean Edward Smith. *Lucius D. Clay: An American Life*. New York: Henry Holt, 1990.

Richard Norton Smith. *Thomas E. Dewey and His Times*. New York: Simon and Schuster, 1982.

W. A. Swanberg. *Luce and His Empire*. New York: Scribner, 1972.

Edward K. Thompson. *A Love Affair with Life and the Smithsonian*. Columbia: University of Missouri Press, 1995.

INDEX

A NOTE ON THE AUTHOR

William B. Pickett is professor of history at the Rose-Hulman Institute of Technology in Terre Haute, Indiana. Born in Crawfordsville, Indiana, he studied at Carleton College and Indiana University, where he began teaching. He has been a Fulbright professor in Japan and an adviser to the *Indiana Magazine of History* and the Indiana University Oral History Project. His other books include *Dwight David Eisenhower and American Power* and *Homer E. Capehart: A Senator's Life*.